An Abridged History of the United States

Volume II

Bob Navarro

2019

Dedicated to my Angel, Espy

Contents

Post-Civil War Issues

The Gilded Age

The gilded age, which occurred after the Civil War ended, was concerned with issues such as the reform of the civil service system, the regulation of the railroads, attempts at temperance, the restriction of further immigration—especially in the west against the Chinese—and the revamping of the monetary system. These proved to be very volatile issues and served to further split the political coalitions between the Democrats and the Republicans. The tariffs were also extended to promote industrial growth, with high wages and a strong domestic market for products being the end result. However, the tariffs caused inflation with higher prices for manufactured goods, created a vast inequity between the rich executives and the poorer classes such as farmers, and inevitably brought about a marked increase in corruption—both in government and in private business.

The Reconstruction, which took place between 1865 and 1877, was the period of readjustment to deal with the South—which was a ruined land. The physical destruction wrought by the invading Union forces was enormous and far-reaching with cities, plantations and farms devastated, lives lost or altered forever, and much of the property either confiscated or destroyed. In addition, the old social and economic order founded on slavery had collapsed completely, with nothing to replace it. The eleven Confederate states were restored into the Union, provided with loyal governments, and helped back into being viable economic entities once again. However, the new role of the emancipated slaves in southern society now had to be clearly defined. Moreover, there was an additional problem of dealing with many white people who were impoverished, hungry and resentful of the occupation army that was in their midst. With a backlash from the South and a weariness from the North, the official end of Reconstruction came in 1877 with the removal of occupying federal troops from the South[1] by President Rutherford B. Hayes, leaving the issue of integration of blacks into white society in abeyance. This action relegated the blacks in the South to inequality and injustice—and essentially placed them in a condition of servitude for the next half-century with the passage of Jim Crow laws.

In foreign policy, President Grant was able to obtain a settlement of the *Alabama* claims against Great Britain—and in the process averted a war with the British over the issue. Thus, no wars happened—except at the end of the gilded-age period—when the Spanish-American War and a lesser-known Philippines-American War occurred in 1898[2]. There was also a brief involvement in the Boxer uprising in China in 1900, when troops were sent from several countries, including the United States, to quell a disturbance that threatened the foreign legations in that country. Thus, the prevailing situation was to a renewed focus on domestic issues, and hence industrialization happened very rapidly— beginning in the 1870s—with the country being transformed into a nation of large cities and many factories. The people were also changed by relocating to urban centers by the attraction of high wages, with their focus now being centered on accumulating money and material possessions. The migration of a significant number of the 5 million blacks from the South into other areas of the country was a shift that had a profound effect on the nation—especially the ones who migrated from the rural parts of the South into the industrial cities of the North like New York City, Chicago and Philadelphia.

Domestically, the biggest challenge for the United States government as President Grant began his term of office was the size of the national debt—something that had swelled because of the cost of conducting the Civil War. President Grant also addressed Indian policy as he tried to resolve the differences between the Native Americans and the white culture. He made a valiant attempt to promote justice in Indian affairs as well as to secure a place for them in American society. But, the westward movement—which had never ceased despite the Civil War—pushed into these new areas that were already inhabited by Indians. As these new settlers moved across the plains of the country, the inevitable result was a series of Indian wars that were fought over the territorial incursions. The disastrous defeat of General George A. Custer with the wipeout of all his forces in 1876 by the Sioux Indians at Little Big Horn, Montana produced a backlash that interfered with the fair treatment of Native Americans for many years after this event. The bitter struggle finally culminated under the administration of President Benjamin Harrison with the Massacre at Wounded Knee Creek, South Dakota in 1890, in which more than 350 Indian men, women and children were shot to death by United States Army forces.

The completion of the transcontinental railroad paved the way for a steady settlement of towns along the railroad route. At the end of the Civil War in 1865, there were 35,000 miles of railroad tracks in the United States. By 1890, there were more than 164,000 miles of track that connected the East coast with the West coast. The railroads replaced the horse, stagecoach and wagon train as the primary mode of transportation, and they created new markets for goods and services.

The Rise of Progressivism

Progressivism arose as a response to the decadence of the Gilded Age, and became a movement favoring reform. It started with the presidency of Theodore Roosevelt who advocated a new direction for both economic and social policies that moved away from conservative stances. Thus, he spoke out about the need for laws to regulate tenement housing, to prevent child labor and to provide better working conditions. He also advocated progressive taxation and opposed the monopolistic influence of large corporations. The progressive movement was continued by Presidents William Taft and Woodrow Wilson, and in the 1912 election, Theodore Roosevelt even formed a Progressive Party to run as a third-party candidate.

The progressive policies included support for organized labor and trade unions— especially with regard to increases in wages, improvement in working conditions and the creation of a universal health care system. The progressive reform endeavored to eliminate corruption in government, improve the environment, deal with health hazards and regulate business practices. Politically, it also strived to provide the public with more control over government such as through the implementation of direct primary systems for the nomination of candidates for public office, and through direct citizen participation in government via initiatives, referendums and recalls.

In terms of the Constitution, four new amendments were adopted as the progressive era evolved. These new amendments authorized an income tax (Sixteenth Amendment), provided for the direct election of senators (Seventeenth Amendment), prohibited the manufacture and sale of alcoholic beverages (Eighteenth Amendment)—which was overturned by another amendment (Twenty-First Amendment)—and extended the right of voting to women (Nineteenth Amendment). In terms of legislative actions, Congress passed new laws that established federal regulation of the meatpacking, drug and railroad industries. Congress also strengthened anti-trust laws, lowered the tariff rates and established federal control over the banking system—especially with the creation of the Federal Reserve System, which acts as a central bank for the United States.

Gunboat Diplomacy

Although gunboat diplomacy[2] was first used by President William McKinley during the Spanish-American War in 1898, it was President Theodore Roosevelt who defined its use by the takeover of Panamanian land to build the Panama Canal through it—and control it afterwards. President William Taft occupied Nicaragua at the end of his term to protect American interests there. President Woodrow Wilson also continued with this gunboat policy by his occupation of Mexico, Haiti and the Dominican Republic during his administration.

Dollar Diplomacy

Dollar diplomacy[3] became prevalent during the administration of President William Taft. President Taft attempted to establish control over Honduras by buying up its debt to British bankers. And, when a revolt broke out in Nicaragua in 1912, the Taft administration sided with the insurgents and sent troops into the country to seize the customs houses. As soon as the United States consolidated its control over the country, Secretary of State Philander Knox encouraged United States bankers to offer loans to the new regime—primarily to keep foreign money from being invested in Nicaragua.

Another area where dollar diplomacy was used was the Caribbean—which was largely dominated by United States interests. The United States government urged American bankers to invest in Haiti in order to keep out foreign funds. The United States would not permit foreign nations to interfere, and consequently felt obligated to intervene to prevent economic and political instability. The United States persuaded four banks to refinance Haiti's national debt, thus setting a policy of further economic intervention.

Technical Achievements

Many notable technical achievements were made at the turn of the century. In 1903, the first Pacific cable was laid between San Francisco, California and Manila in the Philippines. The first airplane flight was also made by Orville and Wilbur Wright at Kitty

Hawk, North Carolina in 1903. And, the first underwater subway was constructed in New York City in 1903. In 1910, Thomas Edison demonstrated the first motion picture. In 1926, Robert H. Goddard invented liquid-fueled rockets—a precursor of the space age. In 1927, Philo Taylor Farnsworth invented the complete electronic television system. In 1932, Polaroid photography was invented by Edwin Land who created a revolution in instant photography.

However, most of the developments came about as a result of WWI, which furthered the development of new weaponry such as powerful howitzers, advanced mortars and improved machine guns. The large number of head-wounds caused by exploding shells and fragmentation forced the development of the modern steel helmet, in particular, the Brodie helmet by Britain and the United States.

The widespread use of chemical warfare also came into use during the conflict. Gases used for warfare that were developed included chlorine, mustard gas and phosgene. As a result, effective countermeasures to gas attacks were created such as gas masks.

Fixed-wing aircraft were used militarily for reconnaissance, and later were used for dropping grenades, for ground attacks by mounting weapons on them, and to take aerial photographs. To shoot down these planes, anti-aircraft guns and fighter aircraft were developed. Zeppelins, balloons, airships, aircraft carriers and improved submarines were also deployed. Consequently, countermeasures against these weapons—especially against submarines—led to the development of depth charges, hydrophones and anti-submarine weapons.

The tank was created and light automatic weapons were introduced, such as the Lewis Gun and the Browning automatic rifle. Flamethrowers increased the savagery of war by its use as powerful and demoralizing weapons that caused terror on the battlefield. The development of anti-personnel projectiles that produced shrapnel in the form of showers of lethal lead pellets as they exploded in midair also increased the brutality of war. And, snipers firing high-powered rifles that were equipped with telescopic sights added a new element—with countermeasures that were developed such as anti-snipers and directed artillery fire when sniper positions became known.

The Changing of the World Order

When Germany attacked Poland in 1939, France and England declared war on Germany to defend Poland against the German invasion. Germany responded by declaring war on France and England, thus starting WWII. Germany then attacked Russia in 1941, extending the conflict to the east. When Japan attacked the American fleet at Pearl Harbor, Hawaii in 1941, the United States declared war on Japan, and then on Germany. The war lasted until Germany was defeated in 1945. Japan surrendered when it was devastated by two atomic bombs that were dropped on Hiroshima and Nagasaki by the United States in 1945. After the war, the United States and Russia became the two most powerful nations in terms of weaponry, with China also evolving into a superpower in recent years.

The Creation of Atomic Weapons

The Manhattan Project was started by the United States in 1939, with the goal being that of creating a nuclear weapon. Three primary research and production sites for the project were established at Hanford, Washington, Oak Ridge, Tennessee, and Los Alamos, New Mexico. The first test explosion of an atomic bomb took place in 1945 near Alamogordo, New Mexico. Two of these bombs were dropped in Japan over Hiroshima and Nagasaki in 1945. 10 other countries have developed nuclear weapons since then, and a few more are working towards that goal. So far all efforts to constrain the nuclear arms race have not been successful, with the result being an accumulation of an enormous stockpile of atomic and hydrogen bombs, especially by Russia and the United States.

The Rise of Communism

Communism took hold in Russia after WWI. It spread into China where after WWII, it emerged as the ruling political party. North Korea, Vietnam and Cuba instituted communist governments through the influence of Russia and China. In the Soviet Union, various countries were assimilated into the communist sphere, including Romania, Poland, Bulgaria, East Germany, Czechoslovakia, Hungary and Latvia. The post-war world saw the beginning of the "Cold War" between the West and the East as democratic governments became allied against the communist governments. Conflicts in Korea and Vietnam pitted the United States government against communist forces, with a third conflict in Cuba being averted by diplomatic efforts. China, North Korea, Cuba, Vietnam and Russia remained as the principal communist countries although both China and Russia have altered their economic systems to incorporate capitalistic enterprises.

The United States as World Policeman

After emerging victorious in WWII, the role of "world policeman" was thrust on and assumed by the United States. Its first test was in the Korean War, a conflict that lasted 3 years and which ended in a stalemate. Its next encounter was in Vietnam where a 25-year conflict occurred that involved the countries of Vietnam, Laos and Cambodia—with the clandestine assistance of North Vietnam from China and Russia. In Cuba, WWIII almost broke out over the shipment of arms and missiles to Cuba by the Soviet Union. The United States was also involved in the Balkan War and the First Gulf War. Recent terrorist events and threats, such as the 9-11 events, have involved the United States in wars against Iraq and Afghanistan, and partially in Yemen, Somalia, Libya, Lebanon and Syria. With the Middle East being a tinderbox of activity, it is certainly possible that the United States may become further involved in another war—most probably against Iran, which is seeking to become a nuclear power. As the leader of the free world, the role of the President of the United States has expanded to combat and contain any territorial aggressions in foreign areas that threaten the interests of the United States.

The Shift in Economic Power

After WWII ended, the United States emerged as a super economic power. Among the many benefits that were derived from the war effort were an increase in skilled workers who labored in the war industries, the creation of the largest industrial plant capacity in the world, the expansion of resources, products and new inventions, the creation of the largest scientific farm plant in the world, and the biggest backlog of housing, transportation, communication and living comforts.

Additional gains that were gotten as derivatives were the growing of good and plentiful food, the creation of adequate hospitals, better schools and good housing, the expansion of rural electrification, a more efficient farm economy with new equipment, an increased demand for goods, the attainment of full employment, the achievement of social objectives, and the elimination of trade barriers

The United States became the country with the highest standard of living. However, this did not mean that all American workers were now living in security, comfort and luxury—especially with regard to miners and agricultural workers, as well as some white-collar employees with low incomes. The evils of bad living conditions in the big cities began to manifest themselves as the population shifted from rural to urban areas as a result of the war with its lure of defense-related jobs in the cities. Thus, slums, crime, inadequate housing, accumulation of waste, poverty, homelessness and other ills became the new focus of attention—even as the nation moved towards a new level of prosperity.

Ulysses Grant

Election of 1868

In the 1868 presidential election, General Ulysses Grant won by getting 214 electoral votes. Schuyler Colfax became Vice President by getting 214 Electoral votes.

Significant Events: 1869

The Public Credit Act was passed by Congress to stipulate that government bond payments be made in gold.

The repeal of the Tenure-of-Office law was considered by the Senate, and was referred to the Committee on the Judiciary.

Congress passed the Judiciary Act, which increased the number of Supreme Court Justices from 7 to 9.

The first transcontinental railroad line was completed at Promontory Point, Utah as the Union Pacific Railroad tracks from the west were joined to the Central Pacific Railroad tracks of the east by the last spike. The coast-to-coast railway reduced journeys of 6 months to only 6 days, and pioneers began to transform the western part of the United States.

In San Francisco, California riots occurred against immigrant Chinese laborers by American laborers who were against them for being willing to work for very low wages.

A financial panic, termed "Black Friday," was experienced on Wall Street as gold manipulation caused a massive sell-off. The collapse of the market was caused by two speculators who attempted to control the supply by purchasing gold and then hoarding it to increase its price, which threw the stock market into confusion. Since it made the prices of commodities fluctuate wildly, President Grant released $4,000,000 of federal gold reserves to be made available for trading to offset the effect, and to make the price of gold come down to $135 an ounce—thus creating the ensuing panic.

The Wyoming Territory became the first area in the United States to pass a law granting women the right to vote.

Significant Events: 1870

Virginia was readmitted to the Union after it accepted the Fifteenth Amendment.

Representative Willard submitted a resolution for economy in public expenditure, given the public debt of over $2.4 billion. The resolution was accepted by the House and was referred to the Committee of the Whole.

In the case of *Hepburn v. Griswold* the Supreme Court decided that the Legal Tender Act could not be applied retroactively. This effectively made all debts contracted prior to 1862 not redeemable by Treasury notes issued under this act.

Congress established the National Weather Bureau.

Representative Benjamin introduced a bill into the House to authorize the cities of Washington, D.C. and Georgetown to levy a tax upon property to support the poor residents therein, but the House tabled the bill.

Mississippi was readmitted to the Union after it accepted the Fifteenth Amendment.

The Utah Territory passed a law granting women the right to vote, becoming the second territory to do so.

Hiram Revels from Mississippi attended the Senate as the first African-American Senator.

President Grant called for the construction of a canal linking the Caribbean and Pacific Oceans, preferably across the Isthmus of Panama.

The Fifteenth Amendment to the Constitution was certified as having been ratified by the state legislatures, and was signed into law by President Grant.

Texas was readmitted to the Union after it accepted the Fifteenth Amendment.

House Representative Butler submitted a bill to amend an act to protect all persons in their civil rights.

The Senate agreed to two resolutions regarding the African slave trade:

- That the President inform the Senate as to what measures were being taken by the government to suppress the traffic in slaves along the coast of Africa.
- That the President transmit the reports to the Senate regarding the extent to which the traffic in human beings was being carried out—and by whom.

The Senate voted against the Santo Domingo Treaty, and did not even consider the leasing of Samana Bay.

Congress passed the Ku Klux Klan Act to enforce the Fifteenth Amendment. It also passed legislation that allowed a person to sue if they were deprived of their rights by someone else.

Congress passed an act to establish the Department of Justice, which would be under the direction of the Attorney General.

The United States attempted to annex the Dominican Republic. However, the Senate refused to approve the treaty of annexation.

The Secretary of State declared that no territory in the Western hemisphere could be handed over to a second European nation, and instead must be set unconditionally free.

Congress passed the Internal Revenue and Tariff Acts. The excise taxes were eliminated and tariff rates were reduced, with only a few items still retaining a duty on them.

The Senate agreed to the treaty between the United States and Great Britain for the suppression of the African slave trade.

Georgia was readmitted to the Union.

A petition to the House was presented from Victoria Woodhull asking for the right of women suffrage under the provisions of the Fourteenth and Fifteenth Amendments to the Constitution.

Significant Events: 1871

Congress enacted a law to federally supervise all elections in cities having over 20,000 in population. The measure was passed to protect black voters in the South.

The District of Columbia was provided with a territorial government. However, in 1874, it was abolished and was replaced by a commission to serve as the government.

President Grant formed a Civil Service Commission to create a merit system for federal jobs. George William Curtis was appointed to head the commission, but Congress failed to make an appropriation. Curtis resigned in 1875 after his recommendations were ignored, and the commission was discontinued.

Congress passed the Illinois Railroad Act to have a commission fix maximum rates on railroads and warehouse use—and to forbid all discrimination that favored giant corporations over small businesses.

Congress passed the Ku Klux Klan Act to enforce the Fourteenth Amendment. The act authorized the President to suspend the writ of *habeas corpus* and to enforce the Fourteenth Amendment through the use of federal troops—as well as to punish criminal acts that were committed by individuals.

In the case of *Knox v. Lee* the Supreme Court decided that the Legal Tender Act of 1862 was constitutional.

The United States Navy bombarded and destroyed 5 Korean vessels in an unsuccessful attempt to force that country to agree to a favorable treaty with the United States.

The Treaty of Washington between the United States and Great Britain was ratified by the Senate. The treaty provided for arbitration of the *Alabama* claims that had resulted from the Civil War, settled the fishing and boundary disputes, and left the question of the ownership of the San Juan Islands to be adjudicated by the German Emperor. In 1872, the United States was awarded $15.5 million in damages for the destruction caused by the Confederate ship *Alabama* and other vessels that had been built by the British. In 1872, the United States was also awarded the San Juan Islands by the German Emperor.

The frauds conducted by William "Boss" Tweed were exposed in a series of articles that were published by the *New York Times*. The fraudulent contracts involving faked leases, padded bills, false vouchers, unnecessary repairs and kickbacks amounted to $200 million and led to New York City being brought to the verge of bankruptcy[5].

The Great Chicago fire in Illinois caused damages of almost $200 million, killed 300 people, destroyed over 18,000 buildings, charred an area equal to 2,125 acres, and left about 100,000 persons homeless. In a devastating fire in Peshtigo, Wisconsin, 600 people were killed and 2,000 acres of forest were burned.

Race riots occurred in Los Angeles, California against immigrants of Chinese descent in which 15 Chinese laborers were lynched. The action was perpetrated by American workers who felt threatened by the competition of Chinese workers who they claimed that employers were using the coolie labor to depress wages.

Significant Events: 1872

Congress passed an act that fixed the date of congressional elections to be on the first Tuesday after the first Monday in November.

The Senate refused to ratify a treaty with the Samoan Islands that would have given the United States the right to have a naval coaling station in Pago Pago.

Congress created the Yellowstone Park as the first public national preserve in Wyoming.

Congress passed the Amnesty Act to remove restrictions of holding elective office, as contained in section 3 of the Fourteenth Amendment, from all except 500 former Confederates.

The General Mining Act was passed by Congress to codify the informal system of acquiring and protecting mining claims on public land. The law applied primarily to precious metals such as gold, platinum and silver, but was also used to cover other metals like copper, lead, zinc, uranium and tungsten.

Congress declared an end to the Freedmen's Bureau.

The Credit Mobilier of America scandal was exposed in the *New York Sun*. The scandal ruined the political career of Vice President Schuyler Colfax, who was replaced on the

Republican ticket in the 1872 election by Henry Wilson—even though Wilson had also been involved in the scandal.

President Grant was re-elected as President by receiving 286 Electoral College votes. Vice President Henry Wilson received 286 Electoral College votes.

A fire in Boston, Massachusetts killed 13 people, burned 65 acres and caused $75 million in property damages.

Significant Events: 1873

Congress passed the Coinage Act that embraced the gold standard and demonetized the silver dollar coin.

The Timber Culture Act was passed by Congress to authorize grants of an additional 160 acres under the homesteading land program if the settlers on these lands planted trees on one-fourth of that additional land.

Congress passed an act by which it increased the salaries of its members to $7,500, and the salary of the President to $50,000, the salary of the Vice President to $10,000 and the salaries of the Supreme Court Justices to $10,000, with the Chief Justice getting $10,500.

Congress passed the Coal Lands Act by which 160 acres could be purchased by individuals, or 320 acres by groups, at $10 to $20 per acre for coal bearing lands.

Congress passed the Comstock Act that prohibited the mailing of obscene literature. The law made it illegal to send any obscene, lewd, and/or lascivious materials through the mail, including contraceptive devices and information, banned contraceptives, and banned the distribution of information on abortion for educational purposes.

The financial Panic began with the failure of the firm Jay Cooke and Company. A 5-year depression resulted from the effects of over-trading, over-production and over-speculation—as well as by excessive issues of paper money, which caused inflation. The stock market crashed and was closed for 10 days as 37 banks and brokerage houses went under. Other businesses were affected, in particular, the Northern Pacific Railroad, which was forced to shut down its operations. The Secretary of the Treasury W. D. Richardson released $26 million in Greenbacks as legal tender to expand credit in an attempt to stabilize the situation. Despite this infusion of liquidity, thousands of businesses failed, hundreds of banks failed and hundreds of thousands of people were left without jobs. President Grant addressed the Congress in an attempt to allay the fears of the economic downturn. He called for legislation, a return to species payments and more mining of gold.

An American steamer *Virginius*, which was headed for Cuba with munitions and men to assist the insurgents there, was captured by a Spanish gunboat. Its 61 passengers, including 8 Americans, were executed before the Spanish government could intervene.

Significant Events: 1874

The government of Hawaii signed a treaty with the United States granting exclusive trading rights.

The Legal Tender Act was passed by Congress, but was vetoed by President Grant, and then was passed over his veto. The law added $18 million of Greenbacks to the money supply, thus adding to the inflationary effect.

The Poland Act was passed by Congress to facilitate the prosecution under the Merill Anti-Bigamy Act.

Congress passed the Anti-Moiety Act that repealed laws giving any shares of fines, penalties or forfeitures to informers or customs officials. The act also curtailed "fishing expeditions" by requiring a court order to produce corporate records.

Significant Events: 1875

The Specie Redemption Act was passed by Congress to provide for the exchange of gold for legal tender beginning in 1879.

The Hawaiian Reciprocity Treaty was signed between the Hawaiian government and the United States. One of its provisions was that no Hawaiian territory would be turned over to any third party—especially any European power.

The Tariff Act was passed by Congress to raise the rates by 10 percent.

The Civil Rights Act was passed by Congress to forbid discrimination in public accommodations and to prohibit exclusion of blacks from jury duty. Ben Butler had proposed an amendment to the original bill that would have compelled racial integration of all schools in the South, but President Grant had the amendment stricken out.

The Page Act was enacted by Congress to deal with immigrants from China and Japan. The law required migrants from Oriental countries to be processed at the point of departure by United States Consulates, with the right of denying entry to America for anyone found to be objectionable, such as prostitutes or forced Coolie laborers.

The Senate ratified a treaty with Hawaii, with a condition being that no third power could acquire any Hawaiian land.

The Supreme Court ruled in the case of *Minor v. Happersett* that the Fourteenth Amendment did not prevent a state from setting up suffrage requirements.

The Whisky Ring scandal was exposed in which several government officials were discovered to have been involved in extorting millions of dollars from distillers and diverting government taxes. The scandal touched President Grant since his personal secretary, Orville Babcock, was involved in the scheme¹.

Vice President Henry Wilson died in office.

Significant Events: 1876

Secretary of War William Belknap was exposed in his receipt of almost $25,000 in bribes for trading post privileges at Fort Sill in Indian Territory. The Senate began impeachment proceedings against him, but Belknap resigned to avoid prosecution since no jurisdiction existed over him once he was no longer in office.

Alexander Graham Bell received a patent for his invention of the telephone, an instrument that would change communication in America—and in the world.

The Supreme Court ruled in the case of *United States v. Cruikshank* that the Fourteenth Amendment only protected blacks from state action—not from individual actions infringing upon their rights.

Colorado became the 38th state to join the Union.

Samuel Tilden won the popular vote in the presidential election of 1876, but disputes over Electoral votes in the South forced the election to be resolved by Congress. In the decision made in h 1877, Rutherford Hayes was declared the winner.

Significant Events: 1877

The Electoral Commission Bill authored by Senator George Franklin Edmunds was passed by Congress² to resolve the disputed presidential election between Rutherford Hayes and Samuel Tilden. Its purpose was to regulate the counting of the Electoral College votes for President and Vice President to determine the winners who would be sworn into office in 1877. The President of the Senate then announced the election of Rutherford Hayes as President and William Wheeler as Vice President.

The Supreme Court ruled in the case of *Peik v. Chicago and Northwestern Railroad Company* that a state has the power to regulate intrastate and interstate traffic, which originates within its boundaries.

The Supreme Court ruled in the case of *Munn v. Illinois* that a state has the power to legislate warehouse and intrastate rates.

The Desert Land Act was passed by Congress to encourage the economic development of arid public lands of the western United States. It offered 640 acres at a cost of $1.25 per acre, with a promise to settle, irrigate and cultivate the land within 3 years of purchase.

Panic of 1873

Overview

The American economy entered a crisis in 1873. This followed a period of post-Civil War economic overexpansion that arose from the Northern railroad boom. The crisis came at the end of a series of economic setbacks: the Black Friday panic of 1869, the Chicago fire of 1871, the outbreak of equine influenza in 1872, and the demonetization of silver in 1873. The Panic of 1873 was the start of a very long and severe economic depression in the United States that lasted until 1879. The downturn in the United States started with the bankruptcy of the Philadelphia banking firm of Jay Cooke & Company in 1873.

The Panic of 1873 hit the country hard, and President Grant never attempted decisive action to alleviate the ensuing distress. The first law that he had signed in 1869 established the value of the greenback currency issued during the Civil War, and pledged to redeem the bills in gold. In 1874, he vetoed a bill to increase the amount of legal tender currency, which in turn defused the currency crisis on Wall Street—but it did not help the economy. The ensuing depression led to Democratic victories in the 1874 elections, and they took control of the House of Representatives. By 1875, the Grant administration was in disarray, and with the Democrats in control of the House, President Grant was unable to get any legislation passed.

Failure of Jay Cooke & Company

In 1873, Jay Cooke & Company, a major financier for the United States during the Civil War, was unable to market several million dollars in Northern Pacific Railway bonds. Cooke's firm, like many others, invested heavily in the railroads by underwriting the construction of railroads—especially the Northern Pacific Railway. At a time when investment banks were anxious for more capital for their enterprises, President Grant's monetary policy of contracting the money supply made matters worse. While businesses were expanding, the money that the company needed to finance that growth was becoming scarcer.

Cooke and other entrepreneurs had planned to build the nation's second transcontinental railroad, called the Northern Pacific Railway. Cooke's firm provided the financing, and ground was broken near Duluth, Minnesota for the line in 1870. But just as Cooke was about to swing a $300 million government loan in 1873, reports circulated that the firm's credit had become nearly worthless. In 1873, the firm suspended payments and then declared bankruptcy.

The failure of the Jay Cooke bank, followed quickly by that of Henry Clews, set off a chain reaction of bank failures and temporarily closed the New York stock market. Factories began to lay off workers as the United States slipped into a depression. The effects of the panic were quickly felt in New York City where prices plummeted on the New York Stock Exchange, which then closed for 10 days in 1873.

The Economic Effect

The economic downturn gradually spread to Chicago, Illinois; Virginia City, Nevada; and San Francisco, California. A total of 18,000 businesses failed between 1873 and 1875, and unemployment reached 14% by 1876. Construction work lagged, wages were cut, real estate values fell and corporate profits vanished. Of the country's 364 railroads, 89 went bankrupt, and hundreds of banks went out of business. The unemployed began to move about the country seeking jobs—in particular, to the west—and bread lines began to appear in the cities. The ensuing wage cuts and poor working conditions among American railroad workers resulted in the Great Railroad Strike of 1877, preventing the trains from moving, especially in Pennsylvania and Chicago. President Rutherford Hayes sent in federal troops in an attempt to stop the strikes. Fights between strikers and troops killed more than 100 and left many more injured.

As the panic deepened, ordinary Americans suffered terribly. Between 1873 and 1877, as many smaller factories and workshops shut their doors, tens of thousands of workers became transients. Relief rolls exploded in major cities, with a 25% rate of unemployment—about 100,000 workers—in New York City alone. Unemployed workers demonstrated in Boston, Massachusetts; Chicago, Illinois; and New York City, New York in 1873, demanding public work. In New York City's Tompkins Square in 1874, police attacked the crowd with clubs and beat up thousands of men and women. The most violent strikes in American history occurred, including those led by the secret labor group known as the Molly Maguires in Pennsylvania's coal fields in 1875. Masked workmen exchanged gunfire with the "Coal and Iron Police," a private force commissioned by the state. A nationwide railroad strike followed in 1877, in which mobs destroyed railway hubs in Pittsburgh, Pennsylvania; Chicago, Illinois; and Cumberland, Maryland.

The Political Effect

The poor economic conditions caused American voters to turn against the Republican Party. In the 1874 congressional elections, the Democrats assumed control of the House. Public opinion during the period made it difficult for the Grant Administration to develop a coherent policy regarding the Southern states. The North began to steer away from Reconstruction, and as the Southern states became controlled by the Democrats, African-Americans found that they could no longer pursue activist policies of reform. Retrenchment was also a common response of Southern states to state debts during the depression. As funds were cut from state governments, education suffered, despite being an integral part of blacks' hopes for social reform. Finally, the election of the Republican Rutherford Hayes as President in the disputed election of 1876 led to the end of Reconstruction in 1877.

Aftermath

Further effects happened in 1877 in the form of a crash in the market for lumber, resulting in the bankruptcy of several leading Michigan lumbering concerns—with the effects of the resulting second business slump reaching California in 1878. The rift between workers and the leaders of banking and manufacturing interests lingered on after the depression ended in 1879.

For the largest manufacturing companies in the United States—those with guaranteed contracts and the ability to make rebate deals with the railroads—the depression years were golden. Andrew Carnegie, Cyrus McCormick, and John D. Rockefeller had enough capital reserves to finance their own continuing growth. However, for smaller industrial firms that relied on seasonal demand and outside capital, the situation was dire. As capital reserves dried up, so did their industries, and they failed. Carnegie and Rockefeller then bought out their competitors at fire-sale prices, and created an industrial concentration of wealth—thus beginning the Gilded Age in the United States.

Rutherford Hayes

Election of 1876

In the election of 1876, Rutherford Hayes was opposed by Samuel Tilden. When the first returns seemed to confirm that Tilden had the lead, Hayes assumed that he had lost. But, the Republican National Chairman wired leaders to stand firm. Key Ohio Republicans like James Garfield and the Democrats agreed at a Washington hotel on the Wormley House Agreement by which Southern Democrats were given assurances, in the Compromise of 1877, that if Hayes became President, he would pull federal troops out of the South and end the Reconstruction effort. The Republicans promised Southern Democrats at least one Cabinet post, Federal patronage, and subsidies for internal improvements. The Electoral votes from 4 disputed states (Oregon, Louisiana, Florida and South Carolina) were thrown out by a special Electoral Commission, with Hayes receiving 185 Electoral votes and Tilden 184 Electoral votes, with Hayed being elected as President in a compromise decision.

Significant Events: 1877

The last federal troops were withdrawn from South Carolina and Louisiana, marking the end of Reconstruction.

Because of continued depredations by Mexican marauders across the Rio Grande River into Texas, orders were issued to General Edward Ord by President Hayes to follow these marauders into Mexico to punish them and to retake stolen property. Although Mexico protested the action, the President of Mexico sent a cabinet minister and troops to the border, and an amicable arrangement was made for cooperation with General Ord in protecting the frontier.

A railroad strike began in West Virginia over a dispute caused by cuts in wages by the Baltimore and Ohio Railroad. The strike spread to Maryland where riots ensued that prompted President Hayes to send in federal troops to stop the violence after 10 strikers were killed by the state militia. The strike also spread to Pennsylvania where strikers in Philadelphia battled the local militia in a riot situation that again had to be quelled by federal troops.

Criminal proceedings were started at New Orleans, Louisiana against 4 members of the returning board for elections for turning in forged and counterfeit returns that had increased the votes for Hayes and decreased the votes for Tilden during the 1876 presidential election. One member was found guilty and was sentenced to 2 years in the penitentiary, but upon appeal to the Supreme Court the verdict was set aside in a ruling delivered by Chief Justice Manning, and he was discharged.

President Hayes asked Congress to revise the rules for Civil Service appointments to avoid the evils of the spoils system.

Significant Events: 1878

The Women's Suffrage Amendment was introduced by Senator Aaron Sargent, but was defeated by the Senate

In the case of *Hall v. Cuir*, the Supreme Court found that railroads did not need to provide equal accommodations for all passengers regardless of race or color.

Congress ratified a treaty between the United States and Samoa by which the harbor of Pago Pago was given to the United States Navy as a coal refueling station.

The Bland-Allison Act was passed by Congress to require the Treasury to buy silver and to place it in circulation as silver dollars'. President Hayes vetoed the act, but Congress passed it over his veto'. This act brought the undervalued silver dollar into the monetary system as the Treasury Department began to purchase $2 million worth of silver on a monthly basis to coin it into dollars.

President Hayes signed the Quarantine Act to give the Marine Hospital Service the responsibility to stop disease from coming ashore via sailors from ships.

Congress passed the Timber and Stone Act to sell land that was deemed unfit for farming to those who wanted to log or mine it. The land was sold as 160-acre parcels at $2.50 an acre.

Congress passed the *Posse Comitatus* Act to limit the federal government powers to use the military for law enforcement—except where authorized by the Constitution or by Congress.

The District of Columbia received a permanent constitution from Congress although its residents would not be permitted to vote in either local or national elections.

Congress established the Life-Saving Service as part of the Treasury Department. Its purpose is to render assistance from the shore to victims of shipwrecks.

The Halifax Commission announced the Halifax Fishery Award by which it granted to Great Britain the sum of $5.5 million from the United States as compensation for fishing privileges in Canadian waters.

Significant Events: 1879:

Congress passed the Arrears of Pensions Act to authorize the back-payment of military pensions starting from the date of discharge, with payments being made to families in cases where the veteran was already dead.

Species payments were resumed by the United States to prevent currency from being in an unsettled state.

President Hayes signed a bill that was passed by Congress that allowed female attorneys to argue cases before the Supreme Court.

Congress created the Geological Survey bureau to study the landscape, natural resources and natural hazards of the United States.

Congress passed a bill to restrict Chinese immigration into the United States because it was deemed detrimental to the best interests of the United States to have an unrestricted flow of immigrants from China. However, President Hayes vetoed the bill on the grounds that it violated the Burlingame Treaty of 1868, which guaranteed the Chinese free access to the United States. Congress failed to overturn the veto.

President Hayes vetoed an army appropriations bill because he was against the use of the army to insure the peace at the polls. President Hayes vetoed another election bill specifically passed by Congress because he was against any military interference at the polls.

Congress created the Mississippi River Commission consisting of 7 members to be appointed by the President to improve the navigability of the river.

President Hayes signed the bill passed by Congress to make appropriations for the legislative and executive expenses of the government.

President Hayes vetoed a bill for appropriations for the judicial department passed by Congress because it made it impossible for him as President to execute laws that he had been sworn to uphold. President Hayes vetoed a second judicial appropriations bill passed by Congress because it excluded payment of fees for United States marshals and their deputies. President Hayes exercised plenary power to execute the law—and to pay the federal marshals and deputies.

President Hayes asked Congress to revise the rules for the reform of Civil Service appointments.

Significant Events: 1880

In the case of *Strauder v. West Virginia* the Supreme Court ruled that it was unconstitutional to exclude blacks from jury duty.

Hayes declared that the policy of United States was for a canal to be constructed across the Isthmus of Panama. The insistence by President Hayes on American control helped shape the policy that eventually produced a Panama Canal that was owned by the United States.

James Garfield won the 1880 election for President with 214 Electoral votes. Chester Arthur was chosen as Vice President.

President Hayes appointed 3 commissioners to Peking, China to meet with commissioners designated by the Emperor of China. As a result of these negotiations, the Chinese Exclusion Treaty was signed by China and the United States to permit the United States to regulate, limit or suspend the immigration of Chinese laborers into the United States. Another treaty was concluded to improve the commercial relations of the two countries, and to forbid the opium trade.

Significant Events: 1881

In the case of *Springer v. United States* the Supreme Court ruled that income tax laws were constitutional.

The End of Reconstruction

Takeover by the Southern States

The end of Reconstruction occurred between 1873 and 1877, and is referred to as Redemption: a period in which Southern conservatives and Democrats—who called themselves "Redeemers"—defeated the Radical Republicans and regained control of each Southern state. Instead of complying with federal requirements, the Southern states disenfranchised blacks through various means. They accomplished this by redistricting voting regions to crowd blacks into a single place, changing polling places to make the locations further away and less accessible, making voter registration very difficult through questionnaires, by imposing literacy tests and complex forms, by the exclusion of blacks through grandfather clauses, imposing residency requirements, and by eliminating black neighborhoods as voting districts. Other ways that were used included delaying voting until almost closing time thereby causing many to not be able to vote, through postponement of elections, by gerrymandering of voting districts to minimize or neutralize black voting impact, and by legal challenges—and even harassment—at the polls. Still other tactics that were used included making local offices appointive rather than elective, by extension of terms of office for white incumbents, and by the introduction of unreasonable poll, education, property or county taxes. In addition, voting was changed to be done on the basis of the white population alone, and only white persons were allowed to vote or to hold office. Also, blacks were not allowed to serve on juries or to testify in court cases where whites were involved.

Actions by Former Confederate States

Almost all actions in Southern states were done from the point of view of renewed white supremacy. Black Codes were instituted in the South to incorporate capital punishment, vagrancy, permission to whip black servants, apprenticeship requirements and employment restrictions—all of which created a caste system for blacks. The Black Codes included the enacting of laws that applied the same penal and criminal laws that had formerly been enacted for slaves. The Black Codes also required that blacks have a home, be employed and have a license to work. Even a pass system was instituted to hold blacks on a plantation or to otherwise restrict their movements. Restrictions against owning firearms were also instituted. Consequently, blacks were forced to leave most of the lands that had been appropriated to them, and to make labor contracts instead with the former landholders. As a result of this fraudulent action, thousands of blacks left the South.

Under the Reconstruction Law of 1867 that was passed by Congress, blacks overwhelmingly voted for a new convention while the vast majority of whites abstained hoping that the new arrangement would fail. New constitutions were adopted for the Southern states. Murderous outbreaks and fraud occurred against freedmen. Blacks were deprived of any opportunity to own land—much less to exercise any political rights. The ruling barons were determined to not even recognize the abolition of slavery, and certainly not to grant any civil rights. The condition of freedmen became worse than when they had been slaves, especially as whites harbored ill will towards blacks as a result of having lost the war. Whites developed an intense dislike for blacks as a substitute for hating the federal government, and as a result many murders, shootings and whippings occurred—none of which were ever punished.

The presence of black troops in the state caused a certain amount of friction, and President Johnson promised to remove them. An explosion of violence ensued in which President Grant refused to use federal troops to fight back, Thus, a return to a second era of serfdom and virtual slavery occurred.

The state legislatures refused to permit intermarriages between blacks and whites, and did not take any action on black suffrage. State legislatures also passed subsequent laws that authorized racial segregation. Secret organizations to promote intimidation towards blacks were formed such as the Knights of the White Camellia, the Ku Klux Klan and the Innocents, with over 2,000 murders being committed against blacks. Political violence became endemic as the white militias formed new military organizations such as the White League. White League chapters arose in many parishes, receiving financing for weapons from wealthy white men to kill black people.

The Ku Klux Klan and the Red Shirts increased their activity, and began to commit murders, conduct whippings, burn buildings such as churches and schools, and otherwise intimidate blacks through terrorism. The Ku Klux Klan operated without any interference until the Ku Klux Klan Law was passed in 1869.

Government Actions

In 1873, President Grant ordered the Attorney General to suspend the prosecution of Ku Klux Klan members in South Carolina and North Carolina as a friendly overture. His hope was that Klansmen would be persuaded to reform by obeying the law and not resorting to violence. In 1874, President Grant pardoned Klansmen who had been sentenced for their atrocities. In 1977, President Hayes withdrew the last remaining Federal troops from the South. Shortly thereafter, the national Compromise of 1877 was reached with the Democrats by which all remaining federal troops were removed from the Southern states.

Since the North was tired of the insurgency, and because Democrats controlled most of the Southern legislatures—along with armed militias, which controlled small towns and rural areas in the South—the Federal government withdrew from enforcing Reconstruction efforts. The removal of the federal troops from the South gave the South free rein to pass disfranchising constitutions and statues. The result was that African-Americans were excluded by Jim Crow laws that imposed segregation in public facilities and transportation. In addition, state legislatures passed laws that reduced voting by blacks by creating new requirements for voter registration—as well as other restrictions on blacks—that catalyzed the movement to once again achieve a ruling white class in the South. The Ku Klux Klan now operated without any opposition and revived racial hatred with the lynching of blacks—a terror tactic that helped to significantly weaken the political power of Southern blacks.

In 1875, Congress passed the Civil Rights Act. The act asserted that no citizen could be denied equal use of public facilities or from serving on juries on the basis of color. This act was the last major reform law that was passed in the interest of equal civil rights. Nevertheless, the rights of blacks were greatly reduced by the actions of the Southern state governments, especially by laws that promoted injustice, condoned violence, and imposed white supremacy again. The Southern states acted with a fierce determination that was intended to reestablish slavery, oppose education for blacks, and re-impose political power that would be based on blacks not having the right to vote or hold office.

The federal government also contributed to the demise of civil rights by various actions taken by the Supreme Court. In 1875, in the case of the *United States v. Cruikshank*, the Supreme Court ruled that the only obligation of the United States government concerning the Fourteenth Amendment was to ensure that the states did not deny the rights and privileges to blacks. In 1876, in the case of the *United States v. Reese*, the Supreme Court ruled that the Fifteenth Amendment did not confer the right of suffrage, but only prohibited its exclusion on racial grounds. In 1882, the Supreme Court declared the Ku Klux Klan Act unconstitutional. In 1883, the Supreme Court declared the Civil Rights Act of 1875 to be unconstitutional, with a ruling that stated that the Fourteenth Amendment only forbid states—but not citizens—from discriminating. The Supreme Court also ruled that the Fourteenth Amendment gave Congress the power only to outlaw public—rather than private—discrimination. In 1896, in the case of *Plessy v. Ferguson*, the Supreme Court ruled that state-mandated segregation was legal as long as the law provided for "separate but equal" facilities. Decisions such as these set the stage for further discrimination in the South by fostering and perpetuating opinions and attitudes that justified these actions, and which contributed to media that perpetuated racial stereotypes. These contributed to an intense hatred of blacks—the remnants of which still persist to this day.

The End of Reconstruction

When whites in the South elected former Confederate leaders and military officers to state legislatures and to Congress starting in 1865, it signaled a beginning of reverting to the former social structure. Vagrant laws and Black Codes were enacted to confine the newfound freedom of blacks, and to restrict their economic labor to a level of peonage. In addition, laws were passed to limit the right of blacks for ownership, to restrict their freedom of movement, to deny them participation in the courts, and to make it very difficult for them to enter into contracts—all of which were intended to make them into second-class citizens. Thus, the end of Reconstruction came about as a result of these and other various events, including the collapse of federal enforcement in elections.

James Garfield

Election of 1880

In the 1880 presidential election, Garfield won by getting 214 Electoral votes Chester Arthur was elected as Vice President.

Significant Events: 1881

Postmaster General James presented President Garfield with the evidence of the star route mail frauds. President Garfield instructed James to prosecute all guilty persons— regardless of their party affiliation.

New York Senators Roscoe Conkling and Thomas Collier Platt resigned in objection to the appointment by President Garfield of Judge W. H. Robertson as New York City Customs Collector. Robertson was approved by the Senate, and the New York Legislature refused to re-nominate both Conkling and Platt as Senators.

President Garfield was shot by a lawyer who had expected to obtain a job in the administration and had been denied. President Garfield suffered from blood poisoning, and experienced severe stomach problems. President James Garfield died from complications of his bullet wound on September 19, 1881. Vice President Chester Arthur succeeded Garfield as President.

The Thumb fire in Michigan destroyed over 1 million acres of forest, caused a damage of almost $2.4 million, and killed 282 people.

Chester Arthur

President

After President Garfield was shot in July 1881, Arthur remained as Vice President, not wanting to assume any of the presidential duties from President Garfield. When President Garfield died on September 19, 1881, Chester Arthur became President.

Significant Events: 1881

Samuel Gompers founded the Federation of Organized Trades and Labor Unions of the United States, an organization that was the forerunner of the American Federation of Labor (AFL).

President Arthur addressed Congress, especially with the rebuilding of the Navy.

Secretary of State Blaine declared the Hawaiian Islands were part of the American system, which meant that they were protected under the Monroe Doctrine.

Significant Events: 1882

The Star Route mail frauds unfolded in the courts, as over 160 phony mail routes were uncovered in schemes that were perpetrated to obtain over $1 million in funds for operations that did not have enough business to warrant those amounts. A grand jury indicted 9 men, but after 2 separate trials, each defendant was acquitted in 1883.

Congress passed the Edmonds Act making polygamy a felony—an act aimed directly at the Mormon Church.

Congress voted for special pensions for the widows of Presidents Polk, Tyler and Garfield, giving each of them an allowance of $5,000 per year, and established a precedent for future widows of Presidents.

The Senate ratified the Geneva Convention of 1864, which provided the guidelines for the care of wounded military personnel who had been captured.

The Chinese Exclusion Act was passed by Congress to restrict Chinese labor immigration into the United States. The law excluded skilled and unskilled laborers as well as Chinese workers employed in mining from entering the country for 10 years. The act also affected Chinese immigrants who were already in the United States by making them permanent aliens—thus excluding 375,000 of them who had emigrated to the United States from becoming citizens.

A 9-man Tariff Commission to be appointed by the President was authorized by Congress to protect American businesses. The Taft Commission recommended tariff reductions averaging between 20% and 25%, and in some cases even 40% to 50%.

A treaty of friendship and commerce between Korea and the United States was signed.

President Arthur vetoed a bill passed by Congress to create safety and health standards for steamships bringing immigrants to the United States.

Congress passed a Bank Charter Extension Act to authorize any national bank, at any time within 2 years prior to the date of the expiration of its corporate existence, to extend its period of succession for 20 years by amending its articles of association.

Congress passed the Immigration Act to levy a 50-cent tax on all aliens landing at United States ports. The act also gave power to port authorities to selectively deny entry to convicts, lunatics, idiots and any other persons considered to have the potential to become public charges.

Congress authorized a $19 million Rivers and Harbors Bill for public works, but it was vetoed by President Arthur as a "pork barrel" project. However, Congress was able to override the veto.

Significant Events: 1883

Congress passed the Pendleton Civil Service Reform Act, which established the United States Civil Service Commission. The act placed federal employees on a merit system with competitive exams to mark the end of the spoils system in awarding federal jobs based on party affiliation.

Congress passed a Tariff Act to reduce the annual Treasury surpluses to discourage reckless government spending. Excise taxes were removed—except for those on liquor and tobacco—but an increase in protective tariffs ensued nevertheless, thus causing Treasury surpluses to continue.

Congress passed The Navy Act, which provided for the construction of 3 protected cruisers and a dispatch boat. This marked the rebuilding of the Navy whose ships were obsolete in a fleet that was diminished by over 90% of what it had been at the end of the Civil War.

In a group of 5 cases' consolidated into a single issue, the Supreme Court declared that the Civil Rights Act of 1875 was unconstitutional. The Supreme Court stated that Congress lacked the constitutional authority under the Thirteenth and Fourteenth Amendments to outlaw racial discrimination by private individuals and organizations, thus vitiating the original intent of the law.

The United States instituted 5 standard continental time zones to create a uniform system across the country: Alaska, Pacific, Mountain, Central and Eastern. The system was created by the railroads to eliminate the confusion caused by printed schedules based on local times. The prime meridian of longitude was also assigned as that passing through the British Royal Observatory located at Greenwich, England.

Significant Events: 1884

The Supreme Court ruled that Congress had the power to make Treasury notes.

Severe riots broke out in Cincinnati because of lax administration of justice. A mob caused the city to be thrown into complete disorder that was finally quelled by state militia—but only after 45 people had been killed and 125 were wounded.

Gold was found in Alaska, which attracted many miners into the territory. Congress extended the laws of Oregon to cover Alaska to establish a government since statehood was not yet an option.

The Bureau of Labor was created as part of the Department of the Interior.

The cornerstone for the pedestal for the Statue of Liberty was laid at Bedloe's Island in New York Harbor.

Secretary of the Navy Chandler ordered the establishment of the Naval War College. It was established at Newport, Rhode Island to train naval officers in naval science and warfare. Chandler also set up the Office of Naval Intelligence.

Grover Cleveland won as President by an Electoral College vote of 219. Thomas Hendricks became the Vice President by getting 219 Electoral votes.

The Frelinghuysen-Zavala Treaty between the United States and Nicaragua was signed to conclude an agreement to build a canal across Nicaragua.

Frelinghuysen and the Hawaiian Minster signed a reciprocity treaty between the United States and Hawaii. But, it was only two years later under the Cleveland administration that an extension of the treaty was arrived at—one that called for a naval base to be established at Pearl Harbor.

Significant Events: 1885

The Senate failed to ratify the treaty to authorize the building of a canal across Nicaragua.

Congress passed the Foran Act to further restrict immigration, which industry had been using to break up strikes. This law did not apply to skilled laborers for new industries, or to other select groups such as servants and actors.

Congress passed an act prohibiting the fencing of public lands in the West.

The Washington Monument was finished and dedicated by President Arthur in Washington, D.C.

President Arthur nominated former President Ulysses S. Grant to be placed on the Army retired list with the rank and full pay of general. Congress passed a bill in 1885 for this, which President Arthur signed.

Grover Cleveland—I

The Election of 1884

In 1884, Grover Cleveland won as President with an Electoral College vote of 219. Thomas Hendricks became the Vice President.

Significant Events: 1885

The United States abrogated the fisheries reciprocity section of the 1871 Treaty of Washington with Great Britain.

Vice President Thomas Hendricks died.

Significant Events: 1886

A Presidential Succession Act was passed by Congress to change the order of succession in case of the death or any other event that would make a President unable to govern. The order was still having the Vice President be first in succession, but then he would be followed by the heads of the executive departments in the order of their creation, making the Secretary of State the first in line after the Vice President.

Riots occurred against Chinese aliens living in Seattle, Washington that necessitated the use of federal troops to restore order. Over 400 Chinese aliens were forcibly ejected from their homes.

In the case of *Yick Wo v. Hopkins* the Supreme Court ruled that municipal ordinances that discriminated against Chinese laundries were a violation of the Fourteenth Amendment.

The Chicago Haymarket Square riot occurred as a result of a labor rally. 8 persons were tried on charges of conspiring to kill, and were convicted for a bomb that had exploded during the riot, which killed 7 officers and wounded 60 others. 4 of these men were hanged, one committed suicide, 2 were sentenced to life imprisonment, and one was given 15 years. In 1893, the Governor of Illinois pardoned the 3 men that were still in jail.

In the case of *Santa Clara County v. Southern Pacific Railroad* the Supreme Court ruled that a corporation is a person under the provisions of the Fourteenth Amendment. The ruling conferred the privileges of citizenship to corporations—but without demanding the moral responsibility expected of a person.

Congress passed legislation to recognize the Division of Forestry, which had been created as part of the Department of Agriculture in 1881 to study forests and the future supply of timber in America.

Congress approved the incorporation of trade unions.

The Statue of Liberty was unveiled and dedicated by President Cleveland in a ceremony that was held on Bedloe's Island in celebration of 100 years of American independence.

In the case of *Wabash, St. Louis and Pacific Railway Company v. Illinois*, the Supreme Court ruled that a state could not regulate an interstate railroad that went through its territory.

The American Federation of Labor was organized by Samuel Gompers and Adolph Strasser.

Significant Events: 1887

The Senate ratified the renewal of an 1875 treaty between Hawaii and the United States, including the guarantee for building a naval base at Pearl Harbor.

President Cleveland vetoed the Dependent Pension Bill passed by Congress to provide a pension for all honorably discharged veterans with at least 90 days of service.

Congress passed the Interstate Commerce Act to set up a commission to regulate railroads.

Congress passed the Dawes Severalty Act to replace the Indian reservation system by parceling out tracts of land to individual Indians.

Congress passed the Electoral Count Act to prevent another disputed election like the Hayes-Tilden election of 1876. The act made each state the absolute judge over appointment or returns in accordance with its own electoral laws. It gave the power for Congress to intervene only in cases where the state was unable to decide an outcome— and only if both the Senate and House agreed; otherwise, the governor of the state in dispute would certify the Electoral count.

The Hatch Act was passed by Congress to provide federal subsidies to establish agricultural research and experiment stations in each state with a land grant college.

The Tenure of Office Act passed was repealed by Congress.

President Cleveland vetoed the Texas Seed Bill that authorized federal assistance to buy seed to help farmers in Texas who had been affected by a drought.

Significant Events: 1888

The Bayard-Chamberlain Treaty was signed to end the fishing dispute between Canada and the United States.

The secret ballot was adopted by Kentucky for elections, and was patterned after the Australian system. All states followed suit except South Carolina.

Congress established the Department of Labor.

Congress forbade the return of any Chinese laborers who had left the United States.

Congress passed a law that allowed the government to offer arbitration and conciliation services in contract/labor disputes.

Benjamin Harrison was elected as President with 233 electoral votes. Levi Morton was elected as Vice President.

Significant Events: 1889

The Department of Agriculture was raised to a Cabinet status by Congress.

The Enabling Act was passed by Congress to authorize the framing of constitutions in North Dakota, South Dakota, Montana and Washington in order to be admitted as states into the Union.

The Statue of Liberty

Liberty Enlightening the World

The Statue of Liberty was presented by France to the United States in 1886 to honor the friendship between the two nations. Since that time it has come to be recognized by the world as a symbol that expresses the concept and ideals of personal freedom. Hundreds of thousands of people in France and the United States contributed hundreds of thousands of dollars to the construction of the statue. Subsequently, millions more have contributed millions of dollars to ensure the continued existence of the statue. The Statue of Liberty is located at Liberty Island in New York Harbor, and has become a welcoming symbol to all visitors, immigrants, and returning Americans. As one of the most recognizable icons of the United States, it represents liberty and escape from oppression.

Background

Discussions near Versailles, France over a suitable gift to the United States to mark the Centennial of the American Declaration of Independence were headed by the French politician Edouard Rene Lefevbre de Laboulaye. It was he who first suggested the idea of a monument as a tribute to American independence—and to provide a beacon of promise to this ideal. One of Laboulaye's guests was an artist, Frederic Auguste Bartholdi who had earned a reputation as a sculptor of monuments. He was inspired by the concept of a project of such magnitude, and he became obsessed[1] by the idea.

While on a visit to Egypt, Bartholdi was inspired by the project of the Suez Canal. He envisioned a giant lighthouse standing at the entrance to the canal and drew plans for it. It would be patterned after the Roman goddess Libertas, modified to resemble a robed Egyptian peasant, with light beaming out from both a headband and a torch thrust dramatically upward into the skies. Bartholdi presented his plans to the Egyptian Khedive in 1867, but the project was never commissioned.

In 1871, Bartholdi was again invited to dinner at Laboulaye's house. Bartholdi reminded his friends of the upcoming centennial of American independence in 1876. He proposed the idea of a monument to be funded by both France and the United States that would be designed to promote the concept of liberty. Bartholdi volunteered to journey to America to explore the possibility and to think of a design for the image of a statue.

Bartholdi traveled to New York City in 1871. As his ship sailed through the Verrazano Narrows into the Upper Bay, he noticed an island that was situated as a gateway to America. The site for what he considered the ideal setting was Bedloe's Island. Through the inspiration gathered from finding the location, Bartholdi visualized the statue and produced a sketch. Originally, his statue portrayed Lady Liberty with a broken vase in her left hand as an ancient symbol of slavery, but later he substituted a tablet instead.

Once he had a design for the statue, Bartholdi visited several influential Americans in the hopes of eliciting their help in actualizing the idea into reality[3]. He returned to France in

1871 to meet with Laboulaye and his friends to tell them what he had decided to build. Through the encouragement of his friends, and with some introductory financial support, Bartholdi was commissioned to design a suitable sculpture for 1876 to commemorate the 100-year celebration of America's independence—a symbol that would denote liberty, truth, justice, reason and the law.

Bartholdi kept refining his models for the statue while Laboulaye extended his influence to create enthusiasm for the project. In 1875, the French-American Union was formed to generate funds so that work could begin on the project. For the next few years the statue was worked on at a Paris company workshop that was experienced in the technique of copper repousse, which is what Bartholdi wanted to use for the statue.

Building the Design

Bartholdi and the engineers that he worked with made extensive calculations for forces concerning gravity, wind resistance and other physical factors that would affect the statue in its proposed location. They determined that a thickness equal to 2 pennies placed face to face would meet all the requirements for the skin. Bartholdi made the decision to build his statue to a height of 151 feet. He first engaged the architect Eugene Emmanuel Viollet-le-Duc whose design was to have supporting elements of compartments filled with sand. Viollet-le-Duc died in 1879 before his idea was implemented, and so Bartholdi consequently hired an engineer, Alexandre Gustave Eiffel, whose reputation was that of building bridges by using iron pylons.

Eiffel designed the interior framework of the statue—the armature—with main components made out of flexible iron pylons. He worked for 4 years figuring out the connections of the pylon to the statue that would provide maximum support, and yet be flexible enough to adjust quickly to variable conditions of heat, cold and wind that the statue would be subjected to in the New York harbor. He conceived of a system of light iron truss work designed like a web that would reach out from the pylon structure to the many points on the skin of the statue. The slender strips of iron would line the inside of the skin, and be riveted to it, such that they would hold everything in place. The ends of the truss work would then be bolted to these strips to link the skin to the armature. However, since the iron and the copper could not be allowed to come into direct contact, since they would interact harmfully through galvanic action, he insulated the iron strap work from the skin with a layer of asbestos that had been impregnated with shellac. And, to deal with the supporting framework for the arm and the torch, Eiffel designed a 65-foot girder that was firmly anchored to the upper level of the pylon structure. The statue was also grounded against lightning. The statue was completed in 1884.

Funding

The funding by the French was for the statue only, an effort that began in 1875. The French-American Union raised 40,000 francs in its initial fund-raiser event. It also sent out 14,000 subscription blanks that returned pledges of almost 200,000 francs. Some 181 French cities and towns contributed, including the city of Paris. In addition, the firm of

Japy Freres provided all of the copper that was needed for the exterior of the statue. Furthermore, a lottery was done that sold 300,000 tickets at the price of one franc apiece. And, even copies of a 4-foot clay model were sold for 3,000 francs apiece. Other fund-gathering events included various forms of entertainment, especially the notable performances of *La liberte eclairant le monde* (Liberty enlightening the world) by the French composer Charles Gounod at the Paris Opera. By 1881, the necessary sum of 2,250,000 francs to build the statue had been acquired.

The funding by the Americans was for the pedestal upon which the statue would rest. Initially there was not much interest for the project in America, and the American Committee for the Statue of Liberty got very little response from the American public in terms of donations. Despite the lack of money, the committee appointed American architect Richard Morris Hunt to design the pedestal. With inputs from Bartholdi concerning the statue, Hunt created a detailed plan. However, because of lack of funds, the plan was not finished until 4 years later.

Initially, the Philadelphia Exposition in 1876, where the completed forearm and torch were exhibited, helped to bring in donations. The forearm and torch were then moved to New York City where they were exhibited for 7 years in Madison Square Park, which also brought in some donations. The lottery in France sold tickets in America too, and copies of the statue were sold in America for $300 apiece. Money was obtained from some wealthy Americans like banker Joseph Drexel, financier John Jacob Astor, philanthropist Peter Cooper, tobacconist Pierre Lorillard, circus tycoon P.T Barnum, industrialist Andrew Carnegie, and Ambassador Levi Morton.

The New York Legislature introduced a bill to authorize aid in building the pedestal in the amount of $50,000, but New York Governor Grover Cleveland vetoed the bill. Congress introduced a grant of $100,000 for the remaining costs that President Chester Arthur had approved as part of a larger appropriations bill. However, in subsequent negotiations to resolve differences between the House and the Senate, the appropriation for the statue was dropped from consideration. By 1884, funds were so low that further work was suspended when the height of the pedestal was only 15 feet—far below its planned height of 75 feet.

The newspaper magnate Joseph Pulitzer initiated his own fund drive in 1883 through his publication, the *New York World*, in which he stated that contributions would be accepted in any amount. This drive did not fare very well, and in 1885 he launched a new drive to raise $100,000 that was needed to finish the job, with the paper giving $1,000 to start things off. To entice contributors, Pulitzer promised that he would print the name of every person who donated—no matter how small the amount. The response proved to be phenomenal as collections were taken up in schools, bars and saloons, and individually by army veterans, immigrants, poker clubs, by members of the stock exchange, and by racing, athletic and entertainment events. Even the *New York Times* pitched in with $150. By 1885, the needed goal of $100,000 was reached—with 80% of the sum being received in separate amounts that were each less than one dollar.

Building the Pedestal

The task of building the pedestal began with the very large excavation of 30 feet in depth into which tons of concrete would be poured to form the foundation. It took 8 months to finish it, with the final form being a stepped pyramid that was 53 feet in depth and which contained 12,000 cubic feet of concrete—the largest concrete block in existence at the time: 65 square feet weighing 24,000 tons. The pedestal, which was to be built partly out of granite and partly out of stone, was to be placed on top of this concrete block, and would have a height of 89 feet.

The design was a square with a Doric frieze, a triple balcony, and 40 shields—each of which represented one of the 40 states that were in the Union at that time. Some of the granite blocks were placed so that they projected slightly from the pedestal's surface to give it a checkerboard appearance. The pedestal walls were built to be 17½ feet thick at the base, and then tapered to a thickness of only 6 feet at the top, covering 45 square feet at the base of the statue. The last block was laid in 1886.

Completing the Project

The work on the statue was completed in 1884. In 1885, Bartholdi announced that the statue was ready to be shipped to America. The parts of the statue were dismantled into 350 different pieces and packed into 214 separate huge crates that were loaded aboard the French warship *Isere*. In 1885, the *Isere* sailed from Rouen, France to the New York harbor. The dismantled statue and support framework required reassembly to be erected on the pedestal—at an additional cost of about $20,000. General Stone asked that one or more wealthy individuals contribute, but it was President Grover Cleveland who asked Congress for funds to set up the statue, and they passed a $56,500 appropriation bill to complete the task.

The iron pylon was erected and the secondary armature was set in place. The copper plates were then riveted to the iron strap work, with 300,000 copper rivets being required for the whole structure. The statue was anchored to the pedestal by 4 massive steel beams at the bottom of the pedestal walls and by 4 more steel beams at the top. The upper and lower beams were themselves connected by powerful steel girders that ran along the inside of the walls. Finally, the pylon was joined to both the upper and lower beams with enormous bolts.

When finished, the statue stood at a height of 154 feet (306 feet from sea level to the tip of the torch), and weighed approximately 225 tons. The gala inauguration took place on October 28, 1886, with almost 20,000 people who took part in a parade along 5th Avenue in New York City. President Grover Cleveland gave the speech of inauguration, and the poet John Greenleaf Whittier provided the dedication. 250 ships from the North Atlantic Squadron passed in review amidst various tugboats, steamers, ferries, yachts, dredges, freighter, dinghies, paddle-wheelers and sailboats that were also in the harbor.

Initial Function

The statue was originally designated to act as a lighthouse. However, a powerful lighting system would be required to illuminate with enough luminosity to be able to be seen from miles away. Edward H. Goff of the American Electric Manufacturing Company donated a plant capable of producing enough power for 20 lamps, each with 6,000 candlepower[11]. However, when the power plant and lighting system were installed, the output turned out to be very dim—and looked more like a glowworm rather than a beacon.

The federal government placed the statue in the care of the Lighthouse Board. The agency announced that it would place a new lens with powerful fixed lights. However, all of its efforts did not produce a viable navigation aid, and the statue remained essentially invisible at night. Congress was also reluctant to provide funds for the lighting system, and an appropriation of $50,000 in 1902 was defeated in the House. In the meantime, the statue was transferred by President Theodore Roosevelt from the Lighthouse Board to the War Department.

In May 1916, Ralph Pulitzer, the new editor of the *New York World*, pledged to raise $30,000 to implement a lighting system that would be specially designed by the General Electric Company. The Senate endorsed the idea and unanimously passed a bill to guarantee maintenance of the new plant. In 1916, President Woodrow Wilson participated in a gala ceremony that unveiled the new lighting system consisting of 246 floodlights placed at the 11 points of the star enclosing Fort Wood. The power was provided by an underwater cable that emanated from electric power sources on the mainland. Inside the torch were 15 electric lamps, each with 500 candlepower, hooked up to a series of flashers that shone through a powerful new lens. The torch was redesigned by Gutzon Borglum, who cut out sheet copper sections that formed the flame of the torch, and replaced them with 600 one-foot pieces of blue, amber, yellow and red tinted cathedral glass.

Symbolism

The Statue of Liberty's classical appearance—that of a Roman stola, with sandals and stoic facial expression—derives from Libertas, the ancient Roman goddess of freedom from slavery, oppression, and tyranny[18]. Her raised right foot is on the move to show that liberty and freedom are not standing still, but are instead moving forward as her left foot tramples the broken shackles at her feet—a symbolism of the freedom from oppression and tyranny. The 7 spikes on the crown (a halo) represent the earth's 7 seas and 7 continents, and her flaming torch in her right hand signifies enlightenment. The stone tablet in her left hand represents knowledge, the rule of law and reason, and it shows the date of the birth of the United States of America: July 4, 1776, which is expressed in Roman numbers (JULY IV MDCCLXXVI). Since 1903, the statue has been associated with Emma Lazarus's poem *The New Colossus*. It has symbolized freedom around the world[21], especially the 4 freedoms as featured in the 1943 stamp as a summation of President Franklin Roosevelt's 1941 summation of the aims of World War II—freedom of speech, of religion, from want and from fear.

Benjamin Harrison

The Election of 1888

Benjamin Harrison was elected President in the 1888 election by getting 233 Electoral votes. Levi Morton was chosen as Vice President.

Significant Events: 1889

Warships from Germany, Great Britain and the United States converged upon the harbor of Apia in the Samoan Islands in a confrontation over the civil war that was ongoing there. The United States backed King Malietoa, but the German forces had declared martial law over the entire area. In 1889, a tripartite protectorate was set up to oversee Samoa, with the treaty being ratified by the Senate in 1890. In 1890, Germany, Great Britain and the United States agreed to restore King Malietoa to the Samoan throne.

The first Pan American Congress was held in Washington, D. C.

The states of North Dakota, South Dakota, Washington and Montana were admitted to the Union.

Significant Events: 1890

The Knights of Labor and the American Federation of Labor consolidated to form the United Mine Workers to fight against the bad working conditions in the mines.

The American Women's Suffrage group and the National Women's Suffrage group consolidated to form the National American Women's Suffrage Association.

In the case of *Chicago, Milwaukee, and St. Paul Railroad v. Minnesota*, the Supreme Court ruled that a state cannot set fees so as to deny a reasonable profit.

In the case of *Leisy v. Hardin*, the Supreme Court ruled as unconstitutional state laws, which forbid package liquor from entering a state.

The Oklahoma Territory was created by Congress by redefining the existing Indian Territory.

The Federal Elections Bill proposed by Henry Cabot Lodge was introduced into the Senate, but failed to pass—even though the House approved it. The intent of the bill was to guarantee black suffrage from state obstruction.

The Sherman Anti-Trust Bill was introduced into the Senate. The bill was approved by the House and became law after President Harrison signed the bill. Its intent was to make illegal every contract, trust combination or other arrangement that would restrain trade of commerce—both foreign and domestic.

The states of Idaho and Wyoming were admitted to the Union.

Congress passed the Sherman Silver Purchase Act. The act called for the government to purchase 4,500,000 ounces of silver each month, with the Treasury issuing legal tender notes in payment for the silver.

Congress passed the Original Package Act to uphold a state's right to subject to its own laws the merchandising of goods from another state.

Congress passed the second Morrill Land Grant Colleges Act to require each state to show that race was not an admissions criterion, or else to designate a separate land-grant institution for persons of color.

Congress established Yosemite Park as a national park to prevent the flora and fauna from being destroyed by hunters and loggers.

Congress established the Sequoia National Park.

Congress passed the McKinley Tariff Act that raised tariffs to their highest level, but did provide for reciprocity agreements with other nations.

Congress created the Weather Bureau as part of the Department of Agriculture.

Significant Events: 1891

Congress established the Circuit Court of Appeals to lessen the workload of the Supreme Court on some of its appellate jurisdictions.

Congress created the Office of Superintendent of Immigration to deal with increasing immigration.

Congress passed the Forest Reserve Act under which President Harrison set aside 13 million acres of public land for use as a national forest reserve.

Congress passed the Land Revision Act that gave the President the authority to set aside and reserve any part of public lands covered with timber or undergrowth.

Congress adopted the International Copyright Act to protect the rights of foreign authors from piracy by American publishers.

An international incident with Chile almost resulted in a war with the United States. The incident happened when American sailors from the *USS Baltimore* went ashore and were attacked by a mob, resulting in 2 sailors being killed and several others wounded. Chile negotiated a settlement of $75,000 as payment to the American families of the slain and wounded.

Significant Events: 1892

Congress passed the Geary Chinese Exclusion Act to require registration of Chinese, adopt deportation regulations for those not authorized to remain in the United States, and to extend the existing exclusion laws for another 10 years.

A labor strike by 5,000 members of the Amalgamated Association of Iron and Steel Workers at the Andrew Carnegie's Homestead Steel Mill on the Monongahela River, Pennsylvania was confronted by 300 hired Pinkerton guards who were brought in to protect the mill. The result ended in 20 persons being killed and hundreds wounded— including all 300 Pinkerton detectives. To quell the disturbance, the Governor of Pennsylvania ordered 7,000 state troopers to step in. The strike then ended when workers were forced to call it off.

Congress authorized a $50 per month pension for all Civil War veterans who were wounded in service.

Congress authorized a pension of $8 per month to survivors of the Indian Wars that occurred between 1832 and 1842.

Congress authorized a pension of $12 per month to all women who served as nurses during the Civil War.

Grover Cleveland won the presidency with an electoral vote of 277. Adlai Stevenson was elected as Vice President.

Significant Events: 1893

United States Ambassador John Stevens and local planters led by Sanford Dole overthrew Hawaiian Queen Liliuokalini's government. Dole set up a revolutionary committee and occupied the government buildings with the help of 300 Marines who had been sent by President Harrison on the cruiser *Boston*. Ambassador Stevens recognized the new government, and negotiated a treaty of annexation with the new government. He then declared Hawaii to be a United States protectorate—without any authorization from President Harrison—and submitted a treaty of annexation of Hawaii to the Senate.

Congress passed the Diplomatic Appropriation Act to create the rank of Ambassador for the Foreign Service.

The End of Indian Civilization

The Forced Removal of the Indians

When President Jackson took office in 1829, over 125,000 Indians were living East of the Mississippi River—largely in the areas comprised by Georgia, Alabama and Mississippi. The question was whether these Indians would be allowed to block further expansion by white settlers, and whether the United States Government would continue to abide by previously made treaties—such as those that had been made with the Cherokees and Choctaws. In 1829, the Chippewa, Ottawa and Potawatomi Indians in the Michigan Territory ceded their lands to the United States. Then, in a precursory move, President Jackson issued an order in 1829 to the Creek Indians to either conform to the laws of Alabama or else to relocate West across the Mississippi River.

Since President Jackson favored the removal of all Indians, he shifted federal Indian policy by having Congress pass the Indian Removal Act of 1830. The purpose of this act was to remove the Indians from the Eastern part of the United States and to settle them West of the Mississippi River in territories that were outside the boundaries of the country, which allowed the United States government to take possession of their lands. In 1830, the Sioux, Sauk and Fox Indian tribes gave up their claim to lands in Iowa, Minnesota and Missouri. In 1830, the Choctaw Indians transferred 8 million acres of land located East of the Mississippi River to the United States in return for land located West of the Mississippi River in Oklahoma. By 1830, President Jackson proposed a policy of extinguishing all Indian title to lands within the national boundaries of the United States, and moving the tribes to an area West of the Mississippi River.

To accomplish the migration, the government militarily forced the Cherokees, Choctaws, Creeks, Chickasaws and Seminoles to move out of their land, and go to the land given to them in Oklahoma. President Jackson negotiated with the various Indian tribes by signing 94 different treaties, and gave them a guarantee of perpetual autonomy in the West as the strongest incentive for migration. The removal of the Indians began during President Jackson's presidency in the 1830s, and was continued under the presidency of Martin Van Buren. In 1838, President Van Buren assigned General Winfield Scott to the task of the removal of the Cherokee Indians by placing him in charge of 5 military regiments consisting of 7,000 soldiers. From 1838 to 1839, 17,000 Cherokee Indians were forcibly relocated, with 4,000 of them dying along the 1,200-mile trail to the Indian Territory in Oklahoma.

The removal was accomplished by apprehending the Indians at their homes by military squads. The military forces searched all possible hiding places where Indians might be located, but a few Indians escaped by moving to locations that could not easily be traversed by military troops. The military seized all weapons that were found, and herded the Indians to march them along miles of trails to designated military stockades where they were temporarily imprisoned. Because of unsanitary conditions at the stockades that were caused by overwhelming numbers of Indians being together, many of them became sick and died.

The surviving members of the 5 tribes were then embarked to the Western lands that had been promised to them on a journey that they termed "The Trail of Tears" because of the many hardships that were endured such as famine, disease and harsh living conditions. The tribes had to walk all day long, got very little rest and were subjected to prolonged exposures to inclement weather. The promised government assistance for food, clothing and transportation failed to arrive, and malnutrition, exposure, dysentery, fever, and a cholera epidemic affected many of their number. Several thousand Indians who traveled the 1,200-mile arduous trek across inhospitable terrain to the Indian Territory died along the way.

By 1840, 70,000 Indians had been moved West across the Mississippi River to be resettled on mostly semi-arid lands that were unsuited for farming. In the relocation of the 5 tribes to the West, 25 million acres of land East of the Mississippi River were opened to settlement by whites. The removal of the Indians by the confiscation of their lands by federal fiat left them hungry, homeless and destitute. Although the 5 affected tribes were severely damaged by the removal, each of them survived the ordeal — although they have struggled since then to attain a viable environment in which to thrive and further their individual cultures.

Other Actions

In 1831, the Sauk Indians made a treaty with the United States, to move out of the Rock River area of Illinois and across the Mississippi River, but a conflict ensued. In 1834, Congress set aside Oklahoma as Indian Territory for the residency of Indian tribes that were to be removed from other parts of the nation. It also established the Department of Indian Affairs, although it marked the ending of the United States government's past policy of education and civilization for the Indians.

In 1835, the Seminole Indians in Florida began the Second Seminole War to resist being removed West of the Mississippi River. In 1836, the Seminole Indians massacred General Wiley Thompson and his troops at Fort King, Florida, killing Major Dade and 100 of his men at Fort Brooke, Florida. In 1837, General Zachary Taylor defeated the Seminole Indians at Okeechobee Swamp, Florida, but the Second Seminole War continued until 1842.

In 1835, the Cherokee Indians agreed to give up all of their lands East of the Mississippi River for a sum of $5 million, and to move to a location West of the Mississippi River.

The tribal lands that were allocated to the Indians in the West were no more secure than Indian lands had been in the East. By 1851, Congress had passed the Indian Appropriations Act, which sought to concentrate the Western Indian population on reservations. This policy was adopted because most Americans regarded the Indian control of land and resources as an obstacle to expansion and as a threat to the nation's security. Only the advent of the Civil War in 1860 impeded any further migration.

In 1862, a Sioux uprising occurred in Minnesota. They burned houses and slaughtered 490 whites. General John Pope was sent in pursuit and he ordered General Henry Sibley to suppress the Sioux uprising. The Sioux Indians were defeated, put on trial in a military court, and 303 of them were sentenced to be hanged. President Lincoln reviewed all of these cases and overruled the execution sentences for all except 38 Indians who were hanged in 1862.

In 1864, a Union Army detachment attacked a Cheyenne Indian village at Sand Creek, Colorado. Several hundred innocent Indians were slain in an act of atrocity, which was geared towards ending the uprising of the Cheyenne Indians.

In 1866, the Sioux Indians defeated the forces of Colonel William Judd Fetterman at Fort Kearney near Bozeman in the Montana Territory, with 80 of his troops being killed, including him.

In 1868, the United States government acknowledged in a treaty with the Sioux Indians that the Black Hills of South Dakota were theirs forever, and that no white man could enter without Indian permission. However, gold was discovered in the 1870s, and white men began to trespass Indian lands without permission in their search for gold. The United States Army also made a reconnaissance for an armed invasion in 1874. By 1875, hundreds of miners were in the Black Hills, and no legal action was ever taken by the United States government to uphold the treaty.

In 1869, Congress passed an act to create the Board of Indian Commissioners to supervise all federal spending for Indian tribes. President Grant appointed a commissioner of Indian affairs, and appointed a Board of Indian Commissioners to provide independent advice on Indian policy. The board advised President Grant to abolish the treaty system as a means of dealing with the Indians, and to instead be a ward for their well-being.

In 1870, a resolution was submitted in the House to inquire whether under the Fourteenth Amendment, American Indians were considered as citizens of the United States. The resolution was referred to the Committee on the Judiciary for resolution, but no action was ever taken until 1924 when the Indians were finally recognized as citizens of the United States.

The Final Push

Until 1871, the federal government treated Indian tribes as sovereign but dependent nations by which the government accepted the responsibility to protect Indian lands. In 1871, Congress decided on a new course of signing no more treaties with the Indian tribes, and instead began a policy of breaking up the existing tribal structures. Thus, Congress passed the Indian Appropriations Act, which nullified all Indian treaties and declared all Indians to be wards of the government. One of the reasons for undertaking this policy was the hidden intent to gradually reduce—and eventually eliminate—the federal budget for Indian people.

Because the West was the last refuge for the Indians, they began to fight back. In 1870, the Piegan tribe in Montana attacked several pioneer settlements. The United States Army retaliated by killing nearly 200 members of the Piegan tribe. In 1872, in the Battle of Lost River in Oregon, Captain James Jackson, the commander of the federal troops, fought against the Modoc Indians, thus starting the Modoc War. In 1873, the First Battle of the Stronghold in California was fought by the Modoc tribe against United States troops, with 35 soldiers being killed. In 1873, in the Second Battle of the Stronghold in California, 7 United States soldiers were killed in a fight against the Modoc Indians. In 1873, the Modoc Indians killed General Edward Canby during peace negotiations in Oregon. The tribe was hunted down by the United States Army and Chief Kintpuash and six of his warriors were captured, tried as criminals and hanged. The rest of the tribe was forced to go to a reservation located in the Dakotas. Finally, after the Battle of Dry Lakes in California in 1873, United States Army troops finally captured the leader of the Modoc tribe and hanged him, The surviving band of Modoc Indians was then exiled to Indian Territory, thus ending the Modoc War.

In 1875, the Yavapai and Tonto Apache tribes were forced from the Verde Valley in Arizona to the San Carlos Apache Indian Reservation in Arizona by the United States Cavalry. In 1875, another Indian war erupted when the Sioux tribe was ordered to relinquish lands that had been given to them by an 1868 treaty north of the Platte River. The conflict ended in 1876 by the United States Army. However, in 1876, at the Battle of the Rosebud in the Montana Territory, Sioux and Cheyenne tribes defeated General United States forces.

In 1876, General George Custer and 209 of his men were ambushed and killed by Lakota, Cheyenne and Arapaho Indians at the Battle of Little Bighorn in the Black Hills of South Dakota. In 1876, United States Army troops attacked the Cheyenne Village at Powder River in the Montana Territory and destroyed the winter food and clothing. In 1877, at the Battle of Wolf Mountain in the Montana Territory, the Lakota and Cheyenne warriors fought against the United States Cavalry in a fight that ended in a draw.

In 1877, Chief Sitting Bull of the Lakota Sioux led his people into Canada to avoid capture by the United States Army who was pursuing him and his band. However, Chief Crazy horse of the Sioux surrendered to the United States troops in Nebraska to avoid the decimation of his people by cold and hunger. Chief Crazy Horse was later bayoneted by a soldier in 1877, and the Sioux were relegated to reservations.

In 1877, warriors from the Nez Perce tribe defeated the United States Cavalry at White Bird Canyon in the Idaho Territory in which 34 soldiers were killed. In 1877, the Nez Perce tribe fought the United States Army at the Battle of the Clearwater in the Idaho Territory. In 1877, in the battle of the Big Hole in the Montana territory, a band of Nez Perce Indians fought against the United States Army in which 29 soldiers and 50 warriors were killed. Later, Chief Joseph was defeated by Colonel Nelson Miles in Idaho, and he surrendered his Nez Perce band to be marched to Oklahoma to a reservation.

In 1877, by the order of Congress, the Secretary of the Interior removed the Ponca Indian tribe from their home in the Dakotas and Nebraska, and placed them in the Indian Territory in Oklahoma. This was done in spite of the fact that their original lands had been assured to them in perpetuity by the United States government as part of the territory set aside for the Sioux Indians in a treaty. A delegation of Ponca Indian chiefs visited Washington, D.C. and presented their cause in person to President Rutherford Hayes. In 1881, President Hayes sent a message to Congress for remedial measures to be done on behalf of the Ponca Indians.

In 1878, the Cheyenne Indians broke out from a reservation in Oklahoma. They were pursued by the United States Army and after several months were forced to surrender in the Wyoming Territory, and were returned to the reservation. In 1879, the Meeker Massacre, an uprising at the White River Ute Indian Reservation in Colorado, resulted in the deaths of several soldiers and agency employees. This event marked the start of the Ute War. Eventually, the Utes were forced to go to a reservation in Utah to avoid further bloodshed.

In 1881, Chief Sitting Bull returned to the United States and surrendered his Sioux Indian tribe to United States troops at Fort Buford, Montana. He was murdered by Indian policemen in 1890, at the Standing Rock Indian Reservation in South Dakota as they were trying to arrest him on orders from General Nelson Miles.

In 1885, President Chester Arthur opened up the Crow Creek Reservation in the Dakota Territory to settlement. The order was later revoked by President Grover Cleveland.

In 1885, President Grover Cleveland ordered a military campaign against the Southwestern Apache tribe that was responsible for killing more than 2,500 United States citizens over a period of 15 years. In 1886, Chief Geronimo of the Apache Indians in Arizona gave himself up, and was sent by General Nelson Miles to a reservation in Florida as a war prisoner. He was relocated to Fort Sill, Oklahoma in 1894, where he died in 1909.

The Dawes Act

In 1887, the Dawes Severalty Act ended tribal ownership by dividing reservations into allotments of 160 acres, with each Indian being given a piece of land to be used for farming. However, the un-allotted lands of the tribal holdings were declared to be surplus lands that were immediately made available for settlement by whites. The funds from the sale of these excess lands were to be used to benefit the Indians, with the process of land distribution being initiated by the President of the United States whenever a particular tribe was ready to benefit under this act. A total of two-thirds of the Indian reservation lands were reduced through these allotments. However, the Cherokees, Choctaws, Chickasaws, Creeks, and Seminoles were made exempt from this original legislation to avoid a change in title to their lands.

The Dawes Act was passed with the intention to aid the Indians, but many abuses were perpetrated in the subsequent expansion period of new settlements by whites. The overall result of the Dawes legislation was the creation of extreme poverty on many of the reservations. Also, 90 million acres of land were taken away from Indian ownership. Later changes to the Dawes Act resulted in the passage of the Burke Act of 1906. This act withdrew the right of citizenship from Indians to whom land had been allotted, and it extended the period after which Indians would be allowed to sell their lands. However, the act still excluded the Cherokees, Choctaws, Chickasaws, Creeks and Seminoles from the provisions of the original Dawes Act of 1887.

The Final Chapter

Wounded Knee

In 1890, the United States government broke a Lakota treaty by adjusting the Great Sioux Reservation of South Dakota into 5 smaller reservations to accommodate homesteaders from the East. Once they were on the half-sized reservations, the Sioux tribes were separated into family units on 320-acre plots, and were forced to farm, raise livestock, and send their children to boarding schools that forbade inclusion of traditional Indian culture and language. To support the Sioux, the Bureau of Indian Affairs (BIA) hired white farmers to teach them agriculture by cultivating crops in the semi-arid region of South Dakota—a land that was unable to produce substantial agricultural yields. The bureau cut rations to the Sioux in half, and since the bison had been nearly eradicated, the Sioux began to starve. Tribal members turned to spiritual revival, and many performed the Ghost Dance religious ceremony. The Ghost Dancers were dancing to high pitches of excitement that frightened the government employees and white settlers. Supervising agents of the BIA were alarmed at the activity, and the Pine Ridge agent requested the deployment of more troops to the reservation.

When Chief Sitting Bull was killed at the Standing Rock Reservation in 1890, refugees from his tribe fled and joined Chief Sitting Bull's half-brother, Chief Big Foot, at a reservation at Cheyenne River. General Nelson Miles ordered Chief Big Foot to move his people to a nearby fort, but Chief Big Foot became seriously ill with pneumonia, and his tribe then sought shelter with Chief Red Cloud at the Pine Ridge reservation. However, Chief Big Foot's band was intercepted by Major Samuel Whitside and his battalion of the 7th Cavalry Regiment, and were escorted back to Wounded Knee Creek to be under the command of Colonel James Forsyth.

A total of 500 troops of the United States 7th Cavalry surrounded the encampment of Lakota Sioux. The Army had orders to escort the Sioux to the railroad for transport to Omaha, Nebraska. Colonel Forsyth ordered the disarmament of the Lakota Sioux before proceeding. However, during the process of disarmament, a deaf tribesman who did not speak English, did not comply with the order to disarm and refused to give up his rifle. Two members of Colonel Forsyth's troops seized him from behind to disarm him and a struggle ensued. During the struggle his firearm rang out, and with the sounding of gunshots, the troops began shooting at the Indians, many of whom were unarmed. This set off a chain reaction of events that led to fighting between both sides. Some of the Indians grabbed rifles they had been hiding for self-defense and opened fire on the soldiers. Some of the soldiers used guns against the women and children as the officers lost all control of their men. By the end of the fighting at least 300 Lakota Sioux men, women and children—including Chief Big Foot—had been killed while Army casualties were 25 dead and 39 wounded.

The military hired civilians to bury the dead Lakota, which the burial party found frozen in contorted positions. They were gathered up and placed in a common grave, with about 160 men, women and children having been killed. About 150 Lakota Sioux fled into the hills, with an unknown number later dying from hypothermia. General Nelson Miles denounced Colonel Forsyth and relieved him of his command for the perpetration of this event. An exhaustive Army Court of Inquiry convened by General Miles criticized Colonel Forsyth for his tactical dispositions, but otherwise exonerated him of all responsibility. The Secretary of War concurred with the decision and reinstated Colonel Forsyth to the command of the 7th Cavalry. Nevertheless, General Miles ignored the results of the Court of Inquiry and continued to criticize Colonel Forsyth whom he believed had deliberately disobeyed his orders. General Miles also promoted the conclusion that Wounded Knee was a deliberate massacre rather than a tragedy caused by poor decisions.

Drexel Mission Encounter

A related encounter between soldiers and the Sioux Indians happened at Drexel Mission after the Battle of Wounded Knee. After news of the Wounded Knee Massacre reached them, Lakota Sioux Indians who had surrendered fled, burning several buildings at the mission as they left. They ambushed a squadron of the 7th Cavalry that responded and pinned it down until a relief force from the 9th Cavalry arrived at the scene. One soldier died and 6 were wounded from the 7th Cavalry.

Additional Actions

In 1889, President Benjamin Harrison opened 2 million acres in central Oklahoma to 50,000 white settlers. This land had been purchased from the Creek and Seminole tribes for the sum of $4 million.

In 1889, Congress passed the Nelson Act to relocate the Anishinabe Indians in Minnesota to the White Earth Indian Reservation—and to expropriate their remaining lands.

In 1890, 11 million acres of Sioux Indian Territory that had been ceded to the United States in 1889 were opened for general settlement.   .

In 1890, Congress created the Oklahoma Territory by redefining Indian reservations and creating an area within Indian lands for white settlers.

In 1891, President Benjamin Harrison opened 900,000 acres of Indian land in Oklahoma to settlers. The land was owned by the Sauk, Fox and Potawatomie Indians, but had been ceded to the United States by treaties.

In 1892, President Benjamin Harrison opened an additional 3 million acres of Oklahoma to white settlers. This was land that belonged to the Cheyenne and Arapaho Indians who had been forced into the Oklahoma Territory.

In 1892, President Benjamin Harrison opened 1.8 million acres of Montana to white settlers. This land had been set aside for the Crow Indian reservation.

In 1893, President Grover Cleveland opened 6 million acres of land between Kansas and Oklahoma for settlement. This was land that had been set aside for the Cherokee Indians, but which had been purchased from the Cherokees in 1891 for $8.5 million.

Grover Cleveland—II

Election of 1892

Grover Cleveland won the presidency with an electoral vote of 277. Adlai Stevenson was elected as Vice President.

Significant Events: 1893

President Cleveland withdrew the treaty of annexation of Hawaii from consideration by the Senate.

The Panic of 1893 began as a crash on the New York Stock Exchange initiated a depression. The panic resulted from gold prices dropping sharply, and from the conflict over silver with regard to having it be an integral part of the money supply. The combined effect created a lack of confidence, which then led to instability in capital movement flows as American securities became unattractive to foreign investors. Four years of depression ensued with the collapse of the New York stock market in 1893.

The Geary Exclusion Act was declared unconstitutional by the Supreme Court.

The Sherman Silver Purchase Act was repealed by Congress.

Significant Events: 1894

The Enforcement Act was repealed by Congress. As a result, individual states now controlled elections, especially with regard to black voters.

A Chinese Exclusion Treaty was signed between China and the United States in which China agreed to exclude Chinese laborers from entering into the United States.

President Cleveland vetoed the Bland Bill, which authorized the coinage of silver bullion.

136,000 coal miners began a strike at Columbus, Ohio to demand higher wages.

Coxey's army arrived in Washington, D. C. as a protest march against unemployment. A total of 300 men led by Jacob Coxey lobbied for the government to issue paper money and to create jobs, which would involve building roads and other public works improvements to create work for the unemployed. Coxey and 2 of his associates were arrested and were jailed for 20 days, by which time interest in the protest declined and the discouraged followers had scattered.

The May Day riots broke out in Cleveland, Ohio among the unemployed who condemned city leaders for their ineffective relief measures.

3,000 Pullman Palace Car Company workers went on a wildcat strike in Illinois. The workers were protesting a recent reduction of 20% in wages. They asked George Pullman for higher wages—and when he refused and fired their spokesman—the workers quit work, thus closing the shops. The workers were also supported by the American Railway Union, which as a result shut down 18 of the 24 railroads entering into Chicago, Illinois.

In the case of *Reagan v. Farmer's Loan and Trust Company*, the Supreme Court ruled that judicial review could determine the reasonableness of rates set by the legislatures and state commissions.

President Cleveland refused to allow Eugene Debs to use the Pullman Strike to shut down most of the nation's passenger, freight and mail traffic. He obtained an injunction in federal court, and when the strikers refused to obey it, he sent in federal troops to Chicago, Illinois and 20 other rail centers to run the railroads. A regiment of United States soldiers clashed with the strikers, and 7 men were killed and dozens were wounded in the encounter.

Congress passed a resolution that declared Labor Day as a national holiday.

Eugene Debs and three other strikebreakers were arrested for obstructing the mails. As a result, the Pullman Strike collapsed.

The Wilson-Gorman Tariff Act was passed by Congress. The act only slightly reduced the United States tariff rates from the numbers set in the 1890 McKinley tariff. The act also imposed a 2% graduated income tax on all incomes over $4,000.

Congress created the Bureau of Immigration to be part of the Treasury Department.

A garment workers' strike by 12,000 tailors in New York City occurred to protest sweatshop conditions and piecework system of payment.

The United States and Japan signed a commercial treaty.

Significant Events: 1895

In the case of *United States v. E. C. Knight Co.*, the Supreme Court ruled against the government in its antitrust action of the E. C. Knight Company that it sought to divest of its monopoly. The court ruled that manufacturing—in this case, refining—was a local activity and thus not subject to congressional regulation of interstate commerce.

In the case of *Pollock v. Farmer's Loan and Trust Company*, the Supreme Court ruled that the income tax clause of the Wilson-Gorman Act is unconstitutional.

In the case of *Re Debs*, the Supreme Court ruled that the Sherman Anti-Trust Act could be used against organized labor.

Significant Events: 1896

Utah was admitted into the Union as the 45th state.

In the case of *Plessy v. Ferguson*, the Supreme Court established the "separate but equal" doctrine, which led to the enactment of Jim Crow laws in the South.

William McKinley was elected as President by getting 271 Electoral votes. Garret Hobart was elected as Vice President.

Significant Events: 1897

The Olney-Paunceforte Convention was signed by the United States and Great Britain to provide for arbitration in case of territorial disputes between the two nations, but the Senate refused its consent.

President Cleveland vetoed the Immigration Bill, which would have made mandatory a literacy test for immigrants coming into the United States.

Panic of 1893

Overview

The Panic of 1893 was an economic depression in the United States that was caused by railroad overbuilding and unsound railroad financing, which set off a series of bank failures. Compounding the problem was a run on the gold supply, plus a government policy of using both gold and silver metals as a peg for the value of the dollar. Unemployment grew, rising from 1 million in 1893 to 2 million by 1894. By the middle of 1894, the figure reached 4 million without jobs—over 18% of the work force—and did not fall to single digit levels until 1899. The financial crisis of 1893 accelerated into a major contraction that spread throughout the American economy.

The Chain of Events

The 1880s had been a period of remarkable economic expansion in the United States, with the expansion being driven by speculation, mostly on railroads. By 1890, the economy was generating one of the highest levels of output per person in the world. Agriculture no longer dominated the economy, having been replaced by manufacturing and mining.

Beginning in the 1890s, railroads were vastly over-built, and many companies tried to take over others, seriously endangering their own stability. Many mines were opened, frequently with rail connections, and their products such as silver began to flood the market. Farmers suffered a series of droughts, which left them short of cash to pay their debts, and which also drove down the value of their land.

Because of this situation, the Free Silver movement arose, gaining support from farmers and mining interests. As a result, the Sherman Silver Purchase Act of 1890 was passed by Congress, which required the government to buy up to 4,500,000 ounces of silver redeemable for gold every month. The panic started in 1893 with the bankruptcy of the Philadelphia and Reading Railroad, which had greatly over-extended itself. As the economy worsened, people withdrew their money from banks and caused bank runs, resulting in a credit crunch. As a consequence, immigration, which had averaged over 500,000 people coming into the United States per year in the 1880s, was also affected and averaged only 270,000 from 1894 to 1898.

A financial panic in the United Kingdom, a recession in France and Germany, the collapse of speculations in Australian, South African and Argentine properties, and a drop in trade in Europe caused foreign investors to sell American stocks to obtain American funds backed by gold. The immediate result was panic in New York City, the nation's financial center. People attempted to redeem silver notes for gold, and ultimately the limit for the minimum amount of gold in federal reserves was reached whereby United States notes could no longer be successfully redeemed for gold. Furthering the crisis was the fact that investments were heavily financed through bond issues with high interest payments. Thus, the National Cordage Company went into receivership as a result of its bankers calling in their loans in response to rumors regarding the company's financial distress. As the demand for silver and silver notes fell, the price and value of silver dropped. Holders of paper lost the face value of bonds, and many became worthless.

A series of bank failures followed, as well as failures of the Erie Railroad, the Northern Pacific Railway, the Union Pacific Railroad and the Atchison, Topeka & Santa Fe Railroad. The markets for ancillary industries, like iron and steel, also felt the impact of the failing railroads since at times in the 1880s the rails had accounted for 90% of the country's rolled steel output. This collapse was followed by the bankruptcy of many other companies, with over 15,000 companies, 600 banks and 156 railroads failing before the depression ended. Coupled with the huge unemployment, and combined with the loss of life savings by failed banks, meant that many homeowners could no longer meet their mortgage obligations, and many walked away from recently built homes. Since the debt covered a comparable proportion of all farmlands, a declining economy brought further foreclosures and tax sales.

The Devastating Effects

The severity of the depression was the greatest in all industrial cities and mill towns, but farm distress was also great because of the falling prices for export crops such as wheat and cotton. Coxey's Army, a march of unemployed laborers from Ohio and Pennsylvania, went to Washington, D.C. to demand relief. A severe series of strikes took place in 1894, some of which led to violence. The Pullman Strike shut down much of the nation's transportation system in 1894. Many of the Western silver mines closed, and a significant number of railroads, which had been built to serve the mines, also went out of business. Many people abandoned their homes and went West to the cities of Seattle, Portland, Salt Lake City, Denver, San Francisco and Los Angeles, which took in the populations—as did many smaller city centers. Nevertheless, hungry, homeless and jobless men roamed the land begging for food—and sometimes resorted to stealing in order to stay alive. Some broke the law just to be arrested and put in jail where they could obtain food and shelter.

The growing credit shortage created panic, resulting in a depression. The depression caused stock prices to reach an all-time low, and many major firms were forced to declare bankruptcy. Some farmers in need of cash to meet debts tried to increase their income by increasing output of crops whose overproduction had already decreased prices and cut farm receipts—thus making the crisis worse by producing more farm foreclosures. Foreclosures of farm mortgages reduced the ability of mortgage companies, banks, and other lenders to convert their earning assets into cash because the willingness of investors to buy mortgage paper was reduced by the expectation that they would not yield a positive return.

The commercial stagnation in Europe affected the flow of foreign investment funds to the United States. The contraction abroad forced European investors to sell substantial holdings of American securities, causing the rate of new foreign investment to fall off.

The repatriation of American securities prompted gold exports, deflating the money stock and depressing prices. A reduced inflow of foreign capital slowed expansion and may have thus exacerbated the declining growth of the railroads. The slowdown in railroad expansion, coupled with the contraction in building construction, plus the reduction of foreign investment opportunities, as well as the fall of agricultural prices caused American exports and commerce to decline. With the successive contractions of credit, many sound firms failed, which otherwise would have survived under normal circumstances.

Investment, commerce, prices, employment, and wages remained depressed for several years. Changing circumstances and expectations, and a persistent federal deficit subjected the treasury gold reserves to intense pressure and generated sharp counter flows of gold. The treasury was driven 4 times between 1894 and 1896 to resort to bond issues totaling $260 million to obtain specie to augment the reserves. But, even the sale of bonds by the Treasury to acquire gold and to encourage capital inflows did not alleviate the situation. Restricted investment, income, and profits translated into low consumption, widespread suffering, and occasionally explosive labor and political struggles.

The Recovery

The government had no plan to end the economic panic. The Sherman Act was repealed, but it did not end the depression³. Most relief for those without jobs was provided by local voluntary organizations, which were overwhelmed by the enormous need. The economy began to recover in 1896. After the election of President William McKinley, confidence was restored, and with the Klondike gold rush the economy began 10 years of growth that did not stop until the Panic of 1907 occurred.

Gold was discovered in South Africa, which led to a sharp increase in the world's supply of gold. This produced a rise in prices that aided both farmers and businessmen in the United States. The development of new machines and methods to increase factory production created an increase in sales by the United States to foreign nations, which then brought more gold into the country. When the war with Spain occurred, the government was forced to borrow, which again increased the amount of money in circulation. The number of immigrants coming into the United States increased, thus providing farmers with a greater market for their products. When the Currency Act of 1900 was passed by Congress, the nation was firmly placed on the gold standard—thus eliminating the threat of "free" silver.

Resulting Changes

The United States economy that emerged from the depression of 1893 differed greatly from that of previous years. Hard times intensified social sensitivity to a wide range of problems accompanying industrialization by making them more severe. Those whom the depression struck the hardest, as well as much of the general public and major Protestant churches, increased their civic consciousness about currency and banking reform, regulation of business in the public interest, and labor relations. Public opinion began to swing toward governmental activism and intervention.

Government responses to depression, while exhibiting complexity, confusion, and contradiction, showed the transitional character of the era and further clarified the role of the business crisis in the economy of America. Hard times characterized by increasingly vast business units and concentrations of financial and productive power, became a major influence on society, thought, politics and government. A new awareness of deep-rooted changes became evident in attending to industrialization, urbanization, and other dimensions of the transformation of the United States economy.

The consolidation and the influence of investment bankers became more advanced. The nation's international trade position also became more advantageous as huge merchandise exports and increased foreign investments in the United States enhanced America's overseas commerce. New industries became dominant, and manufactures replaced farm produce as the leading products and exports of the country. The depression era formed the beginnings of an emerging industrial-urban economic order that foretold of great changes for the United States in the future.

William McKinley

The Election of 1896

In the 1896 election William McKinley was elected as President by getting 271 Electoral votes. Garret Hobart was elected as Vice President.

Significant Events: 1897

In the case of *Trans-Missouri Freight*, the Supreme Court ruled that railroads were subject to the Sherman Anti-Trust Act.

Secretary of State John Sherman and the Hawaiian government signed a Treaty of Annexation.

Congress passed the Dingley Tariff Bill, which raised rates to their highest level in history—with the average being 57%, and in some cases as high as 119%.

Gold was discovered in the Klondike Valley in Alaska.

75,000 coal miners went on strike in Pennsylvania, Ohio and West Virginia. Violence erupted in Hazelton and Latimer, Pennsylvania when deputy sheriffs fired on the men, killing 20 of them. The strike was settled shortly afterward, with the miners obtaining an 8-hour workday, semimonthly pay, the abolition of company stores and biennial conferences.

Significant Events: 1898

The United States battleship *Maine*, which had arrived in Havana, Cuba, suffered an explosion that destroyed the ship and killed 266 members of its crew. The United States claimed that the explosion was caused by an external submarine mine while the Spanish claimed that it was an internal explosion.

In the case of *Holden v. Hardy* the Supreme Court ruled that the Utah statue limiting daily working hours to 8 is valid.

After the *Maine* explosion, President McKinley demanded from Spain with regard to Cuba, a temporary truce with the Cuban rebels, revocation of the order to concentrate civilians in camps, a United States arbitration for a peaceful settlement between Spain and Cuba, and relief to be sent to Cuba

In the case of *United States v. Wong Kim Ark* the Supreme Court ruled that United States citizenship is without respect to race or color.

President McKinley addressed Congress and asked for a resolution of war against Spain. The resolution was adopted by Congress, which authorized the use of American forces to control Cuba. Congress passed the Volunteer Army Act to authorize the organization of a 1st Volunteer Cavalry. President McKinley called for 125,000 volunteers.

Spain broke off diplomatic relations with the United States, and as a result a plan to place a blockade of Cuba was initiated by the United States Navy. Spain declared war on the United States. The United States imposed a blockade on the Northern coast of Cuba, and Admiral William Sampson sailed from Key West, Florida with a fleet to enforce it.

Under the command of Admiral Dewey, the United States attacked the Spanish forces in Manila Bay in the Philippines. In a battle all of the Spanish ships were lost and 381 Spanish sailors were killed in comparison to no losses of ships for the Americans and only 8 men being wounded.

President McKinley requested an additional 75,000 men for the war against Spain.

Congress passed the Edman Arbitration Act to legitimatize government mediation in railroad disputes.

Congress passed the War Revenue Act for duties on tea, tobacco, liquor and legacies. The act also authorized a bond issue in the amount of $400,000,000—although the government only managed to sell $200,000,000 of the 3% interest bonds.

The invasion of Cuba was initiated with the landing of 650 Marines at Guantanamo Bay. It was followed by 17,000 troops for the invasion of Santiago, Cuba.

The entire Spanish fleet was destroyed at Santiago Harbor, Cuba. The Spanish suffered 475 dead or wounded while the United States only had one man killed and one other wounded.

President McKinley signed the Newlands resolution for the Annexation of Hawaii Treaty—one passed by a joint resolution of Congress.

Puerto Rico surrendered to the United States. Manila in the Philippines also surrendered to the United States.

The Treaty of Paris was signed between the United States and Spain, thus ending the war. The Senate ratified the treaty in 1899.

Significant Events: 1899

President McKinley appointed the Philippine Commission for United States rule of the islands in a move to prevent their annexation by Germany.

Congress approved the use of voting machines for federal elections — at the discretion of individual states.

The Philippine revolt against the United States started when guerillas fired on American forces at Manila, Philippines. In just a few days 57 Americans were killed and 257 were wounded while 500 Filipinos were killed, 1,000 were wounded and 500 were captured.

Congress authorized 65,000 additional men for the army, and asked for 35,000 volunteers to assist in the suppression of the Philippine revolt.

Congress established the third Isthmian Canal Commission[2] to investigate the possible routes and the costs for a canal through Central America.

Congress authorized the appropriation of funds for the Navy to build 3 battleships, 3 armed cruisers and 6 protective cruisers.

The first Hague Peace Conference was opened, and at the insistence of the United States, a Permanent Court of International Arbitration was established to deal with international disputes.

Secretary of State John Hay requested an "open door" policy for China to prevent its dismemberment through "spheres of influence" by other nations. In 1900, it was followed up by a broader guarantee of China's territorial integrity.

Vice President Garret Hobart died.

In the case of *Addyston Pipe & Steel Co. v. United States* the Supreme Court ruled that negotiations made between corporations to eliminate competition are violations of the Sherman Anti-Trust Law.

The Anglo-German Treaty divided the Samoan Islands between the United States and Germany, with the United States getting Tutuila and several other islands and Germany getting the islands of Upolu and Savaii. Britain surrendered her claims to the islands in return for rights in West Africa and in the Pacific. Germany also relinquished its rights in certain areas of Samoa. The agreement was signed by England, Germany and the United States, and was ratified by the Senate in 1900. In 1900, President McKinley placed the American Samoan islands under the control of the United States Navy.

Significant Events: 1900

Congress passed the Gold Standard Act, which established gold as the basis of United States money.

Congress passed the Foraker Act that established Puerto Rico as an unconsolidated territory of the United States[3].

Congress granted territorial standing to Hawaii. President McKinley appointed Sanford Dole as governor of Hawaii.

In the case of *Knowlton v. Moore* the Supreme Court ruled that the inheritance tax levied under the War Revenue Act of 1898 was constitutional.

The Boxer Rebellion broke out in China, and 2,500 American troops—along with 11,800 soldiers from Britain, France and Japan—were dispatched to Peking, China to quell the disturbance.

The first primary election was held in the United States in Hennepin County in the state of Minnesota. This model was adopted by the rest of the country for their elective offices, with Wisconsin being the first state to adopt the primary system.

A very powerful hurricane hit Galveston, Texas in which over 6,000 people were killed and almost $12 million of property was destroyed.

Republican William McKinley was reelected in the 1900 presidential election by receiving 292 Electoral votes. Theodore Roosevelt won as Vice President by getting 292 Electoral votes.

The Department of State announced that negotiations with Denmark had been completed for the purchase of the Virgin Islands. However, the appropriations for their transfer were not done by Congress until 1917.

Significant Events: 1901

The Army Appropriation Act was passed by Congress, which included the Platt Amendment that stated that American troops would not be withdrawn from Cuba[8]. Cuba agreed to lease or sell naval stations on Cuba to the United States.

The Americans captured the Philippine rebel leader to end the Philippine insurrection, which was ended by proclamation in 1901.

In the case of *De Lima v. Bidwell*, the Supreme Court ruled that Puerto Rico could have duties levied on goods sent to the United States.

President McKinley declared a free trade policy with Puerto Rico.

The United States and Denmark negotiated a settlement to have the Danish West Indies and 3 small islands near Puerto Rico (St. Thomas, St. John and St. Croix) to be transferred to the United States for the sum of $4 million.

President McKinley was shot[1] on September 6, 1901, and died from the bullet wound on September 14, 1901[3]. Vice President Theodore Roosevelt became President.

Spanish-American War

Overview

The United States had enjoyed good relations with Spain, which had supplied manpower, arms, and money to the Americans during the American Revolution of 1776. There was also a continuing trade between the Spanish islands of Puerto Rico and Cuba and the United States, and by the late 1800s much of the expansion of the sugar agriculture on Cuba and Puerto Rico was due to the investment of American capital. The United States had even approached the Spanish government on several occasions about the possibility of acquiring one or both islands.

Throughout the 1800s, Cuba had sought to wrest itself from the dominance of the Spanish government. After several failed rebellions, the Cubans finally succeeded in the War of 1895, and some Americans saw this as an opportunity to expand the horizons of the United States by exploiting the sugar and tobacco agriculture. In 1898, Spain instituted limited political autonomy in Cuba, but the Cubans rejected it, and conservative elements among the civilians and military in Havana rioted against the limited autonomy.

As a result, the American Consul-General in Havana telegraphed a request to the State Department for protection of American citizens living there because he considered this riot as a threat to the lives and property of the Americans, some of whom had been mauled by mobs. In response to this request, the battleship *Maine* and the cruiser *Montgomery* were sent to Cuba in 1898 by President William McKinley to assert American power. When the *Maine* was sunk by an explosion in 1898, the event gave the United States the excuse to militarily enter Cuba.

The *Maine* Explosion

The *Maine* had been anchored in Havana, Cuba. Without warning, the ship exploded on February 15, 1898. The ship was on fire from stern to stern, and the "abandon ship" order was given. But, the *Maine* sank in less than 5 minutes, with a loss of 266 of the 354 enlisted men and officers who were on board in what was the worst naval disaster in United States history. The Captain of the *Maine* cabled the Secretary of the Navy about the event, and he cautioned against any rush to judgment until the cause of the explosion could be determined. Nevertheless, the newspapers fanned the hysteria, and accused Spain of causing the explosion. As the American population was stirred into a frenzy by the newspapers, Spain knew that it had to protect its possessions from American aggression.

Prelude to the Conflict

Following the sinking of the *Maine*, President McKinley transmitted an ultimatum to the Spanish government in 1898, and demanded an immediate armistice on Cuba, and accession to Cuba's independence by arbitration. The Spanish reply stated that further negotiations would proceed. In 1898, the Washington administration ordered the curtailment of any further discussions with Spain. A joint session of Congress was held in 1898 to hear President McKinley address the issue with Spain. He summarized the situation in Cuba, and asked Congress to authorize him to take measures, but left the decision of what action to take with Congress. Congress voted on an ultimatum that demanded that Spain give up its authority over Cuba, and that it withdraw its land and naval forces from Cuba. Congress also stated that they would wait for a response, which if not given, would then result in the authorization for the President to use the full power of the United States to enforce the ultimatum.

Congress voted for war in 1898, and President McKinley signed the war resolution. The Senate amended the war resolution with the Teller Amendment disclaiming any intention by the United States to acquire Cuba, but to leave the government and control of the island to its people, with the intended aim being to liberate Cuba from Spain. President McKinley proclaimed a blockade of all principal ports in Cuba, with the Atlantic Squadron commanded by Rear Admiral Sampson in Key West, Florida to enforce the proclamation. President McKinley also authorized the call up of 125,000 volunteers and Congress authorized $22.6 million for naval vessels. Admiral Sampson's American fleet left Key West, Florida and began the first phase of the American plan for war with Spain—the blockade of Cuba and Puerto Rico. President McKinley also called for an additional 75,000 volunteers to increase the United States Army.

The Battle of Manila Bay

Spanish Admiral Patricio Montojo y Pasaron, who had been dispatched to the Philippines, was equipped with a variety of obsolete vessels. Additional reinforcements that were promised from Madrid, Spain resulted in only 2 scout cruisers being sent. Admiral Montojo y Pasaron also weakened his position by retreating from the range of Spanish land batteries, and choosing instead to anchor away from the batteries—in deference to wealthy Spanish merchants who wanted to avoid damage to their commercial properties in the city.

The United States ships consisting of 6 cruisers, 1 cutter and 2 cargo ships were assembled at Hong Kong, China, and constituted the American Asiatic Squadron under the command of Commodore George Dewey. These ships embarked from Hong Kong in 1898 to the Philippines, sailing into Manila Bay. The Spanish shore batteries and the Spanish fleet opened fire on them. The cruiser *Olympia* then began the barrage that resulted in the destruction of the Spanish flotilla. The Spanish forces were outgunned, but the Spanish ships and the land batteries fought back. The American ships withdrew, redistributed their ammunition, and then attacked again, and this time most of the Spanish ships were either destroyed or surrendered. Commodore Dewey won the battle with eight officers and men being wounded, and only a single fatality among his crew. The Spanish suffered losses of 380 men who were either killed or wounded. Commodore Dewey then landed a force of Marines who completed the destruction of the Spanish fleet and batteries and established a guard for the protection of the Spanish hospitals. The *Olympia* also turned a few guns on the Cavite arsenal, and its magazine exploded, killing and wounding many—and thus ending the fire from the Spanish shore batteries.

The Conquest of Guam

Spain made no effort to reinforce the island of Guam, and in 1898, elements of the 8th Corps sailed to the Philippines from San Francisco, California aboard three transports that were accompanied by a cruiser. After stopping in Honolulu, Hawaii, their next stop was in Guam.

The *Charleston* came in range of Fort Santa Cruz and opened fire on this fort. The *Charleston* then anchored to control the harbor. A vessel flying the Spanish flag approached the American warship. Two Spanish officers who were on board were declared to be prisoners of war. The two officers were then paroled, and asked to carry a message to the governor that he should surrender. The governor responded that Spanish law forbade him from coming aboard the vessel, but asked the American captain to come to him instead, guaranteeing the captain's safe return.

The Commander sent a Navy Lieutenant to meet the governor and to deliver the ultimatum. A landing party of 30 Marines was also formed and sent to the beach. The lieutenant presented a letter demanding the surrender of the island with threats that a heavily armed vessel and several transports loaded with troops were awaiting offshore. The governor returned a reply acceding to the demands, and Spanish rule in Guam fell. The Marines went into the city of Piti to round up and disarm the 60-man Spanish garrison, thus completing the act of possession.

The Invasion of Cuba

Spain had to protect their possessions in the Caribbean—even though the ships of the Spanish Navy were in a very poor state with defective guns and rusted turrets. The ships of a second squadron were ordered to sail from Cadiz, Spain to Cuba where the fleet went to Santiago. Reports of ships that were being seen off the Eastern seaboard of the United States created a panic. The American people wanted protection, and so Congress insisted that the Navy do something. Another squadron was sent to Hampton Roads, Virginia.

Admiral Sampson arrived with his squadron at the end of 1898, and added to the blockade of the Spanish ships at Santiago. An American squadron of cruisers tightened the blockade around Santiago. President McKinley called for an additional 125,000 volunteers to create an army of 250,000 troops[5]. The objective of the Americans was to protect the United States and her forces, and to eliminate the threat of the Spanish Naval Squadron. If the Spanish Navy could be contained, then the United States would be able to land an almost unlimited amount of troops in Cuba. However, Admiral Sampson did not know the condition of the Spanish navy, and was wary of their potential might.

The Spanish Admiral Cervera did not want to exit the safe haven of the harbor with his fleet to face the American ships' guns. The American Admiral Sampson did not want to go into the harbor past the Spanish land guns and navigate his ships past the harbor mines to force Admiral Cervera's ships out into the open sea. This stalemate forced the United States Army to conduct a mission on land commanded by General William Shafter. The plan was to land troops near Santiago, march towards the city, and then capture it to drive Admiral Cervera and his ships out of the harbor.

In 1898, a contingent of 100 marines, at Guantanamo Bay. The battle for Cusco Hill was taken to control Guantanamo Bay, and to remove the Spanish soldiers from positions where they could sniper at the marine encampment. The remainder of the Spanish resistance disappeared when American ships shelled Caimanera.

Concealed in the chaparral, the Spanish soldiers regularly fired upon the encampment of marines. A detachment of 300 marines and Cubans to drive off the Spanish soldiers was deployed. When Cuban scouts reported that Spanish soldiers were over the next ridge, the American troops were deployed, moved forward, and began firing. About 70 Spanish soldiers were killed and 150 were wounded, while the American losses were 2 Cubans killed and several Cubans and marines wounded.

The first American soldiers from the Fifth Corps 2nd Infantry Division landed 18 miles east of Santiago at the beaches of Daiquri. General Joseph Wheeler also landed his own division, including the Rough Riders. General Lawton then moved Westward to Siboney to secure the area for additional landings, including the 1st Division. When all was ready, a two-pronged assault would be launched against Santiago with General Lawton's troops attacking from San Juan while General Kent's 1st Division and General Wheeler's volunteers and dismounted cavalry attacked at El Caney to cover the flank.

General Lawton's advance guard moved Westward where they encountered Spanish soldiers. The Spanish withdrew and General Wheeler led a reconnaissance force to determine the enemy strength and position, which he found at the fortified positions near Sevilla at Las Guasimas. General Lawton prepared for an assault on Las Guasimas with his First Brigade, which included the Rough Riders. The Rough Riders moved out along the higher ridgelines in support of 2 cavalry squadrons.

They encountered Spanish soldiers who were in defensive pits and others who lay hidden in the heavy jungle surrounding the roads. The American troops opened fire, the troops advanced forward, and the Spanish returned heavy fire until their lines broke and they fled. The Rough Rider regiment continued forward until they encountered a Spanish outpost. When the commander was killed, Theodore Roosevelt took command of the Rough Riders, and they prevailed, but they lost 8 men and suffered 34 wounded.

The Army began preparations for the assault on Santiago with an attack near San Juan. American troops began moving inland, including Colonel Roosevelt's Rough Riders, and by the 1st Infantry Division. San Juan Hill was defended by 750 Spanish soldiers in heavily fortified positions, and was dominated by large blockhouses. The Americans wanted this position so that they would have a tactical advantage over the 10,000 Spanish soldiers who were stationed around the city of Santiago. The forces stormed and captured San Juan Hill. The Rough Riders regiment under Colonel Roosevelt led the assault at both Kettle Hill and San Juan Hill, and forced the Spanish forces to flee from their trenches. Because they were the frontline of the attack, the Rough Riders sustained the highest casualty rate. The American forces suffered over 1,000 dead and wounded in this battle. Then, the main assault force captured Santiago when the Spanish surrendered the Santiago garrison after the Battle of Santiago Bay had wiped out the Spanish fleet.

The Battle of Santiago bay

The United States Army began the drive to Santiago de Cuba, and Admiral Cervera found himself unable to remain safely in the harbor. Finally, the military commander in Cuba ordered Admiral Cervera to steam his ships out of the harbor to save the Spanish fleet. The Spanish ships began their race from the mouth of Santiago Bay. The battle commenced at the blockade line.

Admiral Cervera directly engaged the *Brooklyn*, hitting it more than 20 times in the battle. But the return fire from the *Brooklyn* resulted in the deaths of most of Admiral Cervera's bridge crew and caused major damage to the ship, such that the *Infanta Maria Teresa* began to burn. Admiral Cervera ordered his ship aground in the shallows along the Cuban coast. Admiral Cervera survived and was rescued by being picked up by the crew of the *Gloucester*.

The rest of the Spanish fleet continued its race for the open sea. The *Almirante Oquendo* was hit repeatedly by the *Iowa* and driven out of the battle. The two torpedo boat destroyers made a dash in a direction opposite the rest of the Spanish squadron. The *Gloucester* opened fire on them, and then shelling followed from the battleships *Iowa, Indiana*, and the *New York*, which sunk both boats.

One of the two last remaining Spanish ships, the *Vizcaya*, became locked in a running gun duel with the *Brooklyn*. Almost none of the *Vizcaya's* nearly 300 shots caused any significant damage to the *Brooklyn* due to faulty ammunition, while the *Brooklyn* pounded the *Vizcaya* with lethal effect. The *Vizcaya* was overwhelmed, having been struck as many as 200 times by the fire of the *Brooklyn* and the *Texas*. The *Vizcaya* turned toward the beach to ground herself.

Only one vessel, the *Cristobal Colon*, still survived as it steamed for the West. Although it was the fastest ship in the Spanish fleet, it had no armament installed, except for a secondary battery. There was only one ship in the United States fleet that could maintain the pursuit, the *Oregon*. The *Oregon* dogged the *Cristobal Colon*, forcing it to hug the coast instead of turning toward the open sea. Finally, a peninsula jutting out from the coastline forced her to turn south across the *Oregon's* path. The *Cristobal Colon* toward the mouth of the Tarquino River and the ship was grounded, marking the end of Spain's naval power presence in the Americas.

Spanish casualties numbered nearly 500, and all 6 vessels of the Spanish squadron were lost. Only 150 Spanish sailors made their way back to the Spanish lines at Santiago. The 1,800 Spanish sailors who were rescued or captured, including Admiral Cervera, were sent to the Portsmouth Naval Shipyard in Kittery, Maine where they were confined as prisoners of war. Two of the Spanish ships, *Infanta Maria Teresa* and *Cristobal Colon*, were later re-floated and taken over by the United States. The cruiser *Reina Mercedes*, abandoned in Santiago Bay because of engine troubles, was captured by the United States and was used as a receiving ship.

The Puerto Rico Campaign

President McKinley set forth the conditions for peace negotiations. The evacuation of Cuba by Spanish forces and its transfer to the United States was the prelude to imposition of order and formation of a stable government on the island. McKinley's second demand was the transfer of Puerto Rico from Spanish authorities to the United States without compensation. The Spanish Governor of Puerto Rico believed that a war between the United States and Spain was inevitable, and in 1898, he declared martial law on the island. He also issued a stirring proclamation calling for resistance against the Americans.

Sea Battles

Admiral Sampson sailed with the bulk of the Key West fleet to San Juan, Puerto Rico. Upon arrival at San Juan, Admiral Sampson imposed a blockade on San Juan. Then, he bombarded the city with his warships, concentrating the firepower on the Morro and Cristobal Castles, which had been fortified by the Spaniards. The losses on the American side were one dead and 7 wounded while the Puerto Ricans suffered 20 dead and 50 wounded. The firing of shells by the American fleet at San Juan created a mass exodus of civilians from San Juan.

The Spanish cruiser *Isabel II* and a torpedo boat destroyer *Terror* left the San Juan Harbor to attack the blockading American ship, the *St. Paul*. However, the *Isabel II* was forced to retire from the fight and she returned to San Juan. The *Terror* attempted a torpedo attack, at which time the *St. Paul* commenced firing on the *Terror*, repeatedly hitting it with rounds and shells until she began to sink, and it was beached.

The Spanish ship *Antonio Lopez* faced the blockade replacement ship, the *Yosemite*. The *Yosemite* headed towards San Juan, and shells from the *Yosemite* hit the *Antonio Lopez*. With the *Yosemite* coming closer, the captain attempted to deliver the cargo of ammunition in Puerto Rico, but, the ship grounded, and it was abandoned by the crew.

While the *Yosemite* fired at the immobilized ship, the Spanish ships *Isabel II, General Concha* and *Ponce de Leon* rushed from San Juan Bay and joined the fight by opening fire on the *Yosemite*, but she sped out of range towards the horizon. When the cruiser *New Orleans* arrived at the scene, it fired incendiary shells at the *Antonio Lopez*, causing it to catch fire—and to eventually sink it a few weeks later.

Land Campaign

President McKinley ordered General Nelson Miles to invade Puerto Rico, but he could not comply until the end of the Santiago Bay campaign. General Miles with Army troops departed for Puerto Rico from Guantanamo Bay. A contingent of 3,500 men landed at Guanica Bay, immediately moving to the city of Ponce and other towns located on the southern part of the island. These troops then proceeded north towards San Juan and the main military post of Spanish forces.

Marines and sailors of the *Puritan* landed and attempted to hold the Fajardo lighthouse area on the northeast corner of Puerto Rico. Spanish authorities in Fajardo became aware that the Fajardo lighthouse was in the hands of United States forces and notified Spanish Military Headquarters at San Juan. The Spanish headquarters ordered the evacuation of all Spanish forces from Fajardo. The Americans took over Fajardo. A Spanish captain ordered 200 men to Fajardo, where they entered the town. The troops attacked the Marines around the lighthouse. The United States ships bombarded the lighthouse area and forced the Spanish soldiers back to Fajardo.

The United States Army took 22 cities, but before it could reach San Juan, Spain agreed to sign a peace treaty with the United States, putting an end to hostilities. President McKinley's conditions for a peace agreement were ratified in the Treaty of Paris in 1898. The transfer of Puerto Rico to the United States occurred when the last Spanish troops sailed back to Spain. A military government was established, and in 1900, Congress ratified the Foraker Law, bringing a civilian government to the island.

Aftermath

The war cost the United States 5,000 casualties and 3,000 wounded plus several thousand more who were incapacitated by contracting tropical diseases from which many of them later died. A total of 60,000 troops participated in the action at a cost of over $600 million. The Philippines, Puerto Rico, Guam, and Cuba were ceded by Spain to the United States under the Treaty of Paris signed in 1898, for which Spain was compensated with $20 million. All 4 of these territories were placed under military governments by the United States. Cuba was given its independence in 1902, but fell in 1959 to a communist regime headed by Fidel Castro. The Philippine Islands were given their independence in 1946 after WWII ended. Puerto Rico never gained its independence, but did experience political, social, and economic changes to its national institutions that allowed it to be transformed into a United States territory. In 1952, Puerto Rico was granted commonwealth status under a constitution drawn up by Puerto Ricans. Guam became an overseas naval and air base for the United States.

The Spanish-American War catapulted the United States into a world power with its legacy setting the stage for the involvement of the United States in later conflicts such as WWI, WWII, Korea and Vietnam. The Spanish-American War was the first projection of American military power overseas with the intention of securing and holding islands in the Far East, the Pacific, and the Caribbean as colonial possessions. It was the first American war conducted under a naval-based plan rather than an army plan, and it utilized the planning that was accomplished by the Naval War College. The war provided media coverage to the American public by means of telephone, telegraph, illustrations, stereo views, books, photography, newspapers, and motion pictures. President McKinley had the use of telephones and telegraphs to provide him with access to battlefield commanders and reporters.

The Philippine-American War

The Beginning of Revolt

The Philippine Revolution against Spain began in 1896 by a group called the Katipunan. Rizal was implicated in the outbreak of the revolution and was executed for treason in 1896. The Katipunan then split into two groups, one led by Mariano Alvarez and Andres Bonifacio, and another one led by Emilio Aguinaldo. Conflicts between Bonifacio and Aguinaldo culminated in the assassination of Bonifacio by Aguinaldo's soldiers. Aguinaldo continued in rebellion against the Spanish forces as he fought for land reform, restrictions on the power of the Catholic friars, and for greater participation by Filipinos in the government of the islands. However, with his poorly equipped forces, Aguinaldo was driven back into the mountains.

In 1897, the Spanish decided to negotiate with the insurgents. Aguinaldo agreed to a truce, and some of his fellow revolutionaries were exiled to Hong Kong, China. In return, the Spanish promised to expel the religious orders, give the Filipinos representation in the government at Madrid, grant freedom of press and association, and assure equal treatment of Filipinos in both political appointments and in the administration of justice. Aguinaldo and 40 of his followers were promised 800,000 pesos as an indemnity, with 400,000 pesos being deposited in a Hong Kong bank. Aguinaldo took up residence in Singapore where he conferred with the United States Consul.

The United States also invited the exiled Emilio Aguinaldo to return to the Philippines, which he did in 1898, in the hope that he would rally Filipinos against the Spanish colonial government[1]. However, by the time the American land forces had arrived, the Filipinos had taken control of the entire island of Luzon. In 1898, a proclamation of independence was issued by Aguinaldo, with the establishment of the First Philippine Republic.

Spain and the United States sent commissioners to Paris to draw up the Treaty of Paris to end the Spanish-American War. However, the Filipino representative, Felipe Agoncillo, was excluded from the discussions since the revolutionary government was not recognized by either nation. In 1898, President McKinley issued a proclamation of American sovereignty throughout the Philippine Archipelago through an Executive Order[2]. However, the treaty was not recognized by the proclaimed Philippine Government. In 1899, a Philippine Constitution had been drafted and approved by the legislative assembly. It called for national emancipation, a representative government, separation of church and state and the granting of individual liberties.

The Philippine-American War

Aguinaldo gave approval to Apolinario Mabini, a Philippine revolutionary, to associate the American occupation forces with the Spanish friars. General Elwell Otis, the commander of the American forces in Manila, thought that only a military defeat would subdue the insurgents. In 1899, he appointed Brigadier General R.P. Hughes to negotiate with a Philippine committee headed by Florentino Torres. The committee made its demands known, which was total independence as desired by Aguinaldo. However, Aguinaldo was willing to accept a limited American protectorate. Thus, President McKinley sent the Schurman Commission to investigate the proceedings—but with explicit instructions not to negotiate. Felipe Agoncillo was sent to Washington, D.C. to make a compromise, but President McKinley refused to see him.

Hostilities occurred in 1899, after 2 American privates on patrol killed 3 Filipino soldiers in a suburb of Manila. Aguinaldo sent emissaries to General Otis to ask for a cease fire, but was rebuffed since General Otis wanted the unconditional surrender of all insurgents. Initial successes in battles extended the American control to a distance of 30 miles both East and North of Manila. However, the rainy season bogged down the American offensive although many barrios were burned during the incursions into Luzon, and more than 3,000 Filipinos were killed.

Aguinaldo removed Mabini as head of the revolutionary government, and instead installed Pedro Paterno as its new head. In 1899, the Paterno cabinet sent out messages with the intent of hoping to meet with American General Otis, but the failure to meet caused both sides to continue the conflict. Even with a poorly equipped army, the insurgents were able to slow down the American forces, and thus the American forces were only able to capture 120 square miles from the total area of 42,000 square miles of Luzon.

In 1899, the American forces were divided into 3 main units headed by Generals Arthur MacArthur, Henry Lawton and Lloyd Wheaton. To counter the American offensive, Aguinaldo dissolved the Filipino regular army in 1899, and ordered the establishment of decentralized guerrilla commands in each of several military zones. Aguinaldo fled to the mountain jungles where he and his followers became formidable opponents, especially since they were aided by the native population. The guerrilla strategy protracted the war and made it costly for the United States. By 1900, a total of 70,000 American military personnel were involved in the war.

The archipelago was divided into 4 military districts under Generals Wheaton, John Bates, Robert Hughes and William Kobbe, with a fifth district in Manila being led by General Franklin Bell. However, the countryside remained under the control of the insurgents, and American casualties continued to increase. To discourage the insurgents and their supporters, the United States military began resorting to the "water cure" torture in an effort to shorten the war. In spite of the use of this torture technique, the period in 1900 saw a new wave of raids and ambushes by Filipino guerilla forces.

In 1900, General MacArthur issued General Order No. 100 to authorize the power granted to an occupying army. The new order stated that guerillas dressed in civilian clothes would be considered as war rebels, especially if they refused to offer assistance to the American army. Also, all towns would be occupied by army garrison units with powers of summary punishment over Filipino officials who violated their oath of allegiance. Aguinaldo issued an order proclaiming that military brutality was now the official American policy, and he called for a self-defense strategy of retaliation. American policy became even harsher, and American troops burned barrios that offered asylum to the insurgents.

The Ending of the War

In 1901, the insurgent General Trias surrendered, and the capture of one of Aguinaldo's couriers offered the opportunity to capture Aguinaldo. By subjecting the captured insurgent to torture, the American interrogators discovered that Aguinaldo was in the Isabella province. General Frederick Fulton then instructed the insurgent to dispatch a company of loyal insurgent soldiers as his personal guard along with a detachment of 81 scouts disguised as Tagalog insurgents. General Funston and 4 other American officers pretended to be prisoner-captives of these fake insurgents. The group made their way along 50 miles of jungle trail to where they were marched into Aguinaldo's headquarters. Upon a given signal, the captors opened fire upon Aguinaldo's guards and captured him.

Aguinaldo was taken aboard the USS *Vicksburg*. In 1901, Aguinaldo took the oath of allegiance and agreed to sign a manifesto whereby he called on his compatriots to lay down their arms and offer no further resistance to American forces—and to accept being ruled by the United States. Insurgent generals surrendered their forces in Luzon and Laguna. Only 2 insurgent generals continued the conflict. In 1901, William Taft was inaugurated as the civil governor of the Philippines, and General Adna Chaffee became the commanding general of the archipelago.

In 1901, 38 Americans were killed and 11 others were wounded in a surprise guerilla attack on 74 members of the 9th Regiment of the United States Infantry in a massacre. General Jake Smith was given command of the army and marine units, and he proceeded in a terror policy of destruction by killing and burning villages in retaliation. General Chaffee also ordered General Franklin Bell to conduct a campaign against insurgent forces in Batangas. General Bell herded the civilian population into concentration centers, burned all the crops, slaughtered all the cattle, and executed prisoners of war. By 1902, hundreds of Filipinos had died in the camps, much property had been confiscated, and the guerillas had been starved into submission. Only the Moros in the southern islands continued in the guerilla effort.

In 1902, Congress passed the Philippine Government Act to create a civil government for the Philippines, and President Theodore Roosevelt declared the end of the insurrection, and gave clemency to all of the Filipinos. However, insurgent resistance continued in various parts of the Philippines, especially in the Muslim South, until 1913. The problem of administering a government over islands inhabited by 80 different tribes speaking over 60 different languages proved to be challenging.

The Effects of the War

The Philippine-American War was essentially a colonial war that was undertaken by the United States for the purpose of retaining the area, one that was ceded to the United States by Spain. It lasted for almost 3½ years, cost $400 million, and involved 126,500 American soldiers in the conflict. During the 41 months of fighting, 4,230 Americans were killed and 2,800 more were wounded in battles and by guerilla warfare. A total of 16,000 Filipino guerilla soldiers died, with estimates of civilian deaths suffered during the war being 600,000, largely because of famine and disease.

United States Territory

The colonial rule of the Philippines by the United States began in 1901 with a very limited local rule. A civil government was established, with William Taft being appointed as the American Governor-General of the Philippines. The governor-general acted as head of the Philippine Commission, a body appointed by the United States President with legislative and limited executive powers. The Philippine Commission was responsible for passing laws to establish a judicial system, civil service, and local government. A Philippine Constabulary was also organized to deal with the remnants of the insurgent movement and to gradually assume the responsibilities that had been carried out by the United States Army.

The Philippine Assembly, an elected body, was inaugurated in 1907, and became a lower house of a bicameral legislature, with the appointed Philippine Commission acting as the upper house of the legislature. However, during the early years of territorial administration, the Americans were reluctant to delegate authority to the Filipinos. It was not until 1913 when President Woodrow Wilson adopted a new policy to put into motion a process that would gradually lead to Philippine independence. The Jones Act, passed by Congress in 1916, served as the new law in the Philippines, and promised eventual independence. It also instituted an elected Philippine Senate.

During the 1920s the members of the Philippine legislature lobbied Congress for the immediate and complete independence from the United States, with several independence missions being sent to Washington, D.C. A civil service was also formed and was gradually taken over by Filipinos. The Philippine call for independence was spearheaded by Manuel Quezon, who served as Philippine Senate President from 1916 until 1935.

The Boxer Uprising

Overview

The Boxer Movement was an uprising that occurred from 1899 to 1901. The rebellion was against foreign influence in areas such as trade, politics, religion and technology that occurred in China during the final years of the Manchu rule. The Boxers began as an anti-foreign, anti-imperialist peasant-based movement in Northern China that attacked foreigners who were building railroads, and Christians who were held responsible for the foreign domination of China. In 1900, the Boxers invaded Peking, and killed 230 non-Chinese people. Tens of thousands of Chinese Christians were also killed.

The Chinese government did not act to protect the people who were being attacked. Thus, the diplomats, foreign civilians, soldiers and some Chinese Christians retreated to the legation quarter. From there they held out for 55 days until a multinational coalition consisting of 8 countries rushed 54,000 troops to their rescue. After the foreign troops succeeded in quelling the Boxer uprising, the Chinese government was forced to indemnify the victims and make many additional concessions. During the uprising, 48 Catholic missionaries and 18,000 Chinese Catholics were killed. A total of 222 Chinese Eastern Orthodox Christians were also killed, along with 182 Protestant missionaries and 500 Chinese Protestants. More than 50,000 Chinese civilians who were accused to be boxers were killed by foreign troops. Nevertheless, the Boxer uprising laid the foundation for the end of the Qing Dynasty and the establishment of the modern Chinese Republic—even though it did much violence with acts of murder, robbery, vandalism and arson.

Background

The foreign legations were established in the 1860s following the defeat of the Qing Dynasty of China by the British in the First Opium War that lasted from 1839 to 1842, and in which Hong Kong Island was ceded to the British. The Second Opium War that was fought from 1856 to 1860, resulted in the defeat of the Qing Dynasty again—this time by the British, Irish and French. Japan also defeated China in the Sino-Japanese war that was fought from 1894 to 1895. The resulting treaties permitted foreigners to establish quarters within China.

The Legation Quarter compound that was established by the foreign powers lay within the walls of the Imperial City of Peking. These quarters consisted of embassies that housed ministers, diplomatic representatives and other officials from 11 nations[3]. The area also became a center of commercial districts with banks, shops and offices that stood among the various embassies[4].

The Boxers disliked these foreigners who resided in China, especially the foreign religions: the missionaries and their Chinese converts. The Boxers resented the exemption of missionaries from many of the Chinese laws. The Empress of China shared these feelings, and she wanted to get the Boxers to help drive out the foreigners. She also wanted to address the social and economic grievances of the Boxers to prevent them from turning against her and the Manchu dynasty. The Hundred Days' Reform held in 1898, during which the Guangxu Emperor of China sought to improve the central administration, was reversed by several court decisions. The Boxers were defeated by Chinese Imperial troops in 1898, and consequently they turned their attention to foreign missionaries whom they saw as agents of foreign imperialists.

The Uprising

The first significant trouble began in 1891 when anti-missionary riots took place in the Yangzi Valley. In 1895, anti-Christian riots occurred in Chengdu and Sichuan provinces. The next incident was in 1897 when 2 German missionaries were hacked to death by a band of 30 armed men who broke into the missionary residence. The large Boxer uprising began in Shandong province in 1898 as a response to the German occupation of the Jiao Zhou region, the British seizing of Weihai city, and the failure of the Imperial Court's Self-Strengthening Movement.

By 1898, large bands of Boxers had attacked Christians in the villages of Guan County. Trouble was occurring elsewhere and missionaries from Germany, France, Italy and America were being menaced by the Boxers in the Shandong province. In Pingyuan, a village dispute escalated into a major disturbance in which Chinese government troops were dispatched to battle the Boxers. The leaders of the Boxers were arrested and were executed in Peking—an event that further polarized the two sides and energized the Boxers into forging a greater movement against Christian churches and households.

In 1899, 1,500 Boxers attacked the Senluo Temple near the village of Zhifang. Although the Boxers were only armed with swords, spears and a few rifles, they attacked the temple with such ferocity that they repelled the Chinese government troops and sent them into retreat. However, the government forces were able to regroup with cavalry reinforcements, and they proceeded to counterattack. The government forces inflicted 27 casualties on the Boxers who then fled, thus ending the first major battle between the Boxers and the Qing Dynasty troops. The event inspired the Boxers to change their focus from just being against foreign religions to one that encompassed opposition to all foreigners and foreign influences.

In 1900, a Boxer resurgence occurred as thousands of them came to Peking to block a foreign relief expedition, to besiege the foreign legations and to provoke a full-scale war in the hopes of getting the approval of the Chinese government court. The Imperial Court forced the Empress to issue edicts in defense of the Boxers, an action that elicited strong complaints from foreign diplomats. In 1900, the Boxers slaughtered 60 Chinese men, women and children in the village of Kaolo, but the majority of the foreign ministers still did not comprehend the gravity of the situation—although the French and British Legations did issue calls for troops to be sent. In 1900, the Boxers were joined by elements of the Imperial army, and they attacked foreign compounds in the cities of Tianjin and Peking. They also hunted down and murdered all Chinese who had been connected with the foreigners. In this attack they systematically tortured their victims and then mutilated them in a hideous manner. In addition, they set fire to all the shops that sold foreign goods, incinerating about 4,000 stores.

The Legation Quarter was saved by the barriers of the city walls and by the barricades that had been erected in front of the Legation. The legations of the United Kingdom, France, Belgium, the Netherlands, the United States, Russia and Japan were linked into a fortified compound—one that became a refuge for foreign citizens in Peking. The Spanish and Belgian legations were also able to reach the compound safely, but the German legation was stormed before the staff could escape. When the envoy for the German Empire was murdered by a Manchu fighter, the foreign powers demanded redress from the Chinese government. They also sent the first contingent of troops from America, Britain, Russia, France, Italy and Japan.

The fortified legation compound remained under siege from Boxer forces in 1900. Under the command of the British minister to China the legation staff and security personnel defended the compound—mostly with the use of an old muzzle-loaded cannon. Even with superior numbers, the poorly armed Boxers were unable to break into the compound, which was finally relieved by the international army of the Eight-Nation Alliance in 1900.

The Eight-Nation Alliance

Foreign navies had started building up their presence along the northern China coast in 1900. Before the sieges had started and upon the request of foreign embassies in Beijing, Navy troops from 8 countries (France, Russia, Britain, the United States, Germany, Italy, Japan and Austria) were dispatched by train from Takou to Beijing. These troops joined the legations and were able to contribute to their defense. However, as the situation worsened, a second International force of Marines under the command of the British Vice Admiral Edward Seymour was dispatched from Takou to Beijing in 1900.

The foreign powers demanded the surrender of the Taku forts. When this demand was ignored, British Vice-Admiral Sir Edward Seymour ordered the landing of a British force. He also informed the commanding officers of the other foreign contingents of his intentions. The 2,000 troops were transported by train from Takou to Tianjin, with the agreement of the Chinese government, but the railway between Tianjin and Beijing was severed. Admiral Seymour resolved to move forward and repaired the railway, using progress on foot as necessary, to get to Tianjin. Upon reaching Tianjin, the military convoy was surrounded, the railway behind and in front of them was destroyed, and they were attacked by Chinese irregulars and governmental troops. News arrived regarding the attacks on foreign legations', and so Admiral Seymour decided to continue advancing, this time along the Pei-Ho River, towards Tong-Tcheou. But, they had to abandon the advance due to stiff resistance, and retreated Southward along the Pei-Ho River. They took over the Chinese camps of Hsi-Kou, in which they were surrounded until a regiment composed of Russian troops from Port-Arthur arrived to assist them. They completed their retreat back to Tianjin, but suffered the loss of 350 men as a result of the operation.

The allied forces numbered 2,400 men—a very small army compared to 30,000 Boxers and 16,000 Chinese Imperial troops who were camped near Tientsin. Thus, the Boxers were able to burn down all of the missions in Tientsin. The Boxers also set fire to all houses. With a difficult military situation in Tianjin, the eight allied nations took steps to reinforce their military presence. The allied forces attacked with 9 ships and captured the Taku Forts that were commanding the approaches to Tianjin. The assault resulted in the capture of 4 Chinese destroyers by the United States, which enabled the allies to bring more troops on shore. The international force captured Tianjin.

The allied assault by 6,000 men on Tientsin began against a Chinese force of 30,000 Boxers and Imperial troops. Despite the odds, the Japanese troops blew the South gate to the city open, and foreign troops captured the city. The Chinese troops and the Boxers left, leaving behind over 200 foreigners who had been killed or wounded in the diplomatic quarter. Hundreds of Chinese Christians also perished from the violence, disease and starvation that they had been subjected to before the allies relieved the city. The allies lost about 750 men who were killed, wounded or turned up missing.

The next step in the allied assault was the march to Beijing by the combined allied forces of 20,000 troops. They faced 70,000 Chinese Imperial troops and 50,000 to 100,000 Boxers who were encountered along the way. The international force, with British General Alfred Gaselee acting as the commanding officer, called the Eight-Nation Alliance, eventually numbered 54,000 men—and this massive force encountered only minor resistance. The international force reached and occupied Peking, but again over 400 Chinese and foreigners died there while in other areas over 200 foreigners and tens of thousands of Chinese converts were killed.

In the assault on Peking, the United States was able to play a significant role in suppressing the Boxer Rebellion due to the presence of American ships and troops that had been deployed in the Philippines. These military troops of the 14th Infantry Regiment of the United States Army were used in the suppression of the Boxer Rebellion in what was termed "The China Relief Expedition." They battered their way through a series of courtyards leading to the South gate of the Imperial City, and then to the dwelling place of the Son of Heaven—the Forbidden City.

An international expeditionary force under the command of German General Alfred Graf von Waldersee arrived too late to take part in the main fighting, but nevertheless undertook several punitive expeditions against the Boxers. Boxers who were captured were executed by beheadings carried out by the Chinese government. The Boxers disappeared, shed their red and yellow uniforms and abandoned their weapons—thus ending the uprising. A reign of terror ensued in which over one-half of the population panicked and fled the city. Finally, a victory parade was arranged—one that marched right through the Imperial City as a salutary lesson for China.

The Peace Treaty

In 1901, the Qing court was compelled to sign the "Boxer Protocol" known as the Peace Agreement between the Eight-Nation Alliance and China. The peace treaty was signed in 1901. The protocol ordered the execution of 10 high-ranking officials linked to the outbreak, and the punishment—usually by death—of 100 other minor officials who were found guilty for the slaughter of Westerners in China.

China was fined war reparations of 450 million tael of fine silver (about $333 million, or 67.5 million British pounds) to be paid over a period of 39 years at 4% interest per year. The reparation was for the loss that China had caused, with the United States share being 7%. An increase of the existing tariff to 5%, and a tax on previously duty-free merchandise was also made part of the agreement. However, China was not required to surrender any territory. China eventually paid 670 million taels of silver from 1901 to 1939. Some of the reparation was earmarked by both Britain and the United States for the education of Chinese students at overseas institutions, including the establishment of the Tsinghua University.

The military provisions of the treaty included the destruction of the forts located at Dagu, the stationing of foreign troops along the approaches to the national capital at Beijing, the placement of a permanent legation guard in Beijing, and a stipulation that China could not import any arms for a period of 2 years. The military defeat produced a new wave of 1,000 missionaries that were sent to China under the China Inland Mission, and by 1906, there were 3,500 Protestant missionaries working in China who managed to convert 180,000 Chinese to the Christian religion.

The Annexation of Hawaii

Rulers of Hawaii

In 1872, King Kamehameha V died, and William Lunalilo was confirmed as King of Hawaii by the Hawaiian Legislature after an informal popular vote. King Lunalilo made serious efforts to democratize the constitution, but once again, the question of the treaty of reciprocity with the United States arose. King Lunalilo endorsed the cession of Pearl Harbor to the United States, even though he felt uneasy about the presence of the powerful American giant.

In 1874, King Lunalilo died and King David Kalakaua was elected by the Hawaiian Legislature. King Kalakaua was concerned with the well-being of his Hawaiian people, and he maintained a policy of filling administrative posts with Hawaiians wherever possible. Nevertheless, King Kalakaua insisted that there was room in Hawaii for all kinds of people. Toward the end of his reign, his cabinet was overthrown, a new constitution deprived him of almost all his power, and an insurrection took place favoring the abdication of King Kalakaua and his replacement by his sister, Princess Liliuokalani. Subsequently, she took over as Queen upon the death of King Kalakaua in 1891.

When Queen Liliuokalani came to power, the political and economic climate in Hawaii was extremely complicated. Rivalry was intense between white businessmen who dominated the economy and the Hawaiian politicians who still retained the power to get things accomplished. The annexationists were outnumbered, and the majority of the Hawaiian people were against annexation, but the economic power structure was not intimidated since American businessmen considered Hawaiians incapable of self-government. They firmly believed that the monarchy was too inept to safeguard the interests of property and profits.

Queen Liliuokalani announced her intention to promulgate a new constitution, which would restore the power of the monarchy. In response, a Committee of Safety was formed by annexationists. They created a provisional government and a militia, and then made the move by having armed companies of militia take over government buildings and offices. Marines and sailors from the *USS Boston* landed to keep order in Honolulu and their commander, Captain G.C. Wiltse, openly supported the Provisionals, thus making Queen Liliuokalani essentially powerless. In 1893, Queen Liliuokalani faced the inevitable and surrendered under protest. Minister Stevens, at the request of the Provisional Government's advisory council, raised the United States flag over Honolulu.

Annexation by the United States

Annexation was thought to be a mere formality, but President Cleveland's administration concluded that the monarchy had been overthrown by force with the complicity of the United States minister, and he refused to consider annexation. Nevertheless, in 1894, the Republic of Hawaii was established, with Sanford Dole as President.

In 1895, Hawaiians loyal to the Queen staged a revolt in an attempt to restore Queen Liliuokalani to the throne. The revolt was crushed, the Queen was arrested and she was placed under detention in her Iolani Palace. She was also forced to relinquish any claim to the throne as a condition to obtain amnesty for the Hawaiian rebels. President William McKinley signed the resolution of annexation in 1898. Large numbers of royalists and Hawaiians gathered at the home of the deposed Queen Liliuokalani to console her and to pay homage to the last monarch of the Hawaiian kingdom.

A Hawaiian Annexation Commission headed by Lorrin Thurston had been in Washington attempting to negotiate a union with the United States. The regime, which he represented, was an oligarchy composed of Honolulu businessmen and lawyers. However, they were hated by the Hawaiians because they had overthrown Queen Liliuokalani when they had sought annexation under the administration of President Benjamin Harrison. Although this attempt failed, the republic was nevertheless proclaimed as an interim regime pending annexation in the future. But, the Administration of President Grover Cleveland was hostile to this oligarchy, and Thurston resigned as Hawaiian minister, having become *persona non grata*.

With the election of President William McKinley in 1896, the push for annexation resumed, and the ruling oligarchy sent another annexation committee with Thurston as its chairman. But, President McKinley was unreceptive towards annexation, especially since there was very little interest in Hawaii at the time. Thus, the treaty was resubmitted only to be blocked in the Senate by the sugar trust and by the opponents of imperialism. With the failure of the second treaty, proponents of annexation resorted to a joint resolution — but this was also blocked.

As American interest in Hawaii increased due to its strategic location for the expanding American navy, expansionists such as Theodore Roosevelt and others rejected the isolationist views. In 1898, Consul General William Haywood in Honolulu requested more coal storage space for the United States Navy. His request made the Executive Council of the republic aware that support of the American cause in the Spanish-American War would probably ensure passage of the joint resolution. Therefore, in 1898, the republic of Hawaii granted the temporary use of 4 lots for the storage of coal by the United States Navy.

In 1898, Minister H. Sewall in Honolulu wrote Secretary of State John Sherman that President Sanford Dole had been canvassing to find out what stance Hawaii should take in the event of war with Spain. Many of the sugar planters opposed annexation because they would then be subject to American labor laws and to the Chinese Exclusion Act. Those businessmen whom Dole consulted advised the Executive Council not to declare neutrality in the event of war but to put all of the islands' resources at the disposal of the United States Navy. Sewall reported this to Sherman who in turn gave a copy of the letter to the Chairman of the Senate Committee on Foreign Relations.

When this proposal became known, it was published in the press and was discussed with acrimony. Among the Honolulu newspapers, the *Star* argued that the republic should most certainly not declare neutrality and proposed that the American flag be hoisted. In an opposing view, the *Pacific Commercial Advertiser* insisted that Hawaii should declare neutrality, and that the *USS Bennington*, which was on duty in port should be given 24 hours to depart in the event of war. Their position was that the American flag should not be raised, and that the republic should behave with strict neutrality. They also warned that Spanish cruisers from the Carolines might sail to the islands and bombard Hilo, Hawaii and Lahaina, Maui.

The *Independent* warned that a defenseless Hawaii would be subject not only to attack but to seizure by Spanish privateers. The *Independent* argued that that the Spanish Pacific Squadron was stronger than the American Asiatic Squadron, and also that the 5 major powers of continental Europe supported Spain.

Thus, public opinion in Hawaii was divided, but the vast majority of Hawaiians were against annexation, as evidenced by a petition to Congress not to annex the islands. Although it was signed by 35,000 Hawaiians, the petition was discredited by Thurston on grounds that many names on it were forged. Even so, Thurston conceded that most Hawaiians wanted the islands to remain independent. He knew that the American population generally supported the republic, but that the annexationists were definitely in a minority position since they were only supported by the 500 militiamen of the Hawaii National Guard.

Hawaii's diplomatic representative Minister Francis Hatch sent his secretary to the United States Navy Department to offer the *China* to the Navy as a reserve naval ship. Hatch also recommended that the Navy buy up the entire coal supply in Honolulu. In addition, Hatch advised the Executive Council to make a battalion of the Hawaii National Guard who would be available to the United States Navy if necessary. Subsequently, when war was declared against Spain, Hawaii refused to declare neutrality and instead placed all harbor resources at the disposal of the United States forces.

The Newlands joint resolution to annex Hawaii was passed by Congress and signed by President McKinley in 1898. After annexation, the *Klondike* steamer moored at the Honolulu Harbor with troops of the 1st New York Volunteer Infantry on board plus United States Volunteer Engineers. They were stationed at the American military post in the islands, Camp McKinley, in the lea of Diamond Head. With the annexation of Hawaii came the Palmyra Atoll, which had been annexed by the United States in 1859, but later abandoned, and then later claimed by Hawaii. Also, the Johnston Atoll, which was claimed by the United States and Hawaii in 1858, became undisputed in 1898, after the annexation of Hawaii. In 1900, Hawaii officially became a United States Territory, and Sanford Dole became its first governor.

When President Dwight Eisenhower appointed Samuel Wilder King as governor of Hawaii, the push was on for statehood. William F. Quinn succeeded King as governor, and in 1959, a bill to consider statehood was introduced into Congress. In 1959, Hawaii became the United States' 50th state—although it had to be ratified by the 240 electoral precincts of Hawaii to accomplish statehood.

Theodore Roosevelt

Vice President

President William McKinley won the 1900 election by receiving 292 Electoral College votes. Theodore Roosevelt was elected as Vice President.

On September 6, 1901, Roosevelt was informed that President McKinley had been shot by an assailant, and was requested to come to Buffalo, New York. On September 14, 1901, President McKinley died from his wounds. Theodore Roosevelt became President.

Significant Events: 1901

Great Britain and the United States signed the Hay-Paunceforte Treaty that authorized the United States to build a canal across Central America.

President Roosevelt warned of the growing danger from corporate mergers that were creating monopolies. He requested the establishment of a Bureau of Corporations as part of a new Cabinet-level Department of Commerce to provide information on trusts to present to the DOJ for possible indictments.

Significant Events: 1902

The United States signed a treaty with Denmark for the purchase of the Virgin Islands. The Senate approved the treaty, but the Danish Rigsdag rejected it. It was not until 1917, when a Danish plebiscite agreed to the sale that the transaction was completed for the amount of $25 million for which the United States received the islands of St. Croix, St. Thomas and St. John.

Congress created the Bureau of the Census.

Attorney General Knox invoked the Sherman Anti-Trust Law against Morgan and Harriman Northern Securities Company in New Jersey.

The Chinese Exclusion Act was extended to prohibit the immigration of Chinese laborers into the Philippine Islands.

140,000 members of the United Mine Workers went on strike because of several grievances against the railroads. This action shut down the anthracite coalfields of eastern Pennsylvania. A riot by miners was broken up by the militia at Shenandoah, Pennsylvania.

United States troops from Cuba were withdrawn upon the inauguration of the first President of Cuba as the island nation was given its independence.

Congress passed the Newlands Reclamation Act to authorize the building of irrigation dams across the West.

Congress passed the Spooner Act that authorized the President to buy the rights from France for canal construction across Panama for a sum of $40 million.

President Roosevelt formed a national forest preserve consisting of 150 million acres, and withdrew 85 million acres of Alaska.

Congress passed the Philippine Government Act that declared it as an unorganized territory and authorized a commission to administer the islands, with a civil government to be established by Presidential order.

President Roosevelt threatened to send troops to Pennsylvania to seize the mines and operate them with military personnel. Secretary of State Root convinced J. P. Morgan to agree to arbitration by a 5-member commission after the miners agreed to return to work.

Significant Events: 1903

Columbia and the United States signed the Hay-Herran Treaty for the right of the United States to build a canal through Panama, with a 99-year lease. The Senate approved it with $10 million to be paid by the United States, but Columbia rejected the proposal in 1903.

Congress passed the Expedition Act to provide priority to antitrust cases that were in the circuit courts.

Congress created the Department of Labor and Commerce as a Cabinet post, but did not include a Bureau of Corporations as part of that department.

Congress created the General Staff of the Army to centralize the military.

Congress passed the Elkins Act that declared all rebates on published freights to be illegal.

In the case of *Champion v. Ames* the Supreme Court upheld a federal law that prohibits lottery tickets to be sent through the mails from one state to another.

Wisconsin became the first state to adopt a direct primary system for elections.

2,000 workers, including Mexican laborers, went on strike in Morenci, Arizona to ask for better working conditions from the Phelps Dodge Corporation. The strike was broken up by the use of local territorial militia and by 5 companies of federal troops that were sent by President Roosevelt. The Mexican laborer leaders were rounded up and deported back to Mexico.

The Panamanian Province revolted against the Columbian government and set up a new government. President Roosevelt sent 10 United States warships to the area to prevent Colombia from landing troops in Panama. Secretary of State Hays recognized the new Panamanian government and completed canal negotiations with the Panamanian

Minister, Philippe Buneau-Varilla. The Hays-Buneau-Varilla treaty was signed by Panama and the United States to give the United States permanent rights to a 10-mile wide strip in return for $10 million and a yearly rent payment of $250,000.

Significant Events: 1904

In the case of *Gonzales v. Williams* the Supreme Court ruled that Puerto Ricans were not aliens, and thus could enter the continental United States, although it did not classify Puerto Ricans as citizens of the United States.

President Roosevelt appointed the Panama Canal Commission consisting of 7 members to oversee the construction of the canal.

A fire destroyed 2,600 buildings in an 80-block area, and caused $80 million in property damages in Baltimore, Maryland.

In the case of *Northern Securities Company v. United States* the Supreme Court ruled that the company had violated the Sherman Anti-Trust Law.

A brigand named Raisuli took 2 American hostages in Tangier, Morocco as an act of defiance against the ruling sultan. He demanded ransom for them as well as the release of men being held by Moroccan authorities, which the sultan refused. President Roosevelt sent a United States Navy squadron to Tangier with a contingent of Marines aboard with orders to land and pursue Raisuli. Rather than risk a foreign takeover of his country, the sultan agreed to Raisuli's demands, and the 2 American captives were released.

A fire aboard the steamship *General Slocum* killed 900 persons in New York Harbor.

25,000 textile mill workers went on strike to protest working conditions in the mills at Fall River, Massachusetts.

Theodore Roosevelt won the presidency by getting 336 Electoral votes. His Vice President Charles Fairbanks also got 336 Electoral votes.

The Roosevelt Corollary was articulated by President Roosevelt. It extended the Monroe Doctrine by stating that the United States has the responsibility to redress wrongs that are inflicted by a foreign state to any country within the sphere of influence of the United States.

Significant Events: 1905

Acting under the Roosevelt Corollary, the United States intervened to place Dominican revenues under its jurisdiction to discharge the debt owed to Britain by the Dominican Republic.

In the case of *Swift and Co. v. United States* the Supreme Court ruled in favor of the government's action to break up the beef trust monopoly.

In the case of *Jacobson v. Massachusetts* the Supreme Court ruled that state compulsory vaccination laws were constitutional.

In the case of *Lochner v. New York* the Supreme Court ruled that a state law that limited maximum working hours for bakers was unconstitutional.

President Roosevelt mediated between Japan and Russia in their ongoing war. This led to the Treaty of Portsmouth that was signed in 1905, thus ending the conflict. For his effort, President Roosevelt was awarded the Nobel Peace Prize in 1906.

The Industrial Workers of the World (IWW) was founded at Chicago, Illinois.

A yellow fever epidemic broke out in New Orleans, Louisiana that culminated in 3,000 cases with 400 deaths.

The Niagara movement group led by W. E. B Du Bois, John Hope, Frederick L. McGhee and William Monroe Trotter met on the Canadian side of the Niagara River to discuss civil liberties, racial discrimination and human brotherhood. The Niagara Movement eventually established chapters in 21 states and reached 170 members, but by 1910 had disbanded due to internal dissension. In 1911, the remaining membership of the Niagara Movement formed the National Association for the Advancement of Colored People (NAACP).

President Roosevelt assigned Charles Evans Hughes to investigate the insurance companies. A total of 57 hearings were conducted that unearthed schemes and corruption, which led to the reform of the insurance industry.

President Roosevelt pushed for government centralization by asking for a pure food and drug law, government supervision of insurance companies, an investigation of child labor by the Department of Commerce, legislation to allow the Interstate Commerce Commission to establish maximum railroad rates, and an employer liability law for the District of Columbia.

Attorney General Moody directed the instituting of procedures against companies offering or receiving rebates, including Armour, Swift, Cudahy and the Chicago and Alton Railway.

Significant Events: 1906

In a conference held in Algeciras, Spain, President Roosevelt mediated between France and Germany to avoid a war between these two countries over Morocco.

In the case of *Hale v. Henkel* the Supreme Court ruled that witnesses could be compelled to testify against the corporations they were employed by, as well as to provide papers and documents that were potentially pertinent to the case at hand.

The largest earthquake to strike the United States mainland occurred in San Francisco, California. 500 people were killed and 500,000 people were made homeless.

Congress passed the Hepburn Act to permit regulation of rates charged by railroads, pipelines and terminals.

Congress passed the Meat Inspection Act to provide for government inspection of all meats packing companies.

Congress passed the Pure Food and Drug Act to provide federal inspection of and forbid the manufacture, sale, or transportation of adulterated food products and poisonous patent medicines. It also required a statement of the contents on labels.

A group of armed men shot up the town of Brownsville, Texas, killing one man and wounding another. The 25th Infantry Regiment, which was an all-black unit, was accused of the raid. President Roosevelt ordered all 3 companies discharged without honor, thus blemishing the records of 167 black men.

Race riots occurred in Atlanta, Georgia. 21 people were killed—18 of them black—and many more were wounded. Martial law was declared in the city to quell the disturbance.

The San Francisco Board of Education in California ordered all Japanese children transferred to a segregated school. President Roosevelt met with the board and made an agreement with them to have the segregation order rescinded—in return for President Roosevelt and Secretary of State Root negotiating an agreement with Japan to restrict the immigration of Japanese people into the United States.

President Roosevelt sent troops into Cuba to quell a revolt, and they took over the Cuban government. The Platt Amendment was invoked by President Roosevelt to assume military control of the country.

President Roosevelt requested a graduated income tax, federal supervision of all companies that were engaged in interstate commerce, and legislation to prohibit political contributions by corporations, limit injunctions in railroad disputes, reduction of the hours worked by railroad workers and the forbidding of the use of child labor.

Significant Events: 1907

Congress passed an act that forbid corporations from contributing to election campaigns of candidates for national office.

Congress passed the General Appropriations Bill that increased the salaries of Representatives and Senators to $7,500, and for Cabinet members and the Vice President to $12,000.

Congress passed the Immigration Act that included a provision to restrict immigration by Japanese laborers, which President Roosevelt invoked.

President Roosevelt sent United States Marines to Puerto Cortes, Honduras to quell a revolution instigated by a war with Nicaragua—and to protect the North American bananas trade.

Congress passed the Department of Agriculture Appropriations Bill. To avoid the dilemma of either denying the funds by vetoing or losing control over federal lands by approving it, President Roosevelt issued an executive order to take 16 million acres out of circulation—before approving the bill.

President Roosevelt appointed the Inland Waterways Commission to study forest preservation and commercial waterways.

A downturn in the stock market occurred as a result of a currency shortage, with the biggest casualty being the collapse of the Knickerbocker Trust Company. President Roosevelt asked J. P. Morgan for help, and he responded by importing $100 million in gold from Europe to shore up the United States currency and stem the panic.

Oklahoma was admitted as the 46th state in the Union.

President Roosevelt sent the United States fleet consisting of 16 battleships on a cruise around the world to convince the world that the United States was a major naval power.

The President asked for income and inheritance taxes, a federal incorporation law, the fixing of railroad rates, federal regulation of railway stocks, currency reform, limits on injunctions, enactment of workmen's compensation laws, creation of a postal savings bank and establishing further control of campaign contributions.

A coal mine explosion at Monogah, West Virginia killed 361 persons, and another coal mine explosion at Jacobs Creek, Pennsylvania killed 239 persons. Another explosion and cave-in at Monogah, West Virginia buried 100 miners.

Significant Events: 1908

In the case of *Loewe v. Lawlor* the Supreme Court ruled that the antitrust law applied to labor combinations, and declared union boycotting as illegal.

Congress passed a bill to regulate child labor in the District of Columbia.

Congress passed the Aldrich-Vreeland Act to provide additional currency.

President Roosevelt named the National Commission of Natural Resources with 57 members to discuss conservation of the nation's basic resources.

Race riots broke out in Springfield, Illinois in which several blacks were lynched.

William Taft won the presidential election with an Electoral vote of 321. James S. Sherman won the Vice-Presidency with 321 Electoral votes.

Significant Events: 1909

Joseph Pulitzer, the owner of the *World* newspaper, was indicted by the government on 5 counts of criminal libel on orders from President Roosevelt. The *World* had stated that the $40 million paid by the United States had gone not to the French government as alleged, but to a dummy corporation fronting for J. P. Morgan and Company. It suggested that people close to the President had profited richly and implicated American greed in the Panamanian revolution. The paper accused President Roosevelt of deliberate lies. However, no case could be made against Pulitzer because of lack of evidence, and so no charges could be supported against him, and the charges were dismissed against the *World*. The government appealed the case, and the Supreme Court upheld the decision, thus guaranteeing freedom of the press.

The second occupation of Cuba by American troops ended.

President Roosevelt urged the formation of agencies to conserve resources. His proposals included the creation of a Bureau of Mines and the strengthening of the Inland Waterways Commission.

William Taft was inaugurated as President.

The Panama Canal

Initial Ideas

In 1804, President Thomas Jefferson talked about a possible canal through Central America. He was so enthused about the idea that when he sent the Lewis and Clark expedition for an exploration of the Western United States. One of the objectives that he listed was for them to find a Northwest waterway passage to the Pacific Ocean.

President John Quincy Adams encouraged a small group of American entrepreneurs who founded an isthmian canal company. They became involved in canal diplomacy and dispatched agents to the area, but very little was done.

In 1835, President Andrew Jackson expressed interest in a canal through Central America. He sent Army Colonel Charles Biddle to Central America to evaluate the possibility. However, Colonel Biddle concluded after hiking in the jungle that the building of such a canal in Panama was impractical.

In 1850, the Clayton-Bulwer Treaty between the United States and Great Britain was signed to bind both countries for joint control of any canal built through Nicaragua. However, President Zachary Taylor died, and his successor, President Millard Fillmore, did nothing further.

First Explorations

In 1854, President Franklin Pierce envisioned an Atlantic to Pacific canal route through the Isthmus of Darien across Panama. Secretary of the Navy James Dobbin ordered Lieutenant Issac Strain to form and lead an exploring expedition. Strain commanded the *Cyane* and landed at Caledonia Bay. He took a party of 27 men into the dense jungle where they got lost, ran out of food, suffered from foot soreness and flesh-embedding parasites, were afflicted with tropical diseases, and had their weapons rusted by all the rain. Six of the men died by starvation, and the rest subsisted by eating toads and palm nuts. However, in spite of its failure, the expedition contributed to the possibility that the eventual linking of the Atlantic and Pacific Oceans by a canal was still feasible.

In 1870, President Ulysses Grant instructed Admiral Daniel Ammen to organize a series of expeditions to survey the Central American area for the building of a water corridor. Commander Thomas Selfridge embarked on the first of these journeys aboard the steam-sloop *Nipsic*, along with Commander Edward Lull aboard the store-ship *Guard*. Commander Selfridge arrived at Caledonia Bay to survey the Darien wilderness in Panama while Commander Lull explored Nicaragua. A third expedition headed by Captain Robert Shufeldt explored Mexico. In all, 7 expeditions were authorized by President Grant between 1870 and 1875 to consider the possibility of canal plans and to put forth proposals.

Subsequent Actions

In 1880, President Rutherford Hayes addressed Congress and declared that any canal built in Central America or Mexico must be administered by the American government. This declaration rejected the plan of French diplomat Ferdinand de Lesseps to construct such a canal in Panama.

In 1898, President William McKinley directed Secretary of State John Hay to negotiate a new canal treaty with Great Britain. Hay and the British Ambassador Sir Julian Pauncefote negotiated a treaty, but the Senate refused to ratify it without amendments. Hay threatened to resign, but was induced to stay by both President McKinley and later by President Theodore Roosevelt after he assumed the office of the presidency upon President McKinley's assassination. Hay renegotiated a second treaty with Pauncefote, which was then ratified by the Senate. The pertinent part of the second Hay-Pauncefote Treaty was that the United States was free to do whatever was necessary to protect the canal against lawlessness and disorder.

The Construction of the Panama Railway

In 1846, at Bogota, Columbia, American charge d' affaires Benjamin Alden Bidlack signed a treaty with President Tomas Cipriano de Mosquera. One of the agreements included in the treaty was the granting to the United States the exclusive right of transit across the Isthmus of Panama. In exchange, the United States guaranteed the neutrality of the Isthmus and Panama's right of sovereignty there. With the Bidlack Treaty, the construction of a railway was made possible.

William Aspinwall, the founder of the Pacific Mail Steamship Company of New York, drew up a plan to construct a railway across the isthmus, and with his partners created the Panama Railroad Company. The company raised $1 million from the sale of stock, and then hired companies to do the engineering and route studies. The Panama Railway was built across the isthmus between 1850 and 1855, running 47 miles from Colon by Limon Bay on the Atlantic coast to Panama City by the Bay of Panama on the Pacific coast. Estimates of between 5,000 to 10,000 workers—most of them black—died during its construction from diseases and accidents.

The railway project was a major technological achievement, with over 300 bridges and culverts being built along a route that passed over mountains and through swamps. When completed at a cost of $8 million, the railway carried the heaviest volume of freight per unit length of any railroad in the world. In the process of constructing the railroad, two major facts were discovered:

- A gap in the mountains at a point called Culebra that was significantly lower than previous estimates had indicated
- A difference in the size of the tides between the Pacific and Atlantic Oceans

Negotiations With Colombia

In 1887, a regiment from the United States surveyed possible canal routes in Nicaragua. In 1889, the Maritime Canal Company was asked to begin creating a canal in Nicaragua. However, the company lost its funding during the 1893 stock panic, and all canal work ceased in Nicaragua. In 1897 and in 1899, Congress at the request of President McKinley created a Canal Commission to look into possible construction of a canal, and Nicaragua was chosen as the location. In 1899, the First Isthmian Canal Commission was established to examine the possibilities of a Central American canal and to recommend a route. In 1901, the Walker Commission reported that a canal should be built through Nicaragua—unless the French canal company was willing to sell its assets for $40 million.

When Theodore Roosevelt became President of the United States in 1901, he wanted a canal built across Central America, and for it to be controlled by the United States. In 1902, the House of Representatives authorized the President to build a Nicaraguan canal by allocating $180 million. Congress also appropriated $135 million for the acquisition for continuation of the canal project—with a stipulation that an alternative site through Panama would be considered if the proper negotiations could be obtained from France and Colombia. President Roosevelt tstarted negotiations with Columbia to obtain the rights. The Hay-Herran Treaty, which offered a payment of $10 million and an annual rental fee of $250,000 for a 6-mile wide strip was signed by the United States and Columbia in 1903. The Senate approved the treaty, but the Colombian Senate did not because they considered the payment figure as being too low.

The Takeover by the United States

Instead of renegotiating, President Roosevelt considered another possibility. He promised support to Panamanian rebels if they were to revolt and set up an independent state. President Roosevelt stationed 10 American Navy battleships near the Isthmus, and landed 400 Marines to protect the life and property of Americans in the area, especially the American-controlled Isthmian Railroad. In 1903, Panama declared its independence from Colombia while the American battleship *Nashville* commanded by Commander Hubbard impeded any interference from the Columbian ship *Cartagena*.

The United States recognized the new government of Panama, and began negotiations for the canal, with the outcome being the Hay-Bunau-Varilla Treaty that was signed in 1903, and ratified by the Senate. The treaty granted the United States the rights to the Canal Zone in perpetuity, which was to extend 5 miles on either side of the canal route. In return, Panama was to receive a payment of $10 million, and an annual rental payment of $250,000—plus a guarantee by the United States that it would maintain Panama's independence. In addition, the French Panama Canal Company was awarded $40 million for the transfer of their assets in Panama to the United States. Panama approved the treaty in 1903, and the Senate ratified it in 1904.

Beginning of the Project

In 1904, an Isthmian Canal Commission was created to have authority over the Canal Zone affairs, and John Findley Wallace was appointed as the chief engineer in charge of construction. Wallace arrived in Panama to take over from acting chief engineer Major Black, and in 1904, almost 1,800 workers had started on the task to lay the groundwork for building the canal. He had 3,500 men at work, and installed the first of the 95-ton Bucyrus steam shovels to begin digging at the Culebra Cut.

Wallace experimented with both the leftover old French equipment and the modern American equipment. He also provided Panama City and Colon with their own water systems and sewage facilities. However, there was still a lack of right tools such that railroad spikes were being driven in with axes. In addition, there was the basic problem of what to do with the excavated rock and dirt. There was no comprehensive plan to assemble the necessary equipment, to house and feed the labor force, to deal with the problems of yellow fever and malaria, and to put the Panama Railway in operating order.

Continuation of the Project

In 1905, Wallace resigned, and was replaced by John Frank Stevens. However, many problems challenged the project, including the cataloging of the equipment left behind by the French, the refurbishing of over 2,000 buildings that were uninhabitable, the obtainment of housing for the workers, the decayed state of the existing Panama Railway, the bureaucracy introduced from Washington, D.C., and the health issue caused by the flare-up of yellow fever and malaria.

Stevens realized that an investment in infrastructure was necessary, and he upgraded the railway, improved sanitation in the cities of Panama and Colon, remodeled the old French buildings, and built hundreds of new ones to provide housing. He also undertook the task of recruiting the huge labor force required for the building of the canal by dispatching recruiting agents to the West Indies, Italy and Spain. He improved the drilling and dirt removal equipment at the Culebra Cut, and revised the procedure for the disposal of the vast quantities of excavated soil. He also ordered the initiation of a program for the reduction of all disease.

Dr. William Henry Welch of John Hopkins Medical School had recommended to President Roosevelt to assign a sanitary officer to tackle the sources of disease on the Isthmus. In 1905, Dr. William Crawford Gorgas was named as the army doctor to concentrate on the task, especially the eradication of yellow fever and malaria in Panama. Dr. Gorgas orchestrated a thorough campaign against mosquito breeding places, and ordered houses to be fumigated, screens to be placed on windows, doors and porches, streets to be paved, dirt roads to be covered with oil, swamps to be dried, rivers to be sprayed with pesticides, and cisterns and cesspools to be oiled. He also had exterminators hunt down mosquitoes whenever they entered any habitation. As a result, yellow fever cases disappeared by 1906 while malaria cases were reduced to very low levels.

By 1906, there were almost 24,000 men working on the project. The workers were from 97 different countries, with most of them—about 20,000—being blacks from Barbados.

Stevens hired workers who were skilled in 40 different specialties. To entice them to work on the project, Stevens offered workers free transportation to the Isthmus, free housing and free medical treatment. He also hired several hundred unskilled workers from the Basque region in Spain, and eventually imported more than 8,000 for gang labor such as for moving railroad tracks.

Stevens favored a sea-level canal, and a report submitted to the White House estimated that it would cost $247 million and would take 12 to 13 years to complete. However, a minority proposal written by Alfred Noble advocated a lock canal with a high-level lake and a dam at Gatun. The time to complete a lock canal was estimated to be between 8 and 9 years—at the same cost as for a sea-level canal.

In 1905, President Roosevelt sent a team of engineers to Panama to investigate the relative merits of either a lock canal or a sea-level canal, including estimates of costs and time requirements. The engineers decided in favor of a sea-level canal, but the Isthmian Canal Commission (ICC) opposed this scheme. Stevens considered the consequences of landslides, the effect of the Chagres River, and the amount of digging that had to be done for a sea-level canal—and he changed his mind. His report to President Roosevelt was instrumental in convincing him to proceed with a lock-based scheme instead. The new plan called for a canal with 3 locks on the Atlantic side, 3 locks on the Pacific side, and a lake in the middle created by damming the Chagres River at Gatun. President Roosevelt agreed that this was the best option, the ICC overrode the majority opinion of the engineering advisory board and accepted the minority report for a lock canal written by retired Army engineer Brigadier General Henry Abbot. Congress ratified the lock-based plan, which President Roosevelt signed into law in 1906.

An issue arose as to whether the canal work should be carried out by contractors or by the government. Stevens favored the government approach, and President Roosevelt concurred. President Roosevelt decided that Army engineers should carry out the work, and he appointed Major George Washington Goethals as chief engineer under the direction of Stevens in 1907. Stevens opposed the decision to involve the army and he resigned. President Roosevelt appointed Goethals to replace Stevens.

Completion of the Project

The work that had been done under Wallace and Stevens was not very much in terms of actual construction, but in terms of preparation their efforts proved to be essential. When Goethals assumed command, the infrastructure for the construction effort had been created, the health problem had been solved by Dr. Gorgas, and he was able to start making progress on construction. Promoted to Lieutenant Colonel in 1907, Goethals took 2 Army engineers, Majors David du Bose Gaillard and William Sibert with him to Panama. Gaillard had experience in river-and-harbor work while Sibert had a river-and-canal work background.

Other assignments included Rear Admiral Harry Hardwood Rousseau who was given the responsibility for the design and construction of all terminals, wharves, coaling stations, dry docks, machine shops and warehouses. Lieutenant Frederick Mears was put in charge of relocating the Panama Railroad, a task estimated to take 5 years, and that involved building 40 miles of new track at a cost of $9 million. Goethals placed Army engineer Major Harry Hodges in charge of the ICC office in Washington, D.C. to help select and inspect equipment to be sent to the Canal Zone. Hodges also served as acting chief engineer whenever Goethals was away from the Isthmus.

Goethals divided the canal project into 3 major divisions: Atlantic, Pacific and Central. The Atlantic division under Major Sibert was responsible for construction of the massive breakwater at the entrance to Limon Bay, the Gatun locks and the approach channel, and the huge Gatun Dam. The Pacific Division under Sydney Williamson was responsible for the Pacific entrance to the canal, including the breakwater in Panama Bay, the approach channel, and the Miraflores and Miguel locks and their associated dams. The Central division under Major Gaillard was responsible for everything in between, including the excavation of the Culebra Cut, which involved cutting through 8 miles of the continental divide—with the cut having a bottom width of 300 feet and a top width of one-third mile, the height of the cut being 85 feet.

By 1910, there were almost 40,000 people working on the canal project. The building of the locks, which were done by the McClintic-Marshall Company, began with the Gatun Locks at Limon Bay on the Atlantic side in 1909. However, the Pacific side locks at the Bay of Panama were finished first—the Pedro Miguel Lock in 1911, and Miraflores Lock in 1913. Four dams were also constructed to create the 2 artificial lakes for the canal: Lake Gatun and Lake Miraflores. Two dams were constructed at Miraflores, a third dam at Pedro Miguel, and a fourth dam at Gatun to block the Chagres River. In 1913, steam shovels made a passage through the Culebra Cut at the level of the canal bottom and dry excavation ended in 1913, with the tug *Gatun* making the first trial lockage of the Gatun Locks. In 1913, the temporary dike that had dammed the Chagres River, was blown up by a dynamite charge set off telegraphically by President Woodrow Wilson who was in Washington, D.C. The electrical installation work—all devices of which came from the General Electric Company—was then completed.

In 1914, the crane boat *Alexandre La Valley* became the first ship to make a complete transit of the Panama Canal from the Atlantic to the Pacific side, and was followed later by a cement boat, the *Cristobal*, which made the ocean-to-ocean journey across the canal in 1914. In 1914, an executive order issued by President Woodrow Wilson abolished the ICC, and established the Panama Canal Zone, with George Goethals being appointed by President Wilson as the first Governor of the Canal Zone.

Opening of the Canal

A grand celebration was originally planned for the official opening of the canal, but the outbreak of WWI forced cancellation of the festivities. The Panama Railway steamship *Ancon*, piloted by Captain John Constantine, made the first official transit of the canal in less than 10 hours in 1914. At San Francisco, California a Panama-Pacific International Exposition in celebration of the Panama Canal was held from in 1915, and attracted more than 18 million people during its 11-month run. The theme of the fair honored the canal builders, and sent a message to the world that the United States was a powerful nation who could use science and technology to advance human progress. The star attraction of the fair was a detailed model of the canal that covered almost 5 acres of land, and which could be seen by means of an elevated moving walkway spanning about one-quarter of a mile.

Assessment

The Panama Canal cost the United States $350 million, and was the single most expensive construction project in United States history up to this time. More than 57,000 people worked on the project and relatively few of them died from disease and accidents during the American construction era—about 5,600 of which 4,500 were black. About 230 million cubic yards of dirt and rocks were excavated in the American effort. The total excavation required by the canal was around 260 million cubic yards. More than 60 million pounds of dynamite were used, and 5 million sacks and barrels of cement were used to build the locks, dams and spillways.

The Panama Canal became a strategic and very important economic asset to the United States because it revolutionized world shipping. The canal removed the need for ships to travel the long route via the Drake Passage and Cape Horn at the southernmost tip of South America, and saved almost 8,000 miles in going from New York City to San Francisco by sea. The military significance of the canal was proven in WWII when the United States used it to help restore the devastated Pacific Fleet at Pearl Harbor by sending the largest ships through the canal, such as aircraft carriers.

William Taft

Election of 1908

When President Roosevelt refused to run in the presidential election of 1908, he nominated Taft as his successor for the presidency. Taft won with 321 Electoral votes. James Sherman was elected as Vice President.

Significant Events: 1909

Congress passed the Payne-Aldrich tariff bill, which raised tariffs higher. While it reduced the overall rate to 41%, it also raised the rates on items such as coal, iron ore and animal hides. President Taft argued for reciprocity, but Congress did not grant this until 1911.

President Taft authorized 700,000 acres of land in Washington, Montana and Idaho to be opened for settlement.

Congress proposed the Sixteenth Amendment, which authorized an income tax without apportionment or without regard to any census or enumeration.

President Taft set aside 3 million acres of land for conservation purposes.

President Taft met with Mexican President Porfirio Diaz at Ciudad Juarez, Mexico and in El Paso, Texas. At stake was $2 billion in American investments in Mexico.

Two United States warships were ordered to Nicaragua after reports of executions by the dictator. In the following weeks, more warships and transports carried Marines to the area. A blockade was imposed and a threat of intervention by the United States forced the dictator to retire.

Significant Events: 1910

President Taft established the Bureau of Mines, which was incorporated as part of the Department of the Interior in 1911.

Congress amended the Immigration Act of 1907 to prevent criminals, paupers, anarchists and diseased persons from entering into the United States.

A bill to have the House Committee on Rules be elected by the House rather than be appointed by the Speaker was passed by the House, reducing the power of the Speaker.

The largest oil spill in the United States occurred in Kern County, California when a well gushed out. Its initial flow was 19,000 barrels per day, and its peak flow got as high as 90,000 barrels per day. In the 18 months that it was active, it spewed 9 million barrels of oil into the surrounding land.

Congress passed the Mann-Elkins Act to enable reform by giving the ICC the power to make railroads, telegraph and telephone companies adhere to the law.

The Mann Act was passed by Congress to prohibit interstate or international transport of women for immoral purposes.

Congress established the Postal Savings Bank. This action enabled people in rural areas where there were few banks to deposit money in low interest-bearing accounts.

Congress passed the Publicity Act that requires representatives to report campaign contributions.

The controversy over the North Atlantic fisheries was resolved after the United States and Great Britain agreed to submit the issue to The Hague Tribunal.

Significant Events: 1911

President Taft ordered 20,000 troops to the Mexican border along Texas, New Mexico and Arizona as protection while the Mexican revolution was going on.

In the case of *United States v. Grimand* the Supreme Court ruled that the government has authority over forest reserves.

In the case of *Standard Oil Company of New Jersey v. United States* the Supreme Court found the Standard Oil Company guilty of monopolizing the petroleum industry by conducting unreasonable restraint of trade through a series of abusive and unreasonable anti-competitive actions.

In the case of *United States v. American Tobacco Company* the Supreme Court ruled that the company was in violation of the Sherman Anti-trust Law by the restraint of trade and through an attempt to monopolize the business of tobacco in interstate commerce.

President Taft vetoed statehood for Arizona based on its constitution that permitted the recall of judges.

President Taft informed Russia that the 1832 treaty would be abrogated due to Russia's refusal to recognize United States passports held by Jews, clergymen and others.

Significant Events: 1912

New Mexico was admitted into the Union as the 47th state.

A violent strike against sweatshop operations in the mills of Lawrence, Massachusetts was conducted by workers who were aided by the Industrial Workers of the World (IWW) organization.

United States troops occupied Tientsin, China to protect American interests from the ongoing Chinese revolution.

Arizona was admitted into the Union as the 48th state, but only after it rescinded the provision of recalling judges.

President Taft vetoed a bill to restrict the entry of foreigners into the United States by means of a literacy test.

Congress passed a joint resolution that prohibited the shipment of arms or ammunition to any nation on the two American continents where conditions of domestic violence were found to exist.

The steamship *Titanic* struck an iceberg in the North Atlantic Sea, with over 1,500 lives—including Americans—being lost due to a lack of sufficient lifeboats and safety procedures.

President Taft sent Marines into Cuba to protect American interests.

The Pelagic Sealing Agreement was agreed to by the United States, Japan, Russia and Britain. It outlawed pelagic seal hunting north of the 30th parallel, established a monopoly by the United States for catching these seals, and provided an allocation of profits to Britain, Japan and Russia in return for their withdrawal from pelagic sealing in the area.

Congress authorized the parcel-post system for United States mail.

A force of Marines was landed at Nicaragua to protect American interests.

The Lodge Corollary to the Monroe Doctrine was declared by a Senate resolution. It extended the scope to non-European powers, foreign companies and other foreign nations. The corollary stated that any harbor or other place in the American continent whose occupation by a foreign power would threaten the United States would be subject to occupation by the United States to prevent another government from having control.

President Taft signed the Panama Canal Act that authorized rebates of canal tolls to American coastal ships.

President Taft ordered 750 Marines into Santo Domingo to restore harmony.

Ex-President Theodore Roosevelt was shot by a fanatic in Milwaukee, Wisconsin.

Vice President James Sherman died at Utica, New York.

Woodrow Wilson won the presidential election by getting 435 Electoral votes. Thomas Marshall was elected as Vice President.

Significant Events: 1913

A garment workers' strike by 150,000 workers started in New York City and spread to Boston.

President Taft asked Congress to appropriate $250,000 to continue the investigation of the Commission on Economy and Efficiency.

The Sixteenth Amendment to the Constitution was adopted by the nation. The Sixteenth Amendment provided the basis for a graduated income tax.

Congress upheld the Webb-Kenyon Interstate Liquor Act that had been vetoed by President Taft. The act made it illegal to ship liquor into a state that had outlawed liquor.

Congress passed the Physical Evaluation Act to empower the ICC to investigate property held or used by railroads to establish cost and valuation as the basis for rate making.

Woodrow Wilson became President.

The Sixteenth Amendment

Overview

The Sixteenth Amendment allows Congress to levy an income tax without apportioning it among the states or basing it on census results. The Sixteenth Amendment overruled the Supreme Court case of *Pollock v. Farmers' Loan & Trust Co.* that was decided in 1895, which limited the authority of Congress to levy an income tax. The Sixteenth Amendment was ratified in 1913.

The Sixteenth Amendment reads as follows:

> "The Congress shall have power to lay and collect taxes on incomes, from whatever source derived, without apportionment among the several States, and without regard to any census or enumeration."

The Sixteenth Amendment conferred no new power of taxation, but simply prohibited the power of income taxation possessed by Congress from being taken out of the category of indirect taxation.

Enactment, Ratification and Extent

In 1906, President Theodore Roosevelt endorsed a progressive estate tax aimed at the inheritance or transmission of huge fortunes. In 1907, President Roosevelt urged Congress to consider an income tax, but Congress did not respond. In 1909, President William Taft proposed a 2% federal income tax on net corporate income, and a constitutional amendment to allow the previously enacted income tax to be valid. In 1909, the resolution proposing the Sixteenth Amendment was passed by Congress, and was submitted to the state legislatures for ratification.

In 1913, Secretary of State Philander Knox proclaimed that the Sixteenth Amendment had been ratified by the necessary three-fourths of the states, and thus had become part of the Constitution. Congress could now impose a tax on income from any source without having to apportion the total dollar amount of tax collected from each state according to each state's population in relation to the total national population.

Income subject to taxation includes salaries, wages, bank interest, pensions, retirement funds, royalties, corporate dividends, corporate earnings, undistributed corporate profits, business gains and even income from illicit transactions[3]. However, Congress can grant deductions and exemptions, including depreciations, losses, property taxes, real estate taxes and business expenses.

President Woodrow Wilson, after the ratification of the Sixteenth Amendment, called a special session of Congress in 1913. Congress proceeded to pass the Revenue Act of 1913, which called for an income tax of 1% on incomes that were above $3,000 for single people and $4,000 for couples, and applied surcharges between 2% and 7% on incomes ranging from $20,000 to $500,000.

Several challenges have been filed relating to the income tax, but the Supreme Court has upheld the validity of the income tax on all occasions.

Woodrow Wilson

Election of 1912

In 1912, Woodrow Wilson ran for President and won with 435 Electoral votes. Thomas Marshall was elected as Vice President.

Significant Events: 1913

Congress divided the Department of Commerce into two separate departments: The Department of Commerce and the Department of Labor, with both having Cabinet status.

The Seventeenth Amendment was passed, which established the popular election of Senators, rather than having them appointed by the state legislature.

In the *Minnesota Rate* case, the Supreme Court ruled that an individual state could regulate intrastate commerce as long as it did not violate the interstate commerce authority of the federal government.

Congress enacted the Underwood-Simmons Tariff Act that brought down rates on 958 articles, increased them on 86 articles and left 307 unchanged. The act reduced the average tariff rate to 27%.

Congress passed the Owens-Glass Federal Reserve Act, which created 12 regional Federal Reserve banks managed by a Federal Reserve Board, which became the central regulatory body for the banking system of the United States.

Significant Events: 1914

Congress repealed the Hay-Pauncefote Treaty, which had given the United States the right to build and control a canal across Central America.

President Wilson dispatched the Navy to Vera Cruz, Mexico and authorized Marines to land and take over the city, whereupon Mexico severed diplomatic relations with the United States. The diplomatic intervention of Argentina, Brazil and Chile prevented a war from taking place between the United States and Mexico.

A second Coxey's Army of unemployed workers was organized by Jacob Coxey at Massillon, Ohio to march on Washington, D.C.

Congress enacted a law declaring the second Sunday in May as "Mother's Day."

Congress passed the Smith-Lever Act to provide funds for state agricultural colleges, which were to establish instructional and advisory programs for farmers.

WWI began when Archduke Francis Ferdinand was murdered in Sarajevo, Serbia.

The closing of the London Stock Exchange due to WWI caused the New York Stock Exchange to be closed for several days.

The Bryan-Chamorro Treaty was signed to give the United States a 99-year lease in Nicaragua in return for $3 million.

The Panama Canal was opened to shipping.

President Wilson proclaimed neutrality by the United States in WWI. He imposed a ban on loans to any foreign nations that were at war.

The Treasury Department established a Bureau of War Risk Insurance to provide up to $5 million of insurance for merchant ships.

Congress passed the Federal Trade Commission Act that created the Federal Trade Commission consisting of 5 members to oversee the regulation of corporations that were engaged in interstate commerce in an attempt to prevent monopolies.

The Clayton Anti-trust Act was passed by Congress to allow labor to better bargain with corporations, as well as to make illegal directorates that would create a monopoly.

Congress passed the Revenue Act to impose an income tax on incomes that were over $3,000.

Significant Events: 1915

Congress established the Rocky Mountain National Park.

President Wilson vetoed a bill that would require immigrants to pass a literacy test.

Congress passed a law to establish the Coast Guard. Its duties will be to prevent contraband trade, and to assist persons and vessels in distress.

The Seamen's Act was passed by Congress for the purpose of improving safety, security and working conditions for merchant sailors.

President Wilson created the Naval Petroleum Reserve Number 3 in Wyoming.

The Supreme Court ruled that the "grandfather clause" added to the constitutions of Oklahoma and Maryland was unconstitutional.

Marines were dispatched to Haiti by President Wilson where they began a 19-year occupation. Haiti became a United States protectorate under the terms of a 10-year treaty that was approved by the Senate in 1916.

President Wilson asked for a standing army of 142,000 men, and an army reserve of 400,000 men.

Significant Events: 1916

In the case of *Brushaber v. Union Pacific Railroad Co.*, the Supreme Court ruled that the federal income tax was constitutional.

The first woman to serve in the House of Representatives, Jeanette Rankin, was seated as a Representative from Montana.

The Liberty Loan Act was passed by Congress to authorize the Treasury to issue $2 billion worth of convertible gold bonds.

President Wilson sent Marines to the Dominican Republic where they occupied the country until 1924.

President Wilson ordered a mobilization of troops along the Mexican border.

The Mexican President ordered his troops to attack American soldiers that that had crossed into Mexico. An engagement at Parral, Mexico resulted in 2 American soldiers being killed and 6 wounded while United States forces killed nearly 100 Mexican soldiers. Also, another incident at Carrizal, Mexico resulted in 14 Americans being killed while the Mexican forces suffered 30 killed and 43 wounded.

The National Defense Act was passed by Congress to increase the standing army to 175,000 and the National Guard to 450,000.

The Federal Farm Loan Act was passed Congress to establish a land bank system for loans to farmers to maintain and improve farmland.

Congress passed the Federal Highway Act to enable the government to aid the states in the construction of rural post roads.

The National Park Service was established as part of the Interior Department by Congress.

Congress passed the Warehouse Act to authorize warehouses to issue receipts against specified agricultural products such as grain, cotton, tobacco and wool negotiable as delivery orders, or as collateral for loans in order to assist farmers.

Congress passed the Naval Appropriations Act to authorize the construction of 10 battleships, 6 cruisers and 140 smaller vessels.

Congress passed the Keating-Owens Act to bar any item made by child labor from interstate commerce.

The Adamson Eight-Hour Act was signed by President Wilson to institute an 8-hour day for anyone who worked for the railroads—with pay of time-and-a-half for any overtime.

Congress passed the Workmen's Compensation Act to bring coverage to 500,000 federal workers.

Congress passed the Shipping Act to authorize a Shipping Board to build, purchase, lease or requisition vessels through the Emergency Fleet Corporation.

President Wilson won the presidential election by getting 277 Electoral votes. Thomas Riley Marshall was elected as Vice President.

Significant Events: 1917

The United States purchased the Virgin Islands from Denmark for $25 million.

President Wilson broke off diplomatic relations with Germany.

President Wilson recalled troops that were stationed along the Mexican border. He also ordered General Pershing to stop the hunt for Pancho Villa.

The Immigration Act was passed by Congress who overrode President Wilson's veto. The act provided for a literacy test for immigrants—and excluded Asian laborers, except for the Japanese.

Congress passed the Smith-Hughes Act that created the Federal Board for Vocational Education to provide matching funds to states to be used for trade and agricultural schools.

Congress passed the Jones Act, which made Puerto Rico a United States territory—and declared its inhabitants as being citizens of the United States.

Congress approved the first excess profits tax to pay for military spending.

The Senate adopted a cloture rule that allowed a two-thirds majority to end filibusters in order to terminate a floor debate.

President Wilson issued an executive order to allow merchant vessels to be armed.

President Wilson addressed Congress to ask for a declaration of war against Germany. He also created a War cabinet.

The Selective Service Act was passed by Congress to authorize the drafting of all males between the ages of 21 and 30 for military service. The first registration enrolled almost 9.6 million men.

Congress passed the Espionage Act to prohibit any attempt to interfere with military operations, support America's enemies during wartime, to promote insubordination in the military, or to interfere with military recruitment.

Race riots broke out in East St. Louis, Missouri, which killed over 100 blacks.

A posse in Bisbee, Arizona rounded up more than 1,000 members of the Industrial Workers of the World (IWW), herded them into cattle cars, and dumped them in the middle of the desert—without food, water or shelter.

Congress passed the Lever Food and Fuel Control Act to increase food production and to distribute it.

A riot in Houston, Texas resulted in 15 whites and 3 blacks being killed. The army court-martialed and hanged 13 black soldiers over the incident.

Federal raids were conducted on the headquarters of the IWW in 24 cities. The raids were prompted by labor organization's antiwar activities. Federal agents seized documents and books, and arrested 166 of its leaders.

The War Revenue Act was passed by Congress to authorize a graduated income tax beginning at 4% on personal incomes of more than $1,000. It also raised the corporation tax to 6%, and imposed an excess profits tax ranging from 20% to 60%.

Congress passed a Trading With the Enemy Act to forbid commerce with enemy nations or their associates.

The United States declared war on Austria-Hungary.

President Wilson placed the railways under government operation.

Significant Events: 1918

The Supreme Court declared the Keating-Owens Act to be unconstitutional.

In the case of *Arver v. United States*, the Supreme Court ruled that conscription during war is authorized by the Constitution.

President Wilson set forth his Fourteen Points to establish peace in the world.

To promote food conservation, Herbert Hoover called for one meatless day, 2 days without wheat and 2 days without pork each week to be observed by Americans.

Daylight Savings Time was instituted when President Wilson signed a law by which clocks would be set back one hour ahead in Spring to have more daylight available, and then rolled back one hour in the Fall.

Congress passed the Webb-Pomerene Act to authorize exporters to organize associations for export trade, without becoming liable for violations of anti-trust laws.

Congress passed the Sedition Act, which provided heavy penalties for anyone who hindered the war effort.

The Overman Act was passed by Congress to allow the President to organize, consolidate and manage all executive bureaus, agencies and offices as the President saw fit.

In the case of *Hammer v. Dagenhart*, the Supreme Court declared the Federal Child Labor Law as unconstitutional.

Sugar rationing was reduced to 2 pounds per person per month by the Food Board.

President Wilson issued a statement against the lynching of blacks, and categorized it as being a mob spirit against liberty and justice.

Socialist Party leader Eugene Debs was sentenced to 10 years in prison for violating the Espionage Act.

Germany signed the armistice treaty, thus ending WWI in Europe.

The Spanish influenza epidemic reached its peak, especially in the cities of Boston, New York and Philadelphia. The epidemic spread to 46 states and killed 500,000 people. The disease left many with secondary ailments such as Bright's disease, cardiac problems and tuberculosis.

The Wartime Prohibition Act was passed by Congress to ban the manufacture or sale of liquor, except for export.

President Wilson went to Europe to conduct negotiations in the Peace Conference.

Significant Events: 1919

The Eighteenth Amendment was ratified by the states.

President Wilson presented the draft of the League of Nations covenant to the Paris Peace Conference in France.

In the case of *Schenk v. United States*, the Supreme Court ruled that the Espionage Act did not violate the free speech rights guaranteed under the First Amendment.

Congress passed the Nineteenth Amendment to give women the right to vote, and submitted it to the states for ratification.

President Wilson submitted the Treaty of Versailles and the League of Nations covenant to the Senate for ratification.

Race riots broke out in Chicago, Illinois in which 38 people died and 537 were injured.

President Wilson suffering a cerebral thrombosis. He suffered an occlusion of the right middle cerebral artery that paralyzed his left side, and which incapacitated him for the rest of his term[1]. An infection of the prostate gland caused by urinary blockage put his life in danger for almost a week before he recovered from that ailment. The stroke created a severe disability, but for 17 months his condition was kept a secret from the American people and the rest of the world.

Congress passed the Volstead Act over President Wilson's veto to enforce Prohibition.

In the case of *Abrams v. United States*, the Supreme Court ruled that the distribution of pamphlets expressing dissatisfaction with the American presence in Russia fell under the 1918 Sedition Act.

The Senate refused to ratify the Versailles Treaty.

Significant Events: 1920

Attorney General Mitchell Palmer initiated an attack on Communists by authorizing raids on private homes without any warrants or reasons. More than 4,000 people were arrested in 33 cities. 249 of these being aliens who were deported to Russia, with their guilt being established by accusation, innuendo and association.

Congress passed the Esch-Cummins Transportation Act to create the Railroad Labor Board to supervise railroad regulation, and to intercede in the adjustment of wage disputes.

In the case of *United States v. United States Steel Corporation*, the Supreme Court ruled that the corporation was not a monopoly.

The Senate again rejected the joining of the United States into the League of Nations.

The Senate passed a resolution that expressed sympathy for Armenia's plight after WWI. President Wilson sent a proposal to Congress to establish an American mandate over Armenia, but it failed in the Senate. He later requested an appropriation to underwrite a loan to Armenia, but got no response from Congress.

Congress passed the Water Power Act to create the Federal Power Commission to regulate power plants, and to oversee water power reserves on public lands and navigable streams.

Congress passed the Merchant Marine Act to allow government-owned ships to be sold to United States shipping companies.

The Nineteenth Amendment giving women the right to vote was ratified by the states.

Republican Warren G. Harding won the presidential election by getting 404 Electoral votes. Calvin Coolidge was elected as Vice President.

The Nobel Peace Prize was awarded to President Woodrow Wilson for his efforts in ending WWI.

Term Events: 1921

Congress overrode President Wilson's veto to renew the War Finance Corporation to help depressed farm areas.

The Supreme Court ruled that labor unions could be prosecuted if they restrained interstate trade.

President Wilson vetoed the Fordney Emergency Tariff Act.

Warren Harding became President.

The Seventeenth Amendment

Overview

The Seventeenth Amendment to the United States Constitution was passed by Congress, and was ratified by the states in 1913. The Seventeenth Amendment transferred the election of Senators to a popular vote instead of them being selected by each state's legislature as designated by Articles 1 and 3 and Clauses 1 and 2 of the Constitution. It also added a provision that enabled a state's governor to appoint a Senator in the event of a vacancy until either a special or regular election could be held.

The text of the amendment reads as follows:

> "The Senate of the United States shall be composed of two Senators from each State, elected by the people thereof, for six years; and each Senator shall have one vote. The electors in each State shall have the qualifications requisite for electors of the most numerous branch of the State legislatures.
>
> When vacancies happen in the representation of any State in the Senate, the executive authority of such State shall issue writs of election to fill such vacancies: *Provided*, that the legislature of any State may empower the executive thereof to make temporary appointments until the people fill the vacancies by election as the legislature may direct.
>
> This amendment shall not be so construed as to affect the election or term of any Senator chosen before it becomes valid as part of the Constitution."

History

Originally, the popular election of senators was proposed at the Constitutional Convention of 1787, but received almost no support. Instead, the Senate was explicitly modeled after the British House of Lords, and as such was intended to be an upper class and conservative body that would check the popular nature of the House of Representatives in representing the state. It was thought that state legislatures would serve as intermediaries in identifying and elevating to the Senate the best men who were marked by ability, virtue, and achievement. The Senate would thus be a force that would check the runaway tendencies of popular rule.

This process worked without major problems through the 1850s. But, because of increasing partisanship, many state legislatures failed to elect Senators for prolonged periods. This partisanship led to battles in the legislatures, as the struggle to elect Senators reflected the increasing regional tensions leading up to the Civil War.

After the Civil War ended, the problems multiplied, and Congress passed a law in 1866 regulating how and when Senators were to be elected from each state. While the law helped, there were still deadlocks in some legislatures and accusations of bribery, corruption, and suspicious dealings in some elections. These deadlocks resulted in numerous delays in seating Senators, and in some instances the battles in the state legislatures became so charged that no Senator was elected at all, resulting in a vacancy in that seat.

In the 1870s, voters sent a petition to the House of Representatives for a popular election of Senators. Each year after that a constitutional amendment to elect Senators by popular vote was proposed in Congress, but the Senate resisted these efforts. After the turn of the 20th century, the support of Senatorial election reform grew. Senators were increasingly elected based on state referenda, and by 1912, as many as 29 states were electing Senators either as nominees of party primaries or in conjunction with a general election.

By 1910, 31 states had called for a constitutional convention to propose the Seventeenth Amendment. The intent was to remove control of the Senate from the back rooms of political manipulators and machines, and to replace this corrupt practice with the sovereignty of the people as a commitment to democratic principles and ideals. In 1911, Senator Joseph Bristow offered a resolution proposing the Seventeenth Amendment. The Senate approved the resolution, and the measure moved to the House of Representatives where in 1912, it also passed. The Seventeenth Amendment was sent to the States for ratification, and in 1913, the Seventeenth Amendment was adopted[i].

Calls for Repeal

Since its enactment there have been several calls for the repeal of the Seventeenth Amendment. The reason is that this amendment, along with the Sixteenth Amendment, has been blamed for greatly expanding the authority of the United States government. In 2003, the Montana Judiciary Committee passed a resolution calling for the repeal of the Seventeenth Amendment, but the resolution was defeated in the Montana Senate.

Beginning in 2009, several Democratic Party Senators left the Senate for executive branch positions with the Obama administration. As a result of the controversies surrounding successor appointments, interest in repealing the gubernatorial appointment option has greatly increased—although 46 of the 50 states still retain the option of full gubernatorial appointment. Only Connecticut, Oklahoma, Oregon, and Wisconsin rely on a special election. Eight other states also call for quick special elections, but allow for temporary gubernatorial appointments until the resolution of the special election.

Senators have proposed an amendment to the Constitution, which would repeal the Seventeenth Amendment, removing the allowance for gubernatorial appointment of Senators. In 2009, a joint hearing was held between the Senate and House subcommittees on the Constitution regarding these resolutions, and the Senate Subcommittee on the Constitution also held a separate hearing—but to date no action has emerged.

The Eighteenth Amendment

Overview

The Eighteenth Amendment established Prohibition. Congress passed the resolution calling for the amendment in 1917. Its ratification was certified by the states in 1919, but the Eighteenth Amendment was not effected until 1920. It made the manufacture, transportation, import, export, and sale of alcoholic beverages illegal in the United States—although it did not ban the consumption of alcohol.

The text of the Eighteenth Amendment is as follows:

> "Section 1. After one year from the ratification of this article the manufacture, sale, or transportation of intoxicating liquors within, the importation thereof into, or the exportation thereof from the United States and all territory subject to the jurisdiction thereof for beverage purposes is hereby prohibited.
>
> Section 2. The Congress and the several States shall have concurrent power to enforce this article by appropriate legislation.
>
> Section 3. This article shall be inoperative unless it shall have been ratified as an amendment to the Constitution by the legislatures of the several States, as provided in the Constitution, within seven years from the date of the submission hereof to the States by the Congress."

Proposal and Ratification

A resolution calling for an amendment to accomplish nationwide Prohibition was introduced in Congress and passed by both houses in 1917. In 1919, the Eighteenth Amendment was ratified by the states. Prohibition began in 1920, when the Eighteenth Amendment went into effect.

In 1919, the Volstead Act was passed by Congress to enforce the Eighteenth Amendment[3]. The Volstead Act was passed to define the term "intoxicating liquors"—which it defined as any beverage containing more than 0.5 percent alcohol. Besides prohibiting intoxicating beverages, the Volstead Act regulated the manufacture, production, use and sale of high-proof spirits for other than beverage purposes, such as to insure an ample supply of alcohol and to promote its use in scientific research as well as in the development of fuel, dye and other lawful industries.

Reaction

The effects of Prohibition were largely negative as it allowed the creation of a black market. The production, importation, and distribution of alcoholic beverages were taken over by racketeering criminal gangs who fought over market control—often in violent confrontations, including mass murders that were ordered by Mafia chieftain gangsters to obtain profits of millions of dollars. Enforcement became difficult because the gangs became so rich that they were often able to bribe law-enforcement personnel, corrupt judges, intimidate witnesses, and pay for expensive lawyers to get charges dropped. Many citizens were sympathetic to bootleggers', and were lured by illegal speakeasies.

As bootlegging became rampant, the national government did not have the means to enforce every border, lake, river, and speakeasy in America. By 1925, there were about 100,000 speakeasy clubs in New York City alone. Alcoholic drinks were not always illegal in all neighboring countries. Distilleries and breweries in Canada, Mexico and the Caribbean where alcohol was legal flourished as their products were either consumed by visiting Americans or were illegally imported to the United States. The Volstead Act allowed the making of up to 200 gallons per year at home of wine and cider from fruit. Many people stockpiled wines and liquors for their own use before the sales of alcohol became illegal in 1920. The loosening of social mores during the 1920s included the popularization of private cocktail parties among higher socio-economic groups.

The Nineteenth Amendment

Overview

The Nineteenth Amendment prohibits each state and the federal government from denying any United States citizen the right to vote because of that citizen's sex. It was ratified in 1920.

The Nineteenth Amendment reads as follows:

> "The right of citizens of the United States to vote shall not be denied or abridged by the United States or by any State on account of sex.
>
> Congress shall have power to enforce this article by appropriate legislation."

Proposal and Ratification

WWI provided the final push for women's suffrage in America. After President Woodrow Wilson announced that WWI was a war for democracy, members of the National Woman's Party protested at his public speeches and held up banners saying that the United States was not a democracy.

President Wilson called a special session of Congress, and a bill, introducing the Nineteenth Amendment, was brought before the House. In 1919, the House passed the Nineteenth Amendment bill. In 1919, the Nineteenth Amendment was brought before the Senate, and was also passed. It was then given to the states to ratify. The states ratified the Nineteenth Amendment in 1920.

The Presidential Election of 1920 was the first time that women were allowed to exercise their right of suffrage. As soon as women received the right to vote, they also began running for public office. Women gained positions as school board members, county clerks, state legislators, judges, and as members of Congress.

Challenge to the Nineteenth Amendment

In 1922, in the Supreme Court case of *Leser v. Garnett*, a challenge was made to the Nineteenth Amendment. Cecilia Streett Waters and Mary D. Randolph were registered as voters in the state of Maryland whose constitution limited voting rights to men only. Oscar Leser and others filed suit against the state board of registry to have the women's voter registrations invalidated. However, the Supreme Court ruled that the Nineteenth Amendment had been properly adopted, and that it transcended any limitations sought to be imposed by a state.

WWI—The Beginning

The Beginning of the War

<u>Initial Incident</u>

On June 28, 1914, Archduke Franz Ferdinand made an official visit to Bosnia from Vienna as the inspector general to observe the military exercises. He was the nephew of Hapsburg Emperor Franz Joseph, and was the heir to the Austro-Hungarian Empire. He rode in an open car as the motorcade made its way to the town hall in Sarajevo, Serbia. Six members of Young Bosnia¹—a radical patriotic organization—were in the crowd. One of them threw a pocket bomb at the royal car, but it fell behind it, being deflected by the archduke, and it exploded under one of the other cars in the motorcade. Two of the occupants of that car were seriously wounded, as were a dozen others in the crowd that got hit with shrapnel from the bomb. The motorcade then proceeded to Sarajevo where the mayor gave the archduke a ceremonial welcome.

The archduke requested to be taken to the hospital so that he could visit the people who had been injured by the bomb that was thrown at him. The motorcade set out again, but instead of going to the hospital the driver of the archduke's car took the original route instead because he was not informed of the decision. The military governor of Bosnia, who was riding in the car with the archduke, discovered that they were going the wrong way, and he ordered the driver to stop. The driver halted the car and as he prepared to turn it around, the car stalled. One of the members of Young Bosnia was standing close by, and he shot twice with his pistol, killing Archduke Franz Ferdinand and his wife.

<u>Austrian-Hungarian Response</u>

The Austrian-Hungarian government used the assassination of Archduke Franz Ferdinand as a pretext to deal with the Serbian question, a position in which they were supported by Germany. Austria-Hungary's council of ministers met in Vienna to discuss measures against Serbia. In 1914, an ultimatum was sent by the Austrian-Hungarian government to Serbia with 10 demands, but the Serbian reply agreed to only 5 of the demands. It also included reservations and totally rejected the key demand, which involved a compromise of its integrity by demanding a search in Belgrade for the prosecution of the assassination plotters. The Serbians ordered the mobilization of troops before they delivered the response. Austria-Hungary broke off diplomatic relations and declared war on Serbia, mobilizing 300,000 troops.

<u>Escalation</u>

Russia, which supported Serbia, ordered the mobilization of over one million troops that were directed at the Austrian frontier, and called up the reserves—putting more than 4 million men on duty. Germany declared war against Russia and France in 1914, and mobilized a force consisting of 1.3 million men. France allied itself with Russia, thus creating a war against Germany. Germany violated the neutrality of Belgium by advancing through it on the way to Paris, France, which brought the British Empire into the war as Belgium's defender.

<u>Initial War Strategies</u>

Germany had a plan that involved fighting on two fronts, which meant that Germany had to eliminate one opponent quickly before taking on the other. It called for seizing Belgium, and then crippling the French army by pre-empting its mobilization. After the attack, the German army would go East by railroad, and destroy the Russian forces.

France's plan called for a thrust into the Ruhr Valley, Germany's industrial heartland, which would cripple Germany's ability to wage war. France mobilized 1.8 million men who were joined by volunteers and conscripts.

Russia's plan involved a concurrent mobilization of its armies against Austria-Hungary, Germany, and the Ottoman Empire—with Austria-Hungary being the main target. Russia thus reduced the initial commitment of troops against East Prussia.

WWI: 1914

The German Assault in Belgium

The initial WWI assault began when an advance force of German cavalry moved into Luxembourg, Belgium and seized the railway. Germany made a demand to the King of Belgium for unobstructed passage of its armies through Belgium—something that he refused to do even though he only had 117,000 troops at his command. Nevertheless, his Belgian army blew up bridges and rail lines leading into Belgium from Germany in an attempt to block the German advance. Even though the German army had 750,000 troops, he was still able to hold off the assault until Great Britain and France prepared their defenses, which resulted in the Battle of Marne.

The First Battle of the Marne

The German advance from Belgium towards Paris, France was halted by French and British forces at the First Battle of the Marne. Nevertheless, the German army fought its way inside France and inflicted 250,000 casualties among French and British troops—but also suffered 250,000 casualties. After this encounter, including the First Battle of Artois, both Allied and German forces began a series of outflanking maneuvers in a race to the Atlantic Sea. Britain and France faced entrenched German forces from Lorraine to the Flemish coast, but began to take the offensive. The war turned into a stalemate on the western front, and Germany was relegated to defending its occupied territories.

The Russian Front

The Germans won the Battle of the Frontiers in Belgium, but they were attacked by Russia in East Prussia. Germany diverted its forces intended for the Western front and defeated Russia in a series of battles known as the First Battle of Tannenberg. Russia suffered 250,000 casualties and had 92,000 soldiers captured by German forces while the German army sustained 37,000 soldiers killed. The battle was a decisive event since the Russian army experienced a devastating loss that essentially removed them as a major combatant, especially after they lost again at the Battle of Masurian Lakes.

Other Campaigns

Africa

Clashes against German forces in Africa took place when the French and British troops invaded the German protectorate of Togoland. German forces also attacked South Africa, and sporadic, fierce fighting continued there for the remainder of the war.

Serbia

Serbia was conquered in a month. The attack began when the Central Powers launched an offensive from the North. The Bulgarians then joined the attack from the East. The Serbian army, fighting on two fronts, retreated into Albania, and suffered defeat in the

Battle of Kosovo. After the conquest, Serbia was divided between Austria-Hungary and Bulgaria.

However, the Serbian army still fought the Battle of Cer against Austria, occupying defensive positions on the South side of the Drina and Sava Rivers. Austrian attacks were thrown back with heavy losses, which marked the first Allied victory of the war and prevented Austria from obtaining a victory. The Austrians occupied the Serbian capital, Belgrade, but a Serbian counterattack in the battle of Kolubara succeeded in driving the Austrians back.

The Pacific

New Zealand was occupied by Allied forces, and the Australian Naval and Military Expeditionary Force landed on the island of Neu Pommern, which formed part of German New Guinea. Japan seized Germany's Micronesian colonies and after the Battle of Tsingtao, also seized the German port of Qingdao in the Chinese Shandong peninsula. Later, the Allied forces seized all the German territories in the Pacific.

Asia

Japan declared war on Germany, and Austria-Hungary responded by declaring war on Japan.

Naval Actions

At the start of WWI, Germany had cruisers scattered across the globe, some of which were used to attack Allied merchant shipping. The British Royal Navy hunted these vessels, but were still not able to adequately protect Allied shipping. However, the bulk of the German East-Asia squadron did not have orders to raid shipping and was underway to Germany when it encountered elements of the British fleet. The German flotilla sank two armored cruisers at the Battle of Coronel, but then was almost completely destroyed at the Battle of the Falkland Islands.

Britain initiated a naval blockade of Germany to cut off vital military and civilian supplies. Britain also mined international waters to prevent any ships from entering entire sections of the Atlantic Ocean. In response, Germany conducted unrestricted submarine warfare as its U-boats The United States launched a protest, and Germany modified its rules of engagement.

The Ottoman Empire

The Ottoman Empire joined the Central Powers in the war against the Allied Powers. It threatened Russia's Caucasian territories and Britain's control of India. The supreme commander of the Turkish armed forces, launched an offensive against the Russians in the Caucasus with 100,000 troops, but his frontal attack against Russian positions in the mountains during winter cost him 86,000 of his forces at the Battle of Sarikamis.

WWI: 1915

The European Front

The Germans used chlorine gas at the Second Battle of Ypres, opening a 4-mile hole in the Allied lines as British and French troops retreated. 6,000 metal cylinders of chlorine gas were used, causing excruciating drowning by destroying the ability of the lungs to absorb oxygen as the lungs of the soldiers filled up with fluids. However, the Germans became afraid of catching up with their own chlorine gas, and thus Canadian soldiers were able to close the breach after the chlorine gas mist had cleared.

At the Third Battle of Ypres, Canadian, Australian and New Zealand troops took the village of Passchendaele. French soldiers undertook offensive operations in Flanders, Argonne, Alsace and Verdun. Almost 800,000 soldiers from the Great Britain were on the Western Front, occupying areas from the North Sea to the Orne River, with the front containing about 6,000 miles of trenches. At the Second Battle of Artois, French forces fought German forces to a stalemate in which over 100,000 French soldiers and 50,000 German soldiers were killed.

Italy refused to commit troops, and the Austro-Hungarian government began negotiations to secure Italian neutrality. They offered the French colony of Tunisia to Italy in return for their support, but the Allies made a counter-offer in which Italy would receive the Alpine province of Alto Adige and the territory on the Dalmatian coast. When the Allies invaded Turkey, Italy joined the Allied side and declared war on Austria-Hungary. Austria-Hungary used most of its military reserves to fight Italy. The Italians mounted 11 offensives along the Isonzo River, but were repelled by the Austrian-Hungarian forces.

The Russian Front

Hundreds of soldiers froze to death as Russian soldiers battled the Austrian-Hungarian armies in the Carpathian passes of the Caucasus Mountains. The Russians retreated into Galicia, and the Austrian-Hungarian forces achieved a breakthrough on Poland's Southern frontiers. They captured Warsaw and forced the Russians to withdraw from Poland.

Ottoman Empire

The British and French launched the Gallipoli campaign. The Allied troops attempted an amphibious landing at the Gallipoli Peninsula in Turkey. The aim was to capture the capital city of Istanbul, but the Turkish soldiers successfully repelled the British, French, Australian and New Zealand soldiers. The landing attempt failed, with nearly 500,000 casualties experienced on both sides in a campaign that lasted until 1916.

The Turkish government embarked upon a policy of genocide to purge non-Muslim people from the Ottoman Empire. They targeted Armenia, and in a deliberate and systematic campaign killed over 500,000 Armenians. Using massacres and deportations involving forced marches under conditions of exposure, starvation and exhaustion that were designed to lead to the death of the deportees, the Ottoman military forces uprooted thousands of Armenians from their homes. They forced them to march for hundreds of miles on their way to the deserts of Syria. By 1918, more than 1.5 million Armenians had been killed—with the slaughter continuing after WWI had ended.

Naval Events

German ships steamed into the Black Sea and shelled the Russian cities of Odessa, Feodosiya and Sebastopol. In the English Channel, a German submarine sank the British Warship *Formidable*, killing 546 British sailors. Germany declared the waters around Britain and Ireland as a war zone in which all ships would be considered as targets. German U-boats sank hundreds of thousands of tons of British shipping—although their submarines suffered heavy losses. The American cargo ship *William P. Frye* was torpedoed by the German Navy. The British liner *Falaba* was also sunk, and the American tanker *Gulflight* was hit by a German submarine. In another attack, the American vessel *Cushing* was hit by a German airplane.

The biggest naval event was the sinking of the British ocean liner, the RMS *Lusitania*, by a German U-boat. The sinking resulted in 1,200 deaths, including 128 Americans. President Woodrow Wilson demanded an end to attacks on passenger ships, and Germany called a halt to the torpedoing of passenger liners.

The British passenger ship *Arabic* was hit by a German torpedo, and the Italian liner *Ancona* was sunk by an Austrian submarine.

WWI: 1916

Western Front

Battle of Verdun

German artillery opened up with more than 1,200 guns blasting away at French positions on the bank of the River Meuse. When the Germans ceased firing after 100,000 rounds of explosives, the French came out of their hiding places—and the Germans resumed the bombardment. This was the start of the Battle of Verdun, which became the longest battle of WWI.

The German bombardment continued with a shattering impact on the French positions, causing 23,000 deaths as compared to less than 2,000 casualties for the German forces. However, a thaw occurred that melted the ice and turned all roads into mud. Since the roads had already been damaged severely by French artillery fire, the German advance turned into a quagmire—and the Battle of Verdun turned into a stalemate, with casualties being133,000 for the French and 120,000 for the Germans. There were an estimated 700,000 casualties that were suffered in the trench war battle.

Battle of Somme

The British used their infantry to attack the German forces at the Battle of Somme. Although the British outnumbered the German forces, they sustained almost 60,000 casualties in the first wave of the attack while the Germans suffered 8,000 losses. Despite the advantage in numbers, the battle turned into a quagmire, with the British sustaining 420,000 casualties, the French, 200,000 casualties, and the Germans, 500,000 casualties.

Battles of the Isonzo

Italy began the Seventh Battle of the Isonzo against Germany, which generated thousands of casualties for the Italian army. By the Ninth Battle of the Isonzo, the casualties numbered about 140,000 for both sides—until a blizzard brought the battle to an end.

Naval Engagements

The British and German fleets met at the Battle of Jutland off the Danish coast in the North Sea. The British Navy outnumbered the German ships, and caused severe losses to the German Navy. The remaining German ships withdrew—even though they managed to inflict heavier losses to the British ships. However, the British gained control of the North Sea, and most of the German surface fleet remained confined to their homeports for the duration of the war. Nevertheless, the German submarine warfare continued, with the British liner *Persia* being torpedoed. Also, the French ferry *Sussex* was torpedoed.

Eastern Front

Russia launched an offensive against German forces. Even with 1,000 guns and 26 divisions, the result was a disaster for the Russian army as it sustained 80,000 casualties compared to 16,000 for the German forces.

Romania issued a declaration of war, sending 400,000 troops against 31,000 Austrian-Hungarian soldiers. In spite of the numerical advantage, the Romanians surrendered without a fight, with 80% of their force either captured or having fled. 200,000 Romanians were killed or wounded, and 150,000 were taken prisoner, finishing the destruction of the Romanian army.

The Serbs suffered defeat near Gnjilane in the Battle of Kosovo. Montenegro covered the Serbian retreat toward the Adriatic coast in the Battle of Mojkovac. The Austrians conquered Montenegro.

Serbian forces retook part of Macedonia by recapturing Bitola. The Bulgarians defeated British and Greek forces at the Battle of Doiran, avoiding occupation.

Ottoman Empire

The Russians drove the Turks out of most of the Southern Caucasus Mountains, with a string of victories. The Arab revolts that started with the Battle of Mecca ended with the Ottoman surrender of Damascus in Syria. Along the border of Libya and Egypt, the Senussi tribe waged a small-scale guerrilla war against Allied troops, but their rebellion was crushed.

WWI: 1917

Western Front

France launched an attack against German forces. With 3 armies including 53 divisions consisting of 1.2 million men, the French proceeded against 21 divisions of the German army. The French offensive failed, and the result was 270,000 casualties for the French and 163,000 for the Germans. The French army fell into open rebellion with its troops, refusing to obey orders, assaulting and killing officers, and deserting.

British troops attacked German forces at the Battle of Arras. The British captured Vimy Ridge, and were able to hold the Douai plain.

The Allied forces launched a major offensive known as the Third Battle of Ypres. The German forces attacked the British forces with mustard gas. A continual rain bogged down the offensive and led to a stalemate. The Allied forces incurred 310,000 casualties while the Germans suffered 260,000 casualties.

Australian forces mounted an offensive against German forces at the Battle of Polygon Wood. A British assault started the Battle of Brookseinde in which they inflicted 30,000 casualties on the German side while sustaining 25,000 casualties.

Two more battles were launched at Isonzo by Italian forces. The resulting Battle of Caporetto caused Italian forces to retreat, and ended with thousands of Italian troops surrendering to German-Austrian forces, and culminated in the fall of the Italian government in Rome. Italian forces suffered 320,000 casualties, and then suffered 140,000 more in their stand at the Piave River.

Germany launched an operation against the English Channel ports. The Allies halted the drive with only limited gains being attained by Germany. The German Army conducted operations towards Paris, France, and in response, the Allies launched an operation, attempting to encircle Reims, thus beginning the Second Battle of the Marne. The resulting attack became the first successful Allied offensive, pushing the German forces back to their original starting lines.

Russian Front

Riots and strikes began to break out in Russia, with over 676,000 workers striking in Petrograd. The socialist Alexander Kerensky called for the overthrow of Czar Nicholas II. The Czar was overthrown in a revolution, and the Russian Caucasus Army began to fall apart. Kerensky formed a provisional government at Dumas, but declared his intention to continue the war.

Vladimir Lenin arrived in Petrograd from his exile in Switzerland, being allowed to cross by rail through Germany. Upon his arrival, his Bolshevik followers initiated an antiwar stance, and the Russian military began a movement of withdrawing from the battles. This discontent with the war was led by the Bolshevik party, which was headed by Lenin. He promised to pull Russia out of the war and with the triumph of the Bolsheviks, an armistice and negotiations with Germany took place after Germany had marched across the Ukraine. The Bolshevik government signed the Treaty of Brest-Litovsk in 1918, under which Russia was obliged to pay 6 billion marks as an indemnity to Germany. The settlement also included that Russia relinquish Estonia, Latvia, Lithuania, Belarus and Ukraine to Germany. A civil war ensued in Russia, leading to a Communist government headed by Lenin.

The Balkans

After the forced conscription of the Serbian population into the Bulgarian army, the Toplica Uprising began. Serbian rebels liberated the area between the Kopaonik Mountains and the South Morava River. The uprising, however, was crushed by Bulgarian and Austrian forces.

Ottoman Empire

The disintegration of the Ottoman Empire began taking place. British forces captured the capital of Baghdad. In the Sinai and Palestine Campaign, the British captured Jerusalem.

Entry of the United States into WWI

Germany announced that it was resuming a course of unrestricted submarine warfare, even though President Woodrow Wilson had requested peace terms. Germany also tried unsuccessfully to create a new kingdom of Poland to fight against the Russians. Germany even attempted to entice Mexico into the war by proposing to re-conquer and give back to Mexico the territories of Texas, New Mexico and Arizona.

The American liner *Housatonic* was sunk by a German U-boat. The United States severed relations with Germany. President Wilson requested the approval from Congress to arm American commercial ships with navy guns and gun crews. The House approved the measure, but the Senate filibustered the vote. To bypass the filibuster, President Wilson issued an executive order to arm the American merchant ships. After German submarines had sank 7 United States merchant ships, President Wilson addressed the Congress and asked for a declaration of war against Germany. Congress approved the war resolution, and the draft for soldiers began.

United States Marines were dispatched to France. However, American General John Pershing refused to break up United States units to be used as reinforcements for the British and French units. Instead, he used these American troops to bring over supplies. A Supreme War Council of Allied forces to coordinate planning was formed, with French General Ferdinand Foch being appointed as supreme commander of the Allied forces. Consequently, the American divisions, which General Pershing had sought to field as an independent force, were assigned to the French and British units.

Naval Action

The American ships *Algonquin*, the *City of Memphis*, the *Vigilante* and the *Illinois* were all sunk.

The British naval blockade began to have a serious impact on Germany. In response, the Germans declared unrestricted submarine warfare to starve Britain out of the war, by sinking 500,000 tons per month. But, the convoy system became effective in neutralizing the German U-boat threat. The United States sent a navy battleship group to Scapa Flow to join with the British Grand Fleet in the blockade of Germany. The United States sent destroyers to Queenstown, Ireland and submarines to help guard convoys.

WWI: 1918

The Last German Offensive

German forces attacked the British and French forces near Amiens on the western front in France with 190 divisions consisting of over 3 million men. The German offensive move sought to divide the Allied forces with a series of feints and advances, and then to strike a decisive blow before significant help from the United States arrived. The German forces advanced 40 miles and captured 1,200 square miles of territory and 90,000 prisoners. The British forces were forced to retreat as the German forces moved to within 75 miles of Paris, France. The British suffered 160,000 casualties while the French sustained 70,000 casualties. However, the advance was costly for the German army since it incurred 270,000 casualties.

Three German Krupp railway guns fired 200 shells into Paris, France, causing many of its inhabitants to flee. The German army was at the Marne River, only 50 miles from Paris. However, the offensive was halted because the German army lacked tanks and a motorized artillery, and so the Germans were unable to consolidate their gains. The sudden stop was also a result of the 4 Australian Imperial Forces divisions that stopped the German advance, and who prevented a second German breakthrough in the North.

American troops arrived in France by the thousands and grew to 250,000. The United States Army, commanded by General John Pershing, entered into the combat, and encountered the German forces. In the first major engagement between the Germans and the Americans at Chateau-Thierry, the American troops stopped any further advances by the German army. American Marines also launched an attack at Belleau Wood. German casualties mounted to 350,000 soldiers. The Austrian army lost 142,000 men in an attack by a combined British-French force.

The French forces attacked the German soldiers at Soissons and made them retreat. The American First and Second Divisions also attacked the German forces. The German army was in full retreat, having taken over one million casualties. The British attack at Amiens scattered the German army in all directions, with casualties being over 26,000 men. The Allies grew in size to over 200 divisions, being augmented by ever-increasing arrivals of American troops who now numbered over one million men.

The German High Command faced 6 million Allied forces, and they realized that the war was lost. They made attempts for a satisfactory end by recommending immediate peace negotiations. Germany's Chief of the General Staff Paul von Hindenburg urged peace moves to Emperor Charles of Austria. Germany also appealed to Holland for mediation. Austria sent a note to all belligerents and neutrals suggesting a meeting for peace talks on neutral soil. Germany made a peace offer to Belgium. All peace offers were rejected by the Allies. The Germans continued to fight rear guard actions and launched numerous counter attacks on lost positions, but with only a few succeeding. Numerous towns, villages, heights, trenches and outposts of the Hindenburg Line continued to fall.

An Allied attack on the Hindenburg Line began with 260,000 American soldiers. All initial objectives were captured although the American Army stalled due to supply problems and because of a difficult landscape to go through. French units also broke through in Champagne and crossed the Belgian border. The German army had to shorten its western front and was forced to use the Dutch frontier to fight rear-guard actions.

Ottoman Empire

The British and the Turks continued fighting in the Sinai Desert. Turkish troops unsuccessfully attacked the Suez Canal. Deep probes into Arab territory by small bands led by Lieutenant Thomas Edward Lawrence kept the Turks at bay, and allowed the British forces to conquer Sinai, Palestine and Syria. The Egyptian Expeditionary Force broke the Ottoman forces at the Battle of Megiddo.

The Ottoman Empire surrendered at the Mudros Harbor on the Greek island of Lemnos. The treaty with the Ottoman Empire was followed by strife and a final peace treaty was not signed between the Allied Powers and the country that would become the Republic of Turkey until 1923. Under the terms of the Treaty of Lausanne, the Allied forces left Constantinople in 1923.

Last Actions

The Bulgarians suffered their only defeat of the war at the Battle of Dobro Pole. But, the Bulgarian forces decisively defeated the British and Greek forces at the Battle of Doiran, thus avoiding occupation. Bulgaria then signed an armistice, ending the war in the Balkans.

The Austro-Hungarians failed to win in a series of battles on the Asiago Plateau, and were defeated in the Battle of Vittorio Veneto by an Allied force of 56 divisions. Austria-Hungary surrendered.

A German U-boat sank the steamer *Leinster* off the coast of England, killing 450 people.

The War Comes to an End

Declarations of independence were made in Budapest, Prague and Zagreb. Austria-Hungary asked for an armistice. The terms, arranged with the Allied authorities in Paris, France were communicated to the Austrian Commander and were accepted. The armistice with Austria was signed, with Austria and Hungary signing separate agreements.

Having suffered over 6 million casualties, Germany was now in a state of desperation and moved toward peace. Prince Max von Baden replaced Count Georg von Hertling and took charge of a new government as the Chancellor of Germany to negotiate with the Allies. In a note drafted by German Admiral Paul von Hintze that was addressed to President Woodrow Wilson, a request for armistice was requested under the peace terms that President Wilson had offered in his "Fourteen Points" document. Negotiations with

President Wilson began, in the hope that better terms would be offered than those with the British and French. However, President Wilson demanded the abdication of the Kaiser.

Kaiser Wilhelm II was asked to abdicate—but he refused—until General Hindenburg informed him that his safety could no longer be assured. Kaiser Wilhelm II fled to Holland, and Philipp Scheidemann declared Germany to be a republic, which was the start of the Weimar Republic. A German delegation arrived at Allied headquarters at Compiegne, France and accepted the peace terms. On November 11, 1918, an armistice went into effect. Although opposing armies on the Western Front began to withdraw from their positions, a state of war still persisted for another 7 months until the Treaty of Versailles was signed in 1919.

WWI: Aftermath

Overview

WWI started in 1914 and ended with the cease-fire in 1918, although the peace treaty was not signed until 1919. The war took place mainly in Europe, but was also fought in Africa, the Middle East, China and the Pacific Islands. Initiated by the Central Powers of Germany and the Austrian-Hungarian Empire, and later joined by the Ottoman Empire and Bulgaria, culminated in the victory by the Allied Powers consisting of Britain, France, Russia, Japan, Italy and the United States. At the end of the war, the League of Nations was attempted to be established to prevent future wars of this magnitude.

The incident that triggered WWI was the assassination of Archduke Franz Ferdinand, the heir to the Austro-Hungarian Empire, in 1914. The act was perpetrated by a citizen of Bosnia, Serbia. Austria-Hungary demanded action by Serbia to punish those responsible, and when Austria-Hungary deemed that Serbia had not complied, it declared war on Serbia. The retaliation by the Austrian-Hungarian Empire against Serbia activated a chain reaction of war declarations. Within weeks, major European powers were at war with each other.

A total of 60 million soldiers from Europe took part in the war between 1914 and 1918. The war resulted in over 9.5 million military casualties and left over 15 million wounded as well as over 4.1 million missing and 9 million as prisoners of war. Many civilian casualties were incurred in the conflict, resulting in over 40 million casualties altogether. The war marked the end of the German, Russian, Ottoman, and Austro-Hungarian Empires. It also led to the founding of new countries in Europe and the Middle East as well as the transfer of German colonies to the allied powers.

The war cost the United States $42 billion, 131,000 deaths of soldiers and 203,000 wounded.

WWI Effects

Diseases

WWI caused many ailments, some of them by prolonged exposure to cold and wet conditions in trenches. Trench foot was a fungal infection that led to gangrene and amputation as the infection festered. Trench mouth was a disease that affected the gums and caused teeth to fall out. Trench fever caused by excretions of lice erupted when warm weather appeared. The lice would leave red marks on the skin as they burrowed their way into the flesh. Rats were also a problem, a condition that was exacerbated by the accumulation of garbage and decaying human bodies.

The war had an enormous health consequence on the civilian population as well, primarily as a result of a major influenza epidemic that started in Western Europe in Spain. The outbreak of the Spanish influenza killed millions in Europe and then spread around the world, killing 50 million people.

Post-Traumatic Ailment

A condition known as "shell shock" incapacitated thousands of soldiers on both sides. Men were reduced into trancelike states, were psychologically paralyzed, and remained frozen in different postures. Many were left unable to psychologically see or hear, developed hysteria, sank into a deep depression, or else shook uncontrollably. These mental disorders prevented them from returning to duty, and they were sent home. By the end of the war, Germany had recorded 200,000 cases of shell shock while Britain had reported 80,000 cases, with some of these winding up in insane asylums.

Prisoners of War

About 8 million men surrendered and were held in prisoner of war camps. Their rate of survival was higher than those who were at the front. The most dangerous time was the actual act of surrender when soldiers were sometimes gunned down. Once prisoners reached a camp, conditions were satisfactory due to the efforts of the International Red Cross and inspections by neutral nations. But, conditions were terrible in Russia, and starvation was common for prisoners. The Ottoman Empire treated prisoners very poorly, and many of them died in captivity.

War Crimes: Genocide

The ethnic cleansing of the Christian population by the Turks, including the massacre of Armenians during the final years of the Ottoman Empire, were acts of genocide. The number of deaths was estimated to be as high as 1.5 million Armenians. Even instances of cannibalism were reported in Armenia through desperate acts of survival.

Collective Trauma

The experiences of the war led to a collective trauma for all participating countries. Those who fought in the war became known as the "Lost Generation." Memorials to the fallen were erected in thousands of villages and towns. Many of the soldiers returning home from WWI suffered socially and mentally from the horrors that they had witnessed.

The war had profound economic consequences because it cost $208 billion, with Britain and Germany each spending about one-quarter of this amount. Belgium was badly damaged, as was France, Germany and Russia. Over 40 million casualties resulted from the war. Germany was declared to be responsible for the war and was ordered to pay enormous war reparations, thus causing an incredible hardship for the country, which initiated a runaway inflation. Italy's government was economically compromised by the effects of the war. Industry, transport, currencies and governments were in assorted states of collapse. Territorial, ethnic and dynastic conflicts were underway in the wake of the economic and political shambles that were produced by the war.

Almost all European countries were ravaged by hunger and disease, with one-half of the population being in a condition of famine due to dwindling supplies of food. 10 million to

12 million children were in a state of undernourishment, with Germany being the nation that suffered the most. A death rate of 30% existed in some areas, and to add to the woes, an exceptionally harsh winter blanketed Europe between 1918 and 1919.

<u>Re-arrangement of Nations</u>

The Ottoman Empire disappeared as Britain acquired Iraq while France got Lebanon and Syria. The remaining Turkish territory was reorganized as the Republic of Turkey. The Austrian-Hungarian Empire was dissolved and partitioned, largely along ethnic lines, into several successor states including Austria, Hungary, Czechoslovakia, and Yugoslavia. Transylvania was also added to Romania, and Poland re-emerged as an independent country. The Russian Empire lost its western frontier, with the nations of Estonia, Finland, Latvia, Lithuania, and Poland being carved from it, and with Bessarabia being re-attached to Romania. The republics of Armenia and Georgia also came into being.

<u>Opposition to the War</u>

In the United States, many of those who spoke out against the conflict were jailed, including the Socialist Party leader Eugene Debs. The Espionage Act made free speech illegal and many of these prosecuted under it served long prison sentences for statements of fact that were deemed to be unpatriotic. The Sedition Act was passed that made any statements deemed as being "disloyal" into a federal crime. Publications critical of the government were removed from circulation by postal censors.

The League of Nations

In 1918, President Wilson outlined his Fourteen Points, and pushed for the creation of the League of Nations. The League of Nations that was created was intended to be an international organization, and as a way to avoid future wars by giving nations a means of solving their differences diplomatically. President Wilson hoped that the League of Nations and the disarmament conferences would secure a lasting peace. However, Russia was absent from it because the Allies refused to recognize their Communist government, and Germany was excluded because it was regarded as an outlaw nation.

The League of Nations Committee of the Peace Conference met in Paris, France in 1919. President Wilson had by then made 4 drafts of the covenant for the organization. The principal organs of the League were the Assembly, the Council and the Secretariat. Other bodies included in the organization were the Permanent Court of International Justice, The International Labor Organization, the Health Organization, the Committee on Intellectual Cooperation, the Permanent Central Opium Board, the Slavery Commission, the Commission for Refugees, and the Committee for the Study of the Legal Status of Women. The League's headquarters were established at the Palace of Nations building in Geneva, Switzerland in 1938.

A controversial Article X₇ was met with stiff opposition by the United States Senate, and hence the United States never joined the League of Nations. In 1919, 44 nations signed the League of Nations covenant, which grew to 58 members in 1934. The League resolved several territorial disputes, including those for Upper Silesia, Albania, the Aland Islands, Hatay, Mermel, Mosul, Vilnius, Columbia and Peru, and Saar. It also settled incidents between Greece and Bulgaria, in Liberia, Manchuria, Bolivia and Paraguay, and Italy and Abyssinia. It intervened in the Spanish Civil War, and in the Second Sino-Japanese War. The League of Nations was dissolved in 1946.

Intervention in Russia

Once the Bolshevik Revolution was accomplished in 1917, the vanquished anti-Communist factions united as the counter-revolutionary White Movement in an effort to depose of the Bolsheviks. In 1918, the Allies intervened in the Russian Civil War with a military expedition consisting of 14 nations that was launched in 1918 during the Russian Civil War, with the Allies sponsoring the Whites who were commanded by General Anton Ivanovich Denikin. Other anti-Bolshevik factions were led by Admiral Alexander Kolchak, Grigory Semyonov and Ivan Kalmykov.

In 1918, against the advice of the United States War Department, President Wilson agreed to the limited participation of 5,000 United States Army soldiers to Arkhangelsk, while another 8,000 soldiers were shipped to Vladivostok. The Japanese sent the largest military force, which was 70,000 soldiers, to Siberia. However, a deteriorating situation compelled the Allies to withdraw from Russia in 1920. Without Allied support, the Red Army was able to inflict defeats on the White forces, leading to their eventual collapse. The Red Army, commanded by Leon Trotsky, won the Russian Civil War in 1920.

During the Allied intervention, the presence of foreign troops was used as propaganda by the Bolsheviks who eventually founded the Union of Soviet Socialist Republics (USSR). In 1919, at Moscow, the Bolsheviks, led by Lenin, conferred with the world's socialists, and established the Communist International and renamed themselves as the revolutionary Communist Party. At the end of the Russian Civil War, the USSR annexed Armenia, Georgia and Azerbaijan. To maintain the war-isolated cities, keep the armies fed and to avoid economic collapse, the Bolshevik government established food requisitioning from the peasantry that they resisted with reduced harvests. This resulted in armed confrontations, which the Cheka, the Soviet state security organization, and the Red Army suppressed with shootings, by taking hostages, spraying them with poison gas and by doing labor-camp deportations. The result was the occurrence of the Russian famine of 1921 that killed between 3 million and 10 million people.

The 6-year long civil war fought between 1917 and 1923 reduced Russia to ruin, and provoked rebellion against the Bolsheviks. In 1921, Lenin introduced the New Economic Policy (NEP), a state-oriented mixed economy in which the private and state sectors were successful in rebuilding both the industrial and agricultural sectors. Later, Joseph Stalin reversed the NEP to consolidate his control of the Communist Party and the USSR.

The Banana Wars

Overview

The Banana Wars were a series of occupations, police actions, and interventions involving the United States in Central America and the Caribbean, starting with the Spanish-American War in 1898, and ending with the withdrawal of American troops from Haiti in 1934. The reasons for these conflicts were largely economic since they involved the preservation of American commercial interests in these regions. During these 36 years the United States advanced its political interests and maintained its influence, especially by controlling the Panama Canal that was important to trade and naval power. Other Latin American nations were influenced or dominated by American economic policies and commercial interests to the point of coercion, specifically from 1909 to 1913, when President William Taft pursued a dollar diplomacy foreign policy. However, it was under the administration of President Woodrow Wilson that military interventions were heavily used, and extended for long periods of time. These occupations were carried out by American Marines, sailors and army personnel.

The list of countries that the United States directly intervened in to protect its interests include the following:

- Panama—where American military intervention in 1903 resulted in the building of the Panama Canal
- Nicaragua—which after intermittent landings and naval bombardments was occupied by the United States from 1912 through 1933
- Cuba—which was occupied by the United States from 1899 to 1902, and was effectively governed by the terms of the Platt Amendment until 1934
- Haiti—which was occupied continuously by the United States from 1915 through 1934
- Dominican Republic—which was occupied by the United States from 1916 until 1924
- Honduras—where insertion of American troops took place several times between 1903 and 1925
- Mexico—where several interventions took place, including those in Tampico and Vera Cruz in 1914, and the border incursions in 1916 to 1917 to chase after Pancho Villa
- Guatemala—a brief intervention and then an overthrow of the existing president
- El Salvador—warship support in quelling an uprising

Cuba

After the United States invaded Cuba in 1898 during the Spanish-American War, the War Department divided the island into 7 jurisdictions, with each jurisdiction being headed by an American general. In 1899, President William McKinley named General Leonard Wood as the military governor of Cuba. General Wood prepared the Cubans for independence, and by 1901 the Americans had only a skeletal force in Cuba. In 1902, General Wood stepped down from his post, and the Cubans took charge of their own country—even though General Wood had expressed his preference for annexing Cuba.

In 1906, President Theodore Roosevelt initiated the second Cuban intervention by sending American troops when the Cuban President declared that he could no longer guarantee the safety of foreign property—much of which was owned by American planters. The *Denver* and *Marietta* subsequently landed American sailors in Havana, Cuba. When Secretary of War William Taft arrived in Cuba, he recommended landing more troops to President Roosevelt. The President of Cuba resigned, and Taft took over as head of a provisional government that was imposed by the United States. A total of 2,000 American Marines disembarked from battleships to Columbia, Cuba. Charles Magoon replaced Taft as military governor of Cuba and ran the island for the next 29 months with the help of 60 American officers. In 1908, Magoon departed Cuba after a new president was elected as head of the Cuban government.

In 1912, a revolt by Cuban insurgents prompted President Taft to send Marines to Daiquiri, Cuba to protect American interests in nearby sugar mills and mines that were located close to Guantanamo Bay. However, this intervention ended as the American Marines departed from Cuba. In 1917, Marines were sent by President Woodrow Wilson to Cuba to guarantee sugar exports during WWI.

In 1933, President Franklin Roosevelt sent warships to Cuba to cower the Cuban President who was massacring people to put down nationwide strikes and riots. The president of Cuba resigned, but the provisional government lasted less than 3 weeks. Fulgencio Batista, with President Roosevelt's backing, put down the coup and became Cuba's President.

Colombia and Panama

In 1903, President Theodore Roosevelt sent United States warships to prevent Colombia from landing troops in Panama when it revolted against Colombian rule. An independent Panamanian government was recognized by the United States and negotiations resulted in a treaty to give the United States permanent rights to a 10-mile wide strip in Panama to build a canal. In 1908, American troops intervened in Panama, and then 3 times more during the next 10 years. Between 1918 and 1920, United States Marines occupied the province of Chiriqui in Panama to maintain public order. In 1925, American Army troops occupied Panama City to break a rent strike and to maintain order.

Nicaragua

Between 1850 and 1857, the United States had intervened in Nicaragua on 4 separate occasions. In 1910, President William Taft deployed United States Marines to occupy Nicaragua to help support the regime of the Nicaraguan president. In 1912, Nicaraguan rebel forces captured steamers on Lakes Managua and Nicaragua that belonged to American companies. The American minister, George Weitzel, cabled for American troops to be sent to protect the legation. President William Taft sent 100 sailors from the

Annapolis to Managua. The rebels launched an attack on Managua, and American General Smedley Butler landed an additional 350 Marines to reinforce the American troops. Under the direction of Admiral W. H. H. Southerland, 6 ships² sailed for San Juan del Sur, and disembarked more troops, creating a force of 1,000 men. The rebels were forced to capitulate and to turn over all railroad rolling stock, telegraphs and steamers³, after which the United States troops left Nicaragua.

In 1926, Emiliano Chamorro compelled the President to resign, and replaced him as head of state. A revolt against Chamorro began, and United States Marines from the *Cleveland* landed at Bluefield to protect American lives and interests. More Marines from the *Denver* were also disembarked at Corinto. A civil war ensued in Nicaragua, and President Chamorro resigned. A new president was named by the Nicaraguan assembly. Nevertheless, forces from the *Denver* and *Cleveland* landed at Puerto Cabezas⁴.

Eventually, the Tipitapa accords were agreed to by emissaries from Nicaragua and the United States that allowed a policing force of American Marines and sailors to impose a peace. A rebel denounced the Tipitapa accords, and in 1927, 560 men attacked the American garrison at Ocotal. The Americans suffered a few casualties compared to 300 or more for the rebels who were strafed as they fled by a squadron of 5 American planes. But, the revels were still able to fight a jungle war by hiding in remote mountains that had virtually impenetrable valleys of trees that were ideally suited for guerilla warfare.

When the rebels assembled an army at El Chipote, American Marines launched an air and ground assault there in 1927. The rebels ambushed 2 marine guard units, and in 1928, a devastating bombardment of El Chipote began. 2,000 more Marines were deployed in the pursuit force, which numbered 3,700 men. 5 American cruisers with 1,500 sailors patrolled the Nicaraguan coast to prevent an escape by boat. By 1929, there were almost 5,000 troops chasing rebels—some of whom who had escaped to Mexico.

An election was held in 1928 for a new President. The rebels returned to Nicaragua to wage war again. By 1931, with the ongoing depression, Congress was not eager to maintain a large Marine force in Nicaragua, and plans were made to withdraw most of the Marines. In 1933, the United States Marines left Nicaragua following the inauguration of a new president.

Mexico

In 1911, President Taft sent 20,000 troops to Texas to the Mexican border, and stepped up American naval activity off the Mexican coast, but did not intervene in the Mexican revolution. In 1913, seamen from the American ship *Dolphin* were arrested at Tampico, Mexico for trespassing. The Mexican military governor of Tampico apologized for the incident and ordered the release of the American prisoners. However, the United States Navy Admiral Henry Mayo deemed this as insufficient and wanted some type of retaliatory action.

In 1913, an incident occurred in Vera Cruz, Mexico. In which a sailor from the United States ship *Minnesota* was arrested by Mexican federal soldiers as a suspected Mexican deserter. Another event happened in 1913 that served to heighten tensions between the United States and Mexico. The ship *Ypiranga* carrying 250 machine guns and 15 million rounds of ammunition was reported heading for Vera Cruz—right after a steamer was spotted unloading great quantities of ammunition at Vera Cruz.

President Woodrow Wilson reacted to these events by sending American troops to land at Vera Cruz. Admiral Frank Fletcher landed Marines and sailors from the *Florida* to intercept the cargo aboard the *Ypiranga*. The troops were fired upon and as a result more American troops were sent into Vera Cruz from the *Utah*. Vice Admiral Charles Badger arrived at Vera Cruz with his warships, and together with Admiral Fletcher planned the occupation of Vera Cruz. In the seizing of the city, American troops suffered 17 killed and 61 wounded while the Mexican forces had 175 killed and over 250 wounded, although many more were buried or set on fire by American troops.

Martial law was declared in Vera Cruz, and the restoration of authority was done—with the Americans in charge. President Wilson named General Frederick Funston as military governor of Vera Cruz. General Funston proposed an expedition of 7,000 soldiers and Marines to march to Mexico City, but Secretary of the Navy Josephus Daniels instructed Admiral Fletcher to prevent such an undertaking. The Americans ruled Vera Cruz for 7 months even though a mediation of the issue was attempted by a conference of representatives from Argentina, Brazil and Chile that President Wilson and the Mexican president had agreed to. American forces withdrew from Vera Cruz in 1913, and the United States recognized the new Mexican government.

In 1917, United States troops entered Mexico to pursue Pancho Villa. Villa was enraged that the United States had chosen to recognize Carranza as president of Mexico. In 1916, Villa and his men forced 18 American mining engineers off a train and shot them. In 1916, he crossed into Columbus, New Mexico with 1,500 men where he conducted a raid that resulted in 17 American deaths. He also attacked Glen Springs, Texas where his men wounded 3 American soldiers, and his troops killed 4 soldiers at San Ignacio, Texas. General John Pershing was sent by President Wilson for a punitive expedition that reached 7,000 soldiers, but he was never able to catch Villa in a 2-year-long pursuit—although the United States Army killed 120 Mexican combatants.

Haiti

The United States had landed marines in Haiti on 8 different occasions between 1867 and 1900. During revolutionary disturbances in 1914, 2 American warships carrying 800 Marines went to Port-au-Prince to force Haitian rebels to accept the government of the president. In 1915, Admiral William Caperton, who commanded the Cruiser Squadron, positioned his ships off the Haitian coast, and met with the Haitian president. When the president was killed by rebels in 1915, Admiral Caperton ordered a battalion to land at Bizoton. In 1915, Colonel Eli Cole and his Second Marine Regiment arrived at Haiti, and seized soldiers' barracks and police stations, disarming the Haitian soldiers.

In an election supervised by Admiral Caperton, a new president was elected by the Haitian assembly. Admiral Caperton took over the customhouse at Port-au-Prince and withheld funds in a receivership arrangement. In 1915, Admiral Caperton declared martial law[8]. In 1915, the Haitian-American Treaty was approved by the Haitian House and Senate, and was also approved by the United States Senate. American forces remained in Haiti until 1934, when President Franklin Roosevelt pulled the remaining troops to end the occupation that lasted for 19 years.

Dominican Republic

Beginning in 1904, under the administration of Theodore Roosevelt, the United States had a customs receivership treaty with the Dominican Republic. United States customs agents took over the finances of the country to ensure payment of its external debt, especially to European nations. The treaty was expanded to permit greater involvement in the internal affairs of the country, especially to carry out a reform plan for their government. In 1916, Admiral Caperton moved his command to the Dominican Republic as the American military planned a full-scale intervention. The situation was brought about when the existing president was ousted from power in 1916 by being impeached by the Dominican House. Afterwards, troops seized the capital city of Santo Domingo.

The United States already had 300 Marines ashore from the *Castine* to guard the American legation, and 150 more Marines were being readied to land from the *Prairie*. Four warships were placed near the coast, and Admiral Caperton increased the ground strength to 600 men in Santo Domingo, thus forcing the Dominican army of 300 men to flee. Admiral Caperton augmented his forces by landing 4 companies of Marines and a small contingent of sailors. He moved more troops into the Dominican Republic in preparation for an invasion at Monte Cristi and Puerto Plaza. Admiral Caperton also prevented the Dominican assembly from electing another president.

In 1916, the gunboat *Sacramento* landed 130 Marines and a company of sailors at Puerto Plaza. The *Sacramento* also leveled a fort. The *Panther* was involved in seizing Monte Cristi with a landing party. Admiral Caperton put forth a plan to occupy Santiago, Moca and La Vega by using Marines from the *Rhode Island* and *New Jersey*, which he did in 1916.

In 1916, it was decided that establishing a military government was the best course of action. The legitimate government of the Dominican Republic was overthrown, and Captain Harry Knapp was proclaimed as military governor of the country, being assisted by Marine officers in its administration. Captain Knapp also suspended the Dominican assembly to prevent them from causing trouble, and he began the process of disarming the Dominican army and its citizenry, with guerilla warfare resulting from this decision. Opposition was done by 5,000 men in 1918, with more rebellions occurring in 1919 and 1920.

In 1920, the military governor, Thomas Snowden, announced that the United States would be withdrawing its forces from the Dominican Republic. However, it was not until 1924 that the last Marines departed from the country.

Honduras

Between 1903 and 1925, American troops landed in Honduras on 7 different occasions, including one in 1907 to settle a war with Nicaragua.

Guatemala

In 1920, United States troops were sent in a 2-week intervention against unionists. President Woodrow Wilson suggested the overthrow of the Guatemalan President as being in the best interests of the United Fruit Company, something that the Guatemalans complied with in 1920 to prevent intervention by the United States military.

El Salvador

In 1932, President Herbert Hoover sent United States warships to El Salvador in response to a communist-led uprising. Although he was financed and supported by the United States, the president of El Salvador preferred to put down the rebellion with his own forces. In the process he had over 8,000 people killed, most of them peasants.

Warren Harding

Election of 1920

In the 1920 election, Warren Harding won the presidency with 404 Electoral vote. Calvin Coolidge was elected as Vice President.

Significant Events: 1921

President Harding called for a return to normalcy, which was prompted by the American people who wanted an end to international involvements by the United States. To promote the economy, he advocated emergency tariffs, new immigration laws, regulation of communications, tax reduction, repeal of the wartime excess profits tax, reduction of railroad rates, promotion of agricultural interests, creation of a national budget system, the building of a merchant marine and the creation of a department of public welfare. He also requested the passage of an anti-lynching law.

The United States and Colombia agreed to a settlement regarding the takeover of Panama in 1903 for which the Senate authorized a payment of $25 million to Colombia.

Congress passed the Emergency Tariff Act to increase tariffs, especially on farm products—and to lower taxes.

Congress passed the Per Centum Act that provided for the continued exclusion of Asians, but permitted a limited European immigration that was restricted to 3% of that nation's nationals who were already residing in the United States.

Congress passed the Budget and Accounting Act to bring order to the national accounts. Two offices were created: The Bureau of the Budget and the General Accounting Office.

Congress passed a resolution to create the Joint Commission on Agricultural Inquiry to investigate conditions affecting the farms, and to make recommendations.

President Harding signed the Knox-Porter Resolution, which brought the end to WWI since the Senate had rejected the Treaty of Versailles. The Berlin Treaty was signed with Germany in 1921, and then similar treaties were arranged with Austria and Hungary.

The Soviet Union signed an agreement with the United States to release all Americans held in Russia, and to not interfere with American relief workers. This was in response to a request by author Maxim Gorky to the Secretary of Commerce Herbert Hoover for American aid to assist millions of Russians who were on the verge of starvation.

Congress passed the Packers and Stockyards Act to forbade unfair and discriminatory practices, the manipulation and control of prices, and the denial of devices designed to create a monopoly or restraint of trade.

The Grain Futures Trading Act was passed by Congress to regulate all contract markets authorized to sell grain for future delivery, and to prevent market manipulation, monopoly practices and speculations.

The Sheppard-Towner Act was passed by Congress to promote the welfare and health of maternity and infancy by extending federal aid to the states.

The tomb of the Unknown Soldier was dedicated at Arlington Cemetery in Washington, D.C. by President Harding and Vice President Calvin Coolidge.

President Harding pardoned Eugene Debs, a Socialist Party presidential candidate who had been jailed for seditious antiwar activities during WWI.

Congress passed the Federal Highway Act to enable state highway departments to designate a system of interstate and inter-county roads under which all future federal funds would be spent.

Significant Events: 1922

Harding supported the federal anti-lynching bill, the Dyer Bill, which passed the House. However, the Dyer bill was defeated in the Senate.

Congress passed the Capper-Volstead Act to allow farmers to buy and sell cooperatively without being subject to anti-trust laws.

The Supreme Court declared that the Nineteenth Amendment was constitutional.

Congress created the Federal Narcotics Board by passing the Narcotic Drugs Import and Export Act.

Congress extended the Per Centum Act until 1924.

Congress passed a bill to allow the President to add a sixth member to the Federal Reserve Board who would represent the agricultural sector.

Violence in the oil fields at Herrin, Illinois resulted in 21 deaths.

The Bureau of Agricultural Economics was created to conduct research by collecting, assembling and interpreting agricultural data.

The Supreme Court ruled that the Future Trading Act was unconstitutional because it was an illegal use of taxing power.

Congress passed the Cable Act to clarify citizenship status with regard to marriage. American women who married aliens would not lose their United States citizenship. Also, alien women who married American citizens would not automatically become United States citizens.

Congress passed the Fordney-McCumber Bill that authorized the President to set tariff rates up to 50% of their current value.

President Harding vetoed the Soldiers' Bonus Bill, which Congress had passed. He stated that balancing the budget takes precedence over the nation's debt to veterans of WWI.

Significant Events: 1923

Congress passed the Intermediate Credit Act to provide relief to farmers by authorizing the Federal Reserve Bank to aid in financing agricultural cooperatives.

Congress passed the Government Reclassification Act to raise the pay scales of government employees.

In the case of *Adkins v. Children's Hospital*, the Supreme Court ruled that a District of Columbia minimum wage law for women was unconstitutional.

The Supreme Court ruled that the transportation of liquor into the territorial waters of the United States was illegal. However, it stated that the Volstead Act did not prevent United States ships from carrying and selling liquor outside the 3-mile limit.

President Harding commuted the sentences of 23 members of the Industrial Workers of the World (IWW) who had been jailed for being involved in seditious antiwar activities.

President Warren Gamaliel Harding died on August 2, 1923.

Vice President Calvin Coolidge was sworn in as President.

Calvin Coolidge

Vice President

In the 1920 election, the Warren Harding-Calvin Coolidge ticket won by an Electoral vote of 404.

Vice President Coolidge participated with President Harding in the burial ceremony of the Unknown Soldier at Arlington Military Cemetery in 1921. Calvin Coolidge became President upon the death of President Harding in 1923.

Significant Events: 1923

The Bucareli Conferences that were held in Mexico City, Mexico were concluded. The result was the recognition of the Mexican government by the United States.

The Teapot Dome scandal was revealed by Senator Thomas Walsh.

President Coolidge requested the consolidation of the railroads, rate increases for the railroads, the development of a new reforestation program, and increases in military and naval appropriations.

Significant Events: 1924

Congress passed the Soldiers' Bonus Bill to provide 20-year annuities for veterans. The bill was vetoed by President Coolidge, but was overridden by Congress.

The House approved the sale of the Muscle Shoals complex to Henry Ford. However, the Senate rejected the sale — and Ford withdrew his offer.

The National Origins Act was passed by Congress to severely restrict immigration by establishing a system of national quotas that discriminated against immigrants from Southern and Eastern Europe as well as prohibiting the immigration of East Asians, especially the Japanese, and Asian Indians. It limited the number of immigrants who could be admitted from any country to 2% of the number of people from that country who were already living in the United States in 1890.

Congress passed the Foreign Service Act to reorganize and consolidate the diplomatic and consular services of the United States.

Congress passed the Revenue Act of 1924, which cut the bottom rate on incomes under $4,000 to 1.125 percent, and the surtax to 1 percent on incomes between $10,000 and $14,000.

President Coolidge signed the Indian Citizenship Act, which granted United States citizenship to all Indians, while permitting them to retain tribal land and cultural rights.

Calvin Coolidge was elected President with an Electoral vote of 387. Charles Gates Dawes was elected as Vice President.

President Coolidge asked for further development of internal waterways, for judicial and prison reforms, for cutbacks in military procurement and tax cuts.

Significant Events: 1925

Congress passed the Judiciary Act to provide for most appeals from federal district courts to go directly to the Circuit Courts of Appeals to allow the Supreme Court more discretion over its workload by removing the possibility of a direct appeal to the Supreme Court in most circumstances.

The Isle of Pines Treaty was ratified by the Senate that established possession of the Isle of Pines to Cuba.

In the case of *Gitlow v. New York*, the Supreme Court upheld the original conviction of Benjamin Gitlow who had been arrested under New York's Criminal Anarchy Statute. The Supreme Court agreed that the Fourteenth Amendment forbade a state from impairing rights guaranteed by the First Amendment, but it also stated that Gitlow's provocative publication had been more inflammatory than what the law allowed.

400,000 members of the Ku Klux Klan (KKK) marched in Washington, D. C. at the peak of their organization, which numbered 6 million in various chapters across the United States whose membership included 2 United States Senators.

Significant Events: 1926

Congress passed the Revenue Act that reduced income taxes, surtaxes and other taxes, such as those on passenger cars.

Congress passed the Air Commerce Act that gave the Commerce Department control of civil aviation, including licensing of aircraft and pilots.

Congress established the Army Air Corps, which was the predecessor of the United States Air Force.

The Supreme Court ruled that the President had the power to remove Cabinet members and other appointees.

President Coolidge asked for tax cuts, for legislation to regulate radio and for laws to strengthen the banks.

Term Events: 1927

Congress passed the McNary-Haugen Bill to allow the government to purchase agricultural surpluses from farmers. The bill was vetoed by President Coolidge.

Congress passed the Radio Act, which created the Federal Radio Commission to oversee national and international communications.

Congress passed the McFadden-Pepper Act to extend the Federal Reserve Bank charters. The McFadden-Pepper Act specifically prohibited interstate branching by allowing each national bank to branch only within the state in which it was situated.

The Supreme Court declared the Elk Hills lease in Kern County, California to be invalid.

In the case of *Nixon v. Herndon*, the Supreme Court ruled that the exclusion of blacks from party primaries violated the Fourteenth and Fifteenth Amendments.

The Supreme Court ruled that the lease of the Teapot Dome oil reserve lands in Wyoming to have been fraudulently negotiated.

President Coolidge asked for flood control legislation to provide loans for property owners.

Significant Events: 1928

President Coolidge supported a $180 million flood control program allocated by Congress. However, this was not enough to cover the damages of the Mississippi River flood, which amounted to $1.4 billion. Congress passed the Flood Control Act to control flooding on the Mississippi River, and to cover the entire amount of damages.

Congress passed the McNary-Haugen Bill, which was vetoed by President Coolidge.

Congress passed the Jones-White Merchant Marine Act to provide subsidies to private shipping companies, and to allocate $280 million in construction funds for ships built in American yards.

Congress passed the Muscle-Shoals Bill to provide government ownership of a hydroelectric plant in Tennessee, but it was vetoed by President Coolidge.

Herbert Hoover won the presidential election by getting 444 Electoral votes. Charles Curtis was elected as Vice President.

The Clark Memorandum redefined the Monroe Doctrine as pertaining to Europe—and not against Latin America.

Significant Events: 1929

The Senate ratified the Kellogg-Briand Pact, which was a multinational treaty that prohibited the use of war as an instrument of national policy except in matters of self-defense.

The Federal Reserve Board forbade its member banks to make loans to buy stocks on margin in an attempt to stop speculation on Wall Street.

Congress passed the Cruiser Act to authorize funds to construct 19 new cruisers and one aircraft carrier for the Navy.

Herbert Hoover was inaugurated as President.

Herbert Hoover

1928 Election

In the 1928 election, Herbert Hoover won the presidency by getting 444 Electoral votes. Charles Curtis was elected as Vice President.

Significant Events: 1929

President Hoover requested a special session of Congress to deal with the economy.

President Hoover appointed a National Commission on Law Observance and Enforcement to study the adverse effects of Prohibition. He also ordered the DOJ to move in on Al Capone—an endeavor that resulted in the arrest and conviction of the mobster boss on tax evasion charges.

In the case of *United States v. Schwimmer*, the Supreme Court upheld a lower court decision to deny citizenship to a Hungarian immigrant because of her pacifist views.

The Supreme Court ruled that the pocket veto by a President was constitutional.

Congress passed the Agricultural Marketing Act to establish a Federal Farm Board to aid farmers' cooperatives. It set up a fund of $500 million to lend to farmer-owned cooperatives.

Congress approved the Boulder Canyon Project Act to generate more than 3 million kilowatts of electricity by hydroelectric power, and to curb floods in the Imperial Valley of California. The project was also designed to supply water to Southern California, especially to the Los Angeles area.

A riot by 900 inmates at the Leavenworth penitentiary in Leavenworth, Kansas caused President Hoover to initiate penal reform. He appointed Sanford Bates to head the Bureau of Prisons and had $5 billion allocated by Congress to institute a school for prison guards, set up work camps, improve health care for inmates and build new facilities to relieve overcrowding.

Stock prices collapsed on the New York Stock Exchange as the start of the Great Depression began.

President Hoover summoned leaders of industry, finance construction, public utilities, agriculture and labor to the White House to ask manufacturers to maintain wage rates, and for unions to pledge not to strike or demand wage increases.

President Hoover contacted the governors of the states and encouraged them to accelerate construction. He asked Congress for an appropriation of $150 million for public works, and to enact a tax cut. He asked the Federal Reserve Board to expand the money supply and to make more credit available. In addition, he asked the Federal Farm Board to sustain crop prices.

Significant Events: 1930

President Hoover met with Congressional leaders to discuss a public works program.

Congress passed the Public Buildings Act to allocate $230 million for erecting public buildings.

Congress authorized $300 million for road construction to alleviate unemployment, which was at the 3 million mark.

The Supreme Court ruled that the purchase of intoxicating liquors was not a violation of the Constitution.

Congress passed the Hawley-Smoot Tariff Act to raise duties on imported items—in spite of a petition against it that was signed by over 1,000 economists from 179 institutions of higher learning in 46 states.

Congress passed the Veterans Administration Act to establish the Veterans Administration and to consolidate all federal programs for aiding ex-servicemen.

Congress passed the Rivers and Harbors Bill.

The State Department issued an order prohibiting immigration of all foreign laborers because of the mounting unemployment in the United States.

President Hoover appointed an Emergency Committee for Unemployment Relief. after unemployment passed the 5 million mark.

President Hoover requested $150 million from Congress to construct public works, which Congress reduced by allocating only $116 million.

Significant Events: 1931

The Supreme Court upheld the constitutionality of the Eighteenth Amendment by reversing a ruling in a lower court.

Congress passed the Bonus Loan Bill over President Hoover's veto to allow veterans to get loans up to 50% of the value of their bonus certificates.

President Hoover vetoed the Muscle Shoals Bill for a government operated hydroelectric power plant in Tennessee.

Congress passed the Davis-Bacon Bill, which established the requirement for paying prevailing union wages on public works projects.

President Hoover recommended a one-year moratorium on payments of the war debt to prevent the further deterioration of the international financial system.

England went off the gold standard, with 50 other countries following suit—thus creating a massive withdrawal of gold from the United States, and causing over 500 American banks to fail.

Significant Events: 1932

Congress passed a bill to establish a Reconstruction Finance Corporation (RFC) to authorize $500 million to lend money to banks, insurance companies, building and loan societies, agricultural credit corporations, farm mortgage associations and railroads. The bill also authorized borrowing up to $2 billion by tax-exempt bonds.

Congress passed the Glass-Steagall Banking Act to authorize the Federal Reserve Bank to extend credit.

Congress passed the Norris-LaGuardia Anti-Injunction Act to prohibit the use of judicial injunctions in labor disputes to inhibit strikes, picketing and boycotts.

The Bonus Army consisting of 17,000 veterans marched on Washington, D.C. to demand the cashing of their bonus certificates[1]. Under orders by President Hoover, they were driven out by Army troops. All threats of violence ceased as the marchers were pushed beyond the limits of the District of Columbia by the soldiers.

3,000 persons assembled in Detroit, Michigan for a march to the Ford River Rogue factory in Dearborn, Michigan. When gendarmes from Ford ordered the demonstrators to turn back, they refused and police shot tear gas at the crowd. The demonstrators responded by hurling stones, and police fired into the crowd, killing 4 and wounding 50.

President Hoover forced the Senate to investigate the New York Stock Exchange, which disclosed manipulation, price fixing and thievery on an unprecedented scale.

Congress passed the Revenue Tax Act of 1932[2].

Congress passed the Emergency Relief and Reconstruction Act to enlarge the programs of the Reconstruction Finance Corporation by increasing the amount that it could loan up to $1.5 billion for public works and relief.

Congress passed the Federal Home Loan Bank Act that authorized up to 12 regional banks to provide loans for mortgages and home construction.

Congress passed the Wagner-Garner Bill to extend the work of the federal employment agencies to states, which did not sponsor such units, but President Hoover vetoed the bill.

The Controller of the Currency declared a moratorium on foreclosures of mortgages.

In the case of *Powell v. Alabama*, the Supreme Court ruled that the defendants had not been properly represented by counsel, and thus granted a retrial.

Franklin Roosevelt was elected as President with an Electoral vote of 472. John Nance Garner was elected as Vice President.

Significant Events: 1933

The Twentieth Amendment was adopted by the states to shorten the interregnum from March 4th to January 20th for the transfer of Presidential power.

Franklin Roosevelt was inaugurated as President.

Twentieth Amendment

Overview

The Twentieth Amendment established the beginning and ending of the terms of the elected federal offices, and reduced the amount of time between Election Day and the beginning of Presidential, Vice Presidential and Congressional terms. It also dealt with scenarios in which there is no President-elect. The Twentieth Amendment was ratified in 1933.

Text of the Twentieth Amendment

"Section 1. The terms of the President and Vice President shall end at noon on the 20th day of January, and the terms of Senators and Representatives at noon on the 3d day of January, of the years in which such terms would have ended if this article had not been ratified; and the terms of their successors shall then begin.

Section 2. The Congress shall assemble at least once in every year, and such meeting shall begin at noon on the 3d day of January, unless they shall by law appoint a different day.

Section 3. If, at the time fixed for the beginning of the term of the President, the President-Elect shall have died, the Vice President-Elect shall become President. If a President shall not have been chosen before the time fixed for the beginning of his term, or if the President-Elect shall have failed to qualify, then the Vice President-Elect shall act as President until a President shall have qualified; and the Congress may by law provide for the case wherein neither a President-Elect nor a Vice President-Elect shall have qualified, declaring who shall then act as President, or the manner in which one who is to act shall be selected, and such person shall act accordingly until a President or Vice President shall have qualified.

Section 4. The Congress may by law provide for the case of the death of any of the persons from whom the House of Representatives may choose a President whenever the right of choice shall have devolved upon them, and for the case of the death of any of the persons from whom the Senate may choose a Vice President whenever the right of choice shall have devolved upon them.

Section 5. Sections 1 and 2 shall take effect on the 15th day of October following the ratification of this article.

Section 6. This article shall be inoperative unless it shall have been ratified as an amendment to the Constitution by the legislatures of three-fourths of the several States within seven years from the date of its submission."

Proposal and Ratification

The Congress proposed the Twentieth Amendment in 1932, and the states completed ratifying it in 1933[2]. The first Congressional terms to begin under the Twentieth Amendment were those of the 74th Congress in 1935, and the first terms of President Franklin Roosevelt and Vice President John Garner in 1937.

The Great Depression

Overview

The Great Depression did not happen suddenly with the crash of the stock market in 1929. In fact, the stock market turned upward in 1930, and government and businesses spent heavily in 1930. But consumers, many of whom had suffered severe losses in the stock market in 1929, cut back their expenditures, which along with a severe drought that ravaged the agricultural heartland of the United States, brought things to a halt. There were several causes for the economic downturn, with the main ones being as follows:

- Depressed aggregate demand and under consumption
- Contraction of money supplies
- Strict adherence to the gold standard
- Fluctuating aggregate supply
- Structural weakness of banks
- Failure of the free market
- Failure of government policies
- Overinvestment
- Massive amounts of debt
- Cheap credit that allowed stock trades on margin accounts
- Trade decline due to the tariff act that increased rates
- Lack of government deficit spending
- Inequality of wealth and income
- Malfeasance by bankers and industrialists

In the United States major economic slumps had occurred in 1819, 1837, 1857, 1873 and 1893. Another economic collapse in 1914 was averted when the outbreak of World War I resulted in a revival of the American economy. In the 1920s, the prosperity that ensued was the greatest economic boom in American history. Nevertheless, it was built on a house of cards as it also produced the greatest concentration of wealth among the fewest individuals as more than one-third of all net wealth was owned by less than one-half of one percent of the population.

When the downward slide in the stock market began in 1929, the collapse resulted in a loss of 50% of the value of stocks. The investment trusts and pyramid schemes failed and led to a monetary collapse that produced the onset of the depression. Investment fell by 35% between 1929 and 1930, and again by 35% more between 1930 and 1931. Finally, in 1932, investment practically ceased, dropping by 88% of its 1931 level. At the bottom of the depression in 1933, investment had dropped by 98%. The accompanying business retrenchment resulted in a drastic reduction of demand and an accumulation of unsold inventories. As production was curtailed, people lost their jobs and by 1933, a total of 25% of workers in the United States were unemployed. In some cities the unemployment rate was higher, such as Cleveland with 50%, Akron, Ohio with 60%, East St. Louis with

60%, and Toledo, Ohio with 80%. It was estimated that 34 million men, women and children in America were without any income, and that 11 million farm families were destitute.

The Onset of the Depression

The Stock Market Crash

In September 1929, the stock market peaked after what had been a 3-year bull market run. In October 1929, a steady decline in stock market prices occurred until the stock market collapsed on October 24, 1929, with over 14 million stock shares being traded. The stock market then suffered a second collapse on October 29, 1929, with over 16 million shares being traded and a total loss in value of 880 issues exceeding $8 billion. Thousands of investors saw their fortunes wiped out in a single day. As prices fell the supply of people buying became nil, and the ownership of margin accounts became critical. As the number of people wanting to sell increased further, the market fell even lower. And, since the value of the stocks bought on margin declined, then the collateral for the stock loans that had paid for them also decreased. Thus, the banks requested more cash from the stock speculators to cover their loans. A wave of selling continued to sweep Wall Street, the Chicago and Buffalo Stock Exchanges closed, and finally bankers stepped in an attempt to stem the panic.

However, the effect of the banks was only temporary as margin accounts were liquidated, and the volume of bankers' loans fell by $1 billion—with the corporations and banks calling in an additional $2 billion. The New York banks stepped in again by increasing their loans by $1 billion, but after a brief gain, the market plummeted once more, with firms buying their own worthless stock. By November 1929, the market reached its new low with $40 billion in the value of listed stocks being wiped out. The stock market slide continued to fall gradually, reaching its bottom in 1932.

The Federal Reserve

One of the factors that produced the depression was monetary contraction—the consequence of poor policymaking by the Federal Reserve as the crisis in the banking system worsened. The Federal Reserve allowed the money supply to shrink by one-third from 1929 to 1933. Large, public bank failures, particularly that of the Bank of the United States, produced panic and widespread runs on local banks as bank failures reached 25%. The Federal Reserve did not act while these banks failed, and hence did not create the needed liquidity for new loans or investments.

The Federal Reserve did not act to limit the decline of the money supply because of regulation. The amount of credit that the Federal Reserve could issue was limited by laws, which required partial gold backing of that credit. Since the Federal Reserve had hit the limit of allowable credit that could be backed by the gold in its possession, then any reduction in gold in its vaults had to be accompanied by a greater reduction in credit. The American populace lost faith in the banking system and began hoarding more cash. In turn, the potential for a run on the banks caused local bankers to be more conservative in lending out their reserves.

<u>The Financial Collapse</u>

The effects of the depression were staggering. Massive bank failures, panics, reduction in the money supply and deflation occurred. People and businesses that were deeply in debt cut current spending drastically to keep up time payments, thus lowering the demand for new products. As a result, businesses began to fail as construction work and factory orders plunged. Massive layoffs occurred, resulting in an unemployment rate of over 25% by 1933. Debt defaults and bankruptcies became rampant among borrowers and companies. Outstanding debts became greater as prices and incomes fell by 20% to 50% while the debts remained at the same amount. Thus, the economic problems that were experienced by the financial systems between 1930 and 1933 were due to the loss of confidence in the financial institutions—especially banks—and the widespread insolvency of debtors. National debt expressed as a fraction of gross national product climbed from 20% to 40%.

Banks which had financed debts began to fail as debtors defaulted on debt and depositors attempted to withdraw their deposits through multiple bank runs. Government guarantees and Federal Reserve banking regulations to prevent such panics proved to be ineffective. By 1933, one-half of the banks that were operating in 1929 were no longer around, and the ones that were left had experienced heavy losses[3]. The pervasiveness of debtor insolvency greatly increased as the protracted fall in prices and money incomes continued unabated. The collapse of output, the rise in unemployment, and the monetary retrenchment created a situation where the nation's economy declined drastically in what was the most severe business contraction in the history of the American economy.

<u>Other Effects</u>

In rural areas, the economic situation was much worse. Before the depression happened, overproduction of crops and livestock had already plunged the agricultural sector into its own depression. The lower food prices hit the farmers hard with over one-half of them being delinquent in the payment of farm mortgage debt by 1933. Farm income dropped to very low levels and farm mortgages could not be paid, thus resulting in massive foreclosures—and the eviction of farmers from their lands. One-fourth of American farmers lost their fields, stock, barns and homes.

A great drought that became known as the "Dust Bowl" also started in 1930. The effects of these dust storms ruined over 1 million farms and affected over 20 million animals, thus forcing mass migrations out of the affected areas in freight cars known as "Hoover Pullmans" and the creation of shantytowns in empty lots with shelters made from scrap materials that became known as "Hoovervilles". President Hoover attempted to meet the emergency by inducing railroads to haul feed to draught sufferers at one-half the normal rates, by freeing surpluses held by the Federal Farm Board to the affected areas, and by accelerating construction of highways and waterways in the afflicted regions.

The sharp decline in international trade after 1930 helped to worsen the depression, with the Smoot-Hawley Tariff Act seriously reducing international trade and causing retaliatory tariffs in other countries. Since foreign trade was concentrated mostly in farming, American exports declined and prices fell, with farm commodities such as wheat, cotton, tobacco, and lumber being affected. The collapse of farm exports caused farmers to default on their loans, leading to the bank runs on small rural banks that caused them to fail.

Millions were reduced to begging, and some of them searched garbage dumps for food—and a few ate weeds and wild greens. Programs of relief were attempted when private charity activities such as soup kitchens proved incapable of sustaining the destitute. Bread lines became a fixture in the major cities of the United States. Some people died from hunger and illness while others just seemed to give up on their desire to live, with a few committing suicide. Black people suffered a disproportionate share of the depression. Almost 50% of blacks were unemployed by 1932 as they were discharged from menial jobs such as domestic servants, garbage collectors, waiters, elevator operators, bellhops and street cleaners. Even skilled blacks who kept their jobs lost 50% of their wages.

President Hoover's fiscal policies failed to restore the economy because not enough money was spent, especially on work relief programs. His emphasis was centered on balancing the budget and on restoring confidence. This failure of monetary and fiscal policies prolonged the depression since offsetting actions were not taken once the economic decline was underway. In addition, the Revenue Act of 1932 raised taxes to their highest levels—a counterproductive move in a depressed economy. Since a highly unequal income distribution existed in the United States, this meant that the economy was highly dependent on both a high level of investment and on a high level of luxury consumer spending. When this income was curtailed by the new tax law, the spending stopped, thus spiraling the economy into a tailspin. As a result, people lost faith in the government.

Recovery

<u>Overview</u>

In the most intense period of reform legislation and executive action, President Franklin Roosevelt pushed 16 major laws and executive orders in his first 100 days under the first New Deal in 1933. After the first 100 days, more legislation was passed in 1933 and 1934 to further the New Deal, including the Civil Works Administration (CWA). Under the second New Deal, which occurred in 100 days in 1935, President Roosevelt got still more legislation passed through Congress, including the Social Security Act, the Labor Relations Act, the 1935 Revenue Act, the Banking Act of 1935, and the Public Utilities Holding Company Act. To push the economy, President Roosevelt initiated an expansionary monetary policy, abandoned the gold standard and rehabilitated the banking system. His inflationary policies helped to partially increase employment, which was the critical element in the recovery. But, by 1934, a growing class conflict produced a situation where 1.5 million workers participated in 1,800 strikes—even though jobs were scarce.

By 1934, almost 4.3 million persons had been employed by the various programs, and 20 million Americans were being assisted by federal relief. 500,000 miles of roads were built or improved, 40,000 schools were built or improved, 500 new airports were laid out and 500 existing airports were upgraded. Even so, the depression lasted with varying severity for over a decade in spite of the fact that government spending rose to $9 billion in 1936. Between 1937 and 1938, a major recession occurred, which did not result in an economic rebound until 1939. The stock market collapsed again in 1937 with the Dow Jones average dropping by almost 40%. Also, 4 million more unemployed people were added to the rolls in 1938, thus causing the unemployment rate to rise to 20% as the stock market collapsed again in 1938. To counter this, President Roosevelt asked for $3 billion to expand the Works Project Administration (WPA). Congress responded by voting for an appropriation of $3.75 billion

In 1939, almost 9.4 million people remained unemployed—about 17% of the work force. Not until 1941 did production rise to a level that was above the 1929 figure. This was due to the military buildup that took place between 1940 and 1941, which did more to stimulate the economy and reduce unemployment than did any New Deal program. The unemployment rate dropped to 14½% and then dropped further to less than 10%. By the end of 1941, the industrial production had climbed to 30% above its 1929 level—mostly because of the wartime buildup effect that was the reaction to the Japanese air attack on the United States naval forces at Pearl Harbor in Honolulu, Hawaii. It was only at the height of WWII in 1943, that the average unemployment rate fell below its 1929 level.

WWII

The American military buildup that was initiated by WWII did more to revive industry in the United States and reduce unemployment than any New Deal program initiated by President Roosevelt. Although it was still a continuation of deficit spending, the Nazi threat and the attack by the forces of Japan pushed the United States into an accelerated military boom. Even so, it took time for a reversal of the prevailing economic situation since in 1940 the unemployment rate was still 14.6%, and in 1941, the unemployment rate had only dropped to 10%. In 1942, President Roosevelt called for production goals of 60,000 warplanes, 45,000 tanks, 20,000 antiaircraft guns and 18 million tons of merchant shipping. Labor, farms, mines, factories, trading houses, investment firms, communications, cultural and educational institutions were all enlisted into the war effort. However, it was not until 1943 that the economic situation became better than it had been prior to 1929 before the crash occurred. Also contributing was the draft, which helped bring the armed forces of the United States to more than 15 million members. Thus, 65 million men and women were in uniform or worked in war-related jobs by 1943.

Aftermath

The depression produced new policies and safeguards. Banks became regulated by institutions that were begun during the New Deal such as the Federal Deposit Insurance Corporation (FDIC). Welfare payments, social security and unemployment insurance were also started by the New Deal. The artificial price support systems that were initiated allowed farmers to stay on their lands. Resorting to deficit spending to stimulate the economy became the alternative to supply-side policies. However, the New Deal policies also created a system of welfare and entitlement programs that have fundamentally altered society, and which have increasingly added to the national debt.

Most New Deal regulations were abolished or scaled back in the 1970s and 1980s in a wave of deregulation. However, the Securities and Exchange Commission, Federal Reserve, and Social Security won widespread support and were kept as necessary elements. President Franklin Roosevelt also tried to establish national health insurance, but he met with stiff opposition that rejected this effort. Still, he managed to personalize the Presidency to provide the people of the country with a feeling of intimate contact with the President. This created a new political atmosphere in that the expectation is now for the chief executive to lead in whatever situation that he (or she) is confronted with.

The American Dust Bowl

Overview

The American Dust Bowl, which lasted from 1930 to 1940, is considered to be one of the most significant weather events of the 20th century. The rains in the Great Plains disappeared during these years, and with no sod to hold the earth in place, the soil calcified and began to blow. In its greatest extent, the Dust Bowl covered 100 million acres in the states of Nebraska, Kansas, Colorado, New Mexico, Oklahoma and Texas. Its impact left thousands dead, diseased and destitute. Many people did not believe the initial accounts of predatory dust until a storm in May 1934 carried the windblown soil of the Great Plains over much of the nation. In Chicago, Illinois 12 million tons of dust fell. Off the Atlantic Ocean coast from New York City to Washington, D.C., ships at sea that were 300 miles away from shore were covered with brown dust.

By 1936, more than 850 million tons of topsoil had blown off the southern plains, and over 100 million acres of land were left with almost no chance of being cultivated as productive farmland. To reclaim the land, President Franklin Roosevelt implemented a plan to plant a great wall consisting of 2 million trees in a belt 100 miles wide stretching from North Dakota to Texas. By 1938, the massive conservation effort had reduced the amount of blowing soil by 65%. Nevertheless, the land failed to yield a fruitful result until 1939, when regular rainfall finally returned to the region. In 1941, the rains returned in a plentiful amount to the Great Plains, thus ending the decade-long drought. Farmers once again planted their crops, including wheat. The black dust blizzards disappeared, thus ending the nation's worst prolonged environmental disaster. The dust bowl phenomena provided a new understanding of the role of government in combating natural and man-made disasters.

Beginning of the Drought

In 1929, the United States had a food surplus, with many towns in the plains area having stacks of unsold wheat stored in grain elevators. In response, farmers tore up the natural buffalo prairie grass and planted even more amounts of wheat—actions that furthered exposed the land and made it subject to the winds when the blowing season began. This plowing would combine with wind and the drought to blow away uncovered soil in huge dust storms.

In 1930, a windstorm emerged from Kansas and blew towards Oklahoma and Texas. It rolled with black waves of dust and carried significant static electricity to short out ignition systems of automobiles. In 1931, the first full year of drought was experienced. In 1932, a cloud of dust that was over 10,000 feet high moved from Texas to Oklahoma, and then to Colorado and Kansas. More dusters emerged, with at least over a dozen of these being tracked by weather bureaus. The dry spell became hotter and harsher as winds with coarse sand blew across the land, making it calcified and too dry to plant. The accompanying erosion along with the heat, wind and drought coupled with the farmers' neglect in maintaining a balanced prairie ecosystem created a desert. With the desert, great hordes of insects appeared such as spiders, worms, tarantulas, grasshoppers and centipedes. Wild rabbits proliferated and became an added scourge by devouring crops.

Intensification of Storms

In 1933, at least 70 severe dust storms were recorded. In 1934, even more severe dust storms emerged with accompanying summer temperatures that ranged between 115 and 120 degrees Fahrenheit. On May 9, 1934, a huge duster started in the Dakotas and Montana. It was picked up by the jet stream, and the duster moved toward Illinois and Ohio, winding up in Chicago, Boston, Atlanta, Philadelphia, Buffalo and New York City. The storm was 1,800 miles wide and contained 350 million tons of dust. Brown dirt fell on ships in the Atlantic Ocean that were 300 miles from shore.

Black Sunday

After experiencing 49 dusters in 1935, the greatest dust storm occurred on April 14, 1935. A high-pressure weather system in North Dakota interacted with a cold front from the Yukon such that a ferocious wind started that scooped up and carried dust as it made its way toward South Dakota and Nebraska. When this rolling dust storm crossed into Kansas, it was 200 miles wide with high winds between 60 and 100 miles per hour. The storm traveled at a speed of 50 mph as it made its way through Colorado, New Mexico, Oklahoma and Texas where it became 1,000 miles wide and rose to over 23,000 feet high. The storm dissipated over the Gulf of Mexico where it deposited dirt on ships that were 200 miles from shore.

In a single day this dust storm carried twice as much dirt as was dug out of the earth in 7 years to create the Panama Canal—more than 300 million tons of Great Plains topsoil. As the black wall of dust approached, car radios clicked off and car ignitions shorted out because they were overwhelmed by the static that was produced by the storm. Motorists reported receiving shocks by touching door handles and other metal objects in their cars. Waves of sand swept over roads. The black dust storm turned day into night, and it caused visibility problems that grounded airplanes[4] and resulted in cars crashing into ditches, and even derailed a train. Hundreds of ducks, geese and other kinds of birds were observed flying in front of the storm trying to get away—and afterwards many small dead birds were seen on the ground.

Effects of the Storms

The effects of the storms were many, including the making of secondary roads impassable because of the accumulation of dunes caused by the blowing drifts. When the storms hit, dust clouds boiled up, rose to more than 10,000 feet in the sky, and rolled with a terrific force. When the dust fell, it penetrated everything: hair, noses, throats, kitchens, bedrooms and water wells—with a scoop shovel being needed to clean a house after each storm. Darkness ensued during the day, with chickens roosting in mid-afternoon, horses running madly against the storms, and people tying themselves to ropes before going to a barn just a few hundred feet away from their house.

The soil was like fine-sifted flour, and the accompanying heat made it dangerous to go outside as temperatures went above 100 degrees Fahrenheit for several consecutive days. Many cattle suffocated to death from the dust, and when farmers cut them open, they found their stomachs filled with fine sand. Children coughed and gagged, sometimes dying of what doctors called "dust pneumonia". Others suffered from associated ailments such as strep throat, silicosis, sinusitis, laryngitis, bronchitis and tuberculosis.

Even the act of hugging a loved one or shaking someone's hand was something that could shock and knock both people down because the static electricity from these dust storms was so strong. The dust was like a nail file having grit strong enough to cut the skin. Many people rubbed Vaseline in their nostrils as a filter, and the Red Cross handed out respiratory masks to children in the schools. Families put wet towels beneath their doors or taped the doors, stuffed wall cracks with rags and newspapers, and covered their windows with fresh-dampened bed sheets in futile attempts to keep the dust out. Attics had to be shoveled out to keep the roofs from collapsing from the weight of the sand.

The effect of the dust storms on farming was devastating as crops withered and died. Rivers and wells ran dry, leaving no water for irrigation or personal use. The soil hardened and cracked, and resulted in a dry dirt that was carried away by the winds, which created huge dust storms that were referred to as "black blizzards." In the dust bowl area, one-third of all farms foreclosed, two-thirds of the banks closed, and shelves in grocery stores went bare.

Exodus

The Dust Bowl forced 3 million people to leave their homes and caused whole towns to die. The Works Project Administration (WPA) hired many of these farmers, schoolteachers and merchants to renovate schools, post offices and other buildings, to construct 600 new airports, to pave over 650,000 miles of new roads, to build or repair 125,000 bridges and to refurbish over 8,000 parks.

More than 250,000 people moved out from the areas of Texas, Oklahoma and Arkansas, with the majority of them settling in California where they hoped to earn a living by picking fruits and vegetables[5]. However, many Californians did not have sympathy for these migrants, and instituted extra-legal methods in an effort to keep them out. The ones who did make it through settled mainly in the San Joaquin Valley to pick the crops and pack them for shipments around the country[7]. They settled in makeshift camps that produced unsanitary living conditions and which resulted in thousands of cases of influenza. Along with malnutrition and poor diets, the unhealthy conditions caused many other ailments, particularly in children.

Government Response and Recovery

Government programs were implemented to conserve soil and restore the ecological balance of the region. The Agricultural Adjustment Act (AAA) of 1933 was the beginning of a grand scheme for agriculture. President Franklin Roosevelt appointed the National Planning Board under the Public Works Administration in the Department of the

Interior. The Secretary of the Interior established the Soil Erosion Service in 1933. In 1935, the organization was transferred and reorganized under the Department of Agriculture as the Soil Conservation Service.

The government also put forth a plan to kill as many farm animals as possible—in particular, cows and hogs—by offering farmers money for each animal that was slaughtered. It was a desperate move, especially since cattle were subsisting mainly on gathered tumbleweeds that had been salted to serve to them as feed. In addition, the Federal Surplus Relief Corporation (FSRC) was created after more than 6 million pigs were slaughtered to stabilize prices. The FSRC diverted agricultural commodities to relief organizations, and apples, beans, canned beef, flour and pork products were distributed through local relief channels. Contracts were also offered to farmers if they agreed not to plant anything the following year.

In 1935, the federal government formed the Drought Relief Service (DRS) to coordinate relief activities. The DRS bought cattle in counties, which were designated emergency areas, and animals that were deemed as unfit for human consumption were destroyed. The remaining cattle were given to the Federal Surplus Relief Corporation (FSRC) to be used in food distribution to families nationwide. Although it was difficult for farmers to give up their herds, the cattle slaughter program helped many of them avoid bankruptcy.

In 1936, President Roosevelt ordered the Civilian Conservation Corps (CCC) to plant a huge belt of more than 200 million trees from North Dakota to Texas to break the wind, hold the water in the soil, and hold the soil in place[s]. More than 20,000 CCC enrollees were sent into the area. The administration also began a program to educate farmers on soil conservation techniques, including crop rotation, strip farming, contour plowing, terracing and other farming practices. The federal government began an aggressive campaign to encourage Dust Bowlers to adopt planting and plowing methods that conserved the soil. President Roosevelt signed an executive order that granted the federal government the power to buy back land that had been given away by the Homestead Act during the previous 73 years.

A few dusters still occurred during 1937 and 1938, but they were of less severity, especially since the rains started coming back. In 1939, 20 million acres in the Dust Bowl were under strict conservation management. In 1940, the healing of the land began with new green plants and replanted buffalo grass to keep the sod in place. However, some of the land stayed sterile with drifting sand and dusty farms.

Franklin Roosevelt

Election of 1932

In the 1932 presidential election, Franklin Roosevelt won by getting 472 Electoral votes. John Nance Garner was elected as Vice President.

After the election, Roosevelt refused President Herbert Hoover's requests for a meeting to come up with a joint program to stop the economic downward spiral and calm investors, claiming that it would tie his hands. Thus, the economy continued to spiral downward until the banking system began a complete nationwide shutdown due to the spreading panic as President Hoover's term was ending. Even so, President Hoover refused to temporarily close all banks to prevent a total collapse. He did offer to execute an order preventing the withdrawal of deposits and gold, but Roosevelt declined to be part of the joint action, and President Hoover did not act on this either.

Significant Events: 1933

Franklin Roosevelt was sworn in as President.

President Roosevelt issued a proclamation that declared a 4-day bank holiday for the nation. This declaration also stopped and put an embargo on all exports of gold, silver and currency from the United States. Violations of the order were made punishable by a fine of $10,000 or 10 years imprisonment.

President Roosevelt summoned Congress to a special session that marked the beginning of the "100 days" in which President Roosevelt asked Congress to pass special legislation that became known as the New Deal.

Congress passed the Emergency Banking Act to validate the presidential proclamation that closed the banks, and to give the President broad powers over all banking transactions as well as foreign exchanges. The act made gold hoarding and exports of gold illegal under a penalty of 10 years in jail and a $10,000 fine.

Congress passed the Economy Act, which reduced the salaries of federal employees up to 15%, and reduced pension payments to veterans based on non-service connected disabilities. The act also mandated the reorganization of federal agencies to economize the structure of government.

Congress passed the Beer and Wine Revenue Act to allow beer and wine with an alcoholic content of 3.2% by weight or 4% by volume to be made and sold legally in the United States. The act also placed a tax of $5 per barrel on both beverages.

Congress passed the Reforestation Act that established the Civilian Conservation Corps (CCC). The act was meant to provide jobs for 250,000 men between the ages of 18 and

25 in reforestation projects—as well as soil erosion, flood control, national park development and road construction projects.

President Roosevelt issued a proclamation that took the United States off the gold standard for backing of the currency. The proclamation was issued to make more money available to Americans and to stimulate the economy by means of inflating the money supply.

President Roosevelt asked Congress to modify the Volstead Act to provide for the sale of 3.2% beer. Congress complied and legalized beer.

Congress passed the Federal Emergency Relief Act to authorize an appropriation of $500 million for grants to states for relief projects. The act was meant to alleviate unemployment, which had reached a level of 17 million.

Congress passed the Agricultural Adjustment Act (AAA) to provide relief for the farmers by establishing parity prices for certain agricultural products. The act justified the plowing under of crops, about 10 million acres in all, and the killing of livestock—pigs and cattle, of which 6 million pigs were slaughtered.

Congress established the Tennessee Valley Authority (TVA) as a public corporation to construct dams and power plants in the Tennessee Valley, and to provide electricity to residents and enterprises, with the goal of raising the economic standards of people in the area.

Congress passed the Federal Securities Act to provide for the registering and approval by the government of all issues of stocks and bonds. The issuers of the commodities were to fully disclose all information about their firms to the public.

Congress passed the National Employment System Act to provide a federal employment service to cooperate with the states, and to provide matching funds to state agencies.

Congress passed the Home Owners Refinancing Act to provide $2 billion for mortgages and to provide other aid to homeowners such as for taxes and repairs.

Congress passed the National Industrial Recovery Act to establish the Public Works Administration (PWA) and the National Recovery Administration (NRA). The PWA was to construct roads, public buildings and other projects to increase employment. The NRA was to stimulate competition by establishing fair trade practices.

Congress passed the Farm Credit Act to help farmers obtain mortgages at low interest rates.

Congress passed the Banking Act to set up the Federal Bank Deposit Insurance Corporation that insured deposits up to $5,000.

Congress passed the Emergency Railroad Transportation Act to create a coordinated rail transport system by using economies of scale, through consolidation of lines and routes, and by regulatory reform. The act placed railroad holding companies under the supervision of the ICC.

President Roosevelt issued an executive order to set up the National Labor Board to enforce the right of organized labor to bargain collectively.

President Roosevelt authorized the Reconstruction Finance Corporation to purchase newly minted gold at $31.36 an ounce, thus devaluing the United States dollar by one-third of its market value.

President Roosevelt issued an executive order to incorporate the Commodity Credit Corporation as a government corporation to stabilize, support, and protect farm income and prices.

President Roosevelt announced the resumption of diplomatic relations with the Soviet Union.

President Roosevelt issued an executive order to establish the Civil Works Administration (CWA). The CWA was to provide construction jobs by improving or constructing buildings and bridges.

The Twenty-First Amendment went into effect when the states ratify it, thus ending Prohibition in the United States.

Significant Events: 1934

Congress passed the Gold Reserve Act to require that all gold and gold certificates held by the Federal Reserve Bank be surrendered and vested in the sole title of the Department of the Treasury.

Congress passed the Farm Mortgage Refinancing Act to issue up to $2 billion in bonds to assist farmers in refinancing their mortgages with easier credit terms.

President Roosevelt issued an executive order to establish the Export-Import Bank. The bank was to provide short-term credits for exporting agricultural products, long-term credits for exporting industrial products, and loans to American exporters when foreign buyers could not obtain enough exchange to pay in United States dollars.

Congress passed the Civil Works Emergency Relief Act to provide $950 million for new programs of civil works.

Congress passed the Crop Loan Act and set up an initial fund of $40 million through which farmers were given loans for their crop production and harvesting.

Congress passed the Tydings-McDuffie Act to guarantee the Philippines independence within 10 years.

Congress passed the Vinson Naval Parity Act to authorize the building of a full-strength navy.

Congress passed the Independent Offices Appropriations Act to restore the cuts made by President Roosevelt, and overrode the veto by President Roosevelt.

Congress passed an act that forbid loans to any government in default on payments to the United States.

Congress passed the Cotton Control Act to place mandatory controls on cotton crops, with a tax of 5 cents on every pound over the quotas allocated to the farmers.

Congress passed the Jones-Connally Farm Relief Act to extend the list of commodities subject to the Agricultural Adjustment Act, including barley, flax, peanuts, grain sorghums, rye, beef and dairy cattle.

Congress passed the Home Owners Loan Act with a guarantee of $2 billion in bonds to stimulate home building.

Congress passed the Jones-Costigan Sugar Act to control cane and beet sugar production in the United States as well as to place quotas on the amount of sugar imported.

A severe dust storm blew an estimated 100 million tons of topsoil from Texas, Oklahoma, Arkansas, Kansas and Colorado all the way to the Atlantic Ocean.

Congress passed 6 bills, the Crime Control Acts, which were aimed at controlling crime, including the Lindbergh Act for kidnapping that involved the crossing of state lines.

In the treaty with Cuba, the Platt Amendment that gave the United States the right to intervene in Cuba's internal affairs was abrogated. The new agreement retained the right for the United States to maintain a naval station at Guantanamo Bay.

Congress passed the Municipal Bankruptcy Act to permit cities and other local government units to petition the federal courts to approve plans for readjusting their debt, provided that 51% of the holders of outstanding obligations would give their consent.

Congress passed the Securities Exchange Act to establish the Securities and Exchange Commission (SEC) to regulate exchanges and transactions of stocks, bonds and notes of debentures, and to prohibit price manipulation.

Congress passed the Corporate Bankruptcy Act to allow a corporation facing bankruptcy to reorganize upon approval of two-thirds of its creditors.

Congress passed the Farm Mortgage Foreclosure Act to allow loans to farmers to enable them to recover property they had owned before foreclosure took place.

Congress passed the Reciprocal Trade Agreement Act to allow the President to negotiate trade agreements with other nations—without the consent of the Senate.

Congress passed the National Guard Act to make the National Guard a part of the United States Army in time of war or national emergency.

Congress passed the Federal Communications Act to establish the Federal Communications Commission (FCC) to supervise radio, telegraph and telephone communications in the United States, and all international communications originating or terminating in the United States.

Congress passed the Silver Purchase Act to authorize the President to increase the Treasury's silver holdings up to one-third the value of gold holdings.

Congress passed a joint resolution to officially establish the National Labor Relations Board that had been set up by a presidential executive order in 1933.

Congress passed the National Housing Act to establish the Federal Housing Administration (FHA). The FHA was to insure loans made by banks and other lending institutions for construction, renovation and repairs of private homes.

Congress passed the Taylor Grazing Act to set aside 8 million acres of public land for grazing.

Congress passed the Tobacco Control Act to provide for mandatory quotas on tobacco crops, with a tax on excess production.

Congress passed the Farm Bankruptcy Act to place a moratorium of 5 years on farm mortgage foreclosures to allow farmers to regain their properties.

In the case of *Railroad Retirement Board v. Alton R. R. Co.*, the Supreme Court declared the Railroad Retirement Act as being unconstitutional.

President Roosevelt issued a proclamation to nationalize silver and purchase it at 50.01 cents an ounce.

In the case of *Hamilton v. Regents of the University of California*, the Supreme Court upheld the right of land-grant colleges to require military training for students.

Significant Events: 1935

The Senate rejected a proposal to ratify the participation of the United States in the World Court.

President Roosevelt proposed legislation, which became the second New Deal.

Congress passed the Emergency Relief Appropriation Act to allocate $5 billion for a large-scale public works program for the jobless to be administered by the WPA.

Congress established the Soil Conservation Service as part of the Department of Agriculture to promote better use of farmlands and to deal with the "Dust Bowl" effects.

President Roosevelt created the Resettlement Administration to combine the various agricultural relief programs under one agency.

President Roosevelt issued an executive order to establish the Resettlement Administration to relocate struggling urban and rural families to communities that were planned by the federal government.

President Roosevelt issued an executive order to establish the Rural Electrification Administration (REA) to bring electrical power to rural and remote areas where private utility companies had not provided service.

President Roosevelt vetoed the Patman Bill, which would have allowed WWI veterans to cash in bonus certificates because he viewed it as inflationary. However, Congress overrode his veto.

In the case of *Schechter Poultry Company v. United States*, the Supreme Court ruled that the National Industrial Recovery Act that had been passed in 1933 was unconstitutional.

President Roosevelt signed an executive order to create the National Youth Administration (NYA) to provide relief work for youths between the ages of 16 and 25, with grants to high school and college students in return for work.

Congress passed the National Labor Relations Act to limit the means with which employers may react to workers who voted for their own collective bargaining units.

Congress passed the Social Security Act to set up a system to guarantee pensions to those retiring at age 65, with contributions being obtained from employees and employers.

Congress passed the Banking Act to revise the operations of the Federal Reserve System do that it could adjust the supply of money to the fluctuations in the business cycle to maintain a steady level of economic activity.

Congress passed the Public Utilities Act to require public utility holding companies to register with the SEC, and to counteract monopolistic tendencies by gas and electric companies.

Congress passed the Revenue Act to increase taxes on inheritances and gifts as well as on the higher incomes of individuals.

President Roosevelt signed the Neutrality Act to forbid the shipment of arms and munitions to belligerent nations where war is involved.

Congress passed the Motor Carrier Act to place buses and trucks that were engaged in interstate commerce under the authority of the ICC.

Congress passed the Farm Mortgage Moratorium Act to provide a 3-year moratorium against seizures of farms to allow farmers to keep possession of their properties.

Congress passed the Railroad Retirement Act to provide pensions for employees after retirement.

Congress passed the Coal Stabilization Act to administer production quota, price-fixing and labor regulations for soft coal operations.

In the case of *Colgate v. Harvey*, the Supreme Court ruled that a state tax upon income is not to be deemed an interference with interstate commerce merely because the income is derived from a source in another state.

Significant Events: 1936

In the case of the *United States v. Butler*, the Supreme Court ruled that the Agricultural Adjustment Act was unconstitutional because it attempted to regulate and control agricultural production, an arena that was reserved to the states.

Congress passed the Adjusted Compensation Act over President Roosevelt's veto to allow for immediate cash redemption of bonus certificates held by veterans of WWI.

Congress passed the Second Neutrality Act to add a provision against granting any loans or credits from the United States to belligerent nations.

Congress passed the Soil Conservation and Domestic Allotment Act to pay farmers for withdrawing land planted with soil-depleting crops such as cotton, tobacco, corn and wheat.

Congress passed the Robinson-Patman Act to prohibit stores and firms from engaging in price-lowering practices and other methods intended to diminish competition to establish monopolies.

Congress passed the Merchant Marine Act to establish the United States Maritime Commission.

In the case of *Morehead v. New York*, the Supreme Court ruled that a New York minimum wage law that empowered the state labor commission to fix wages in relation to the class of service rendered was unconstitutional.

Congress passed the Revenue Act to place an undistributed profits tax on corporate income.

Congress passed the Government Contracts Act to provide for all persons employed by a contractor dealing with the government to not be paid less than the prevailing minimum wages as determined by the Secretary of Labor.

Franklin Roosevelt won the presidency by getting 523 Electoral votes. John Nance Garner was elected as Vice President.

Significant Events: 1937

Franklin Roosevelt was inaugurated as President.

President Roosevelt sent a message to Congress to propose a reorganization of the federal judiciary, including the Supreme Court. The Senate Judiciary Committee issued an adverse report, and the court-packing scheme was defeated by Congress.

Congress passed the Supreme Court Retirement Act, which allowed justices to retire at age 70 with full pay.

In the case of *West Coast Hotel v. Parrish*, the Supreme Court upheld the principle of minimum wages for women.

The Supreme Court ruled that the National Labor Relations Act was constitutional.

Congress passed the Third Neutrality Act to prohibit American ships from carrying arms into the belligerent nations' zones.

Congress passed the Guffey-Vinson Bituminous Coal Act to re-enact all of the provisions of the previous Guffey-Snyder Act for regulating the coal industry, which had been ruled unconstitutional by the Supreme Court.

The Supreme Court ruled that the Social Security Act was constitutional.

10 people were killed and 90 were wounded when police attacked a peaceful march outside the Republic Steel plant in South Chicago, Illinois after the beginning of a strike involving 85,000 steelworkers against Republic Steel and two other companies.

Congress passed the Bankhead-Jones Farm Tenancy Act to create the Farm Security Administration (FSA) to assist tenant farmers to purchase land, and to acquire damaged lands to rehabilitate and use them for various purposes.

Congress passed the Miller-Tydings Enabling Act to allow certain fixed priced items to be sold without violating federal antitrust laws.

Congress passed the Judicial Procedure Reform Act that made some changes to the federal courts—but only in the lower courts.

Congress passed the Revenue Act to close loopholes in the income tax laws, which had permitted evasion of tax payments.

President Roosevelt issued an executive order to bar United States ships from carrying arms to China and Japan.

Congress passed the Wagner-Steagall Housing Act to establish the United States Housing Authority to make loans for the construction of low-cost dwellings in rural and urban areas.

Japanese planes bombed and sank the United States gunboat *Panay* in the Yangtze River, China, killing two of the sailors. Japan apologized for the incident and paid an indemnity.

Significant Events: 1938

President Roosevelt submitted a recommendation to Congress that called for increased spending to build up the armed forces, especially the Navy. He asked for funds of $8.8 million for anti-aircraft purposes and $6.08 million for defense industry tools.

Congress passed the second Agricultural Adjustment Act to stabilize agricultural prices and farmers' incomes by establishing controls on acreage planted on quotas of crops to be marketed, and on the storage of surpluses.

Mexico nationalized all oil properties of the United States in a dispute between the government of Mexico and the Standard Oil Company of New Jersey as to who owned the rights to exploit a portion of Mexico's oil reserves. The appropriated oil company properties were worth $500 million.

Congress passed the Revenue Act of 1938 to reduce corporate income taxes in order to stimulate the economy.

The House Committee to Investigate Un-American Activities (HUAC) was formed to investigate Nazis, Communists and other organizations deemed as being "un-American."

Congress passed the Naval Expansion Act to authorize the expenditure of $1.1 billion for capital ships, cruisers and aircraft carriers.

Congress passed the Emergency Relief Appropriations Act to deal with the economic recession in the United States.

Congress established the Civil Aeronautics Authority (CAA) to provide federal regulation of air traffic.

Congress passed the Chandler Act to amend the Federal Bankruptcy Act of 1898 by setting forth new procedures for Chapter XI filings to avoid liquidation in the settlement of debts.

Congress passed the Food, Drug and Cosmetic Act to supersede the Pure Food Act of 1906. It called for detailed disclosures of the ingredients for food, drugs and cosmetics on the labels to prevent misbranding and false advertising.

Congress passed the Fair Labor Standards Act to set a minimum wage of 40 cents an hour and the maximum workweek at 44 hours, but only to businesses that were engaged in interstate commerce.

Congress passed the Flood Control Act to support work on rivers and harbors in the United States.

Events: 1939

President Roosevelt requested $1.319 billion for national defense.

In the case of *Tennessee Electric Power Company v. Tennessee Valley Authority* (TVA), the Supreme Court upheld the constitutionality of the TVA to compete with private utility companies.

In the case of *National Labor Relations Board v. Fansteel Metallurgical Corporation*, the Supreme Court ruled that sit-down strikes were unconstitutional.

Congress passed the Administrative Reorganization Act to empower the President to reorganize executive agencies.

The Food Stamp Plan was established to dispose of surpluses of agricultural commodities to persons who were on relief.

President Roosevelt requested Congress to repeal the arms embargo.

President Roosevelt established the Federal Works Agency to consolidate five existing agencies.

Congress passed the Hatch Act to restrict federal employees from participating in political campaigns.

Congress passed the Social Security Amendment to start monthly payments in 1940, and to extend coverage, such as for wives of workers.

A letter written by Albert Einstein and Enrico Fermi and addressed to President Roosevelt urged the development of nuclear research.

WWII started with the invasion of Poland by Germany. In response, both England and France declared war on Germany.

President Roosevelt declared a limited national emergency because of WWII. He also asked Congress to repeal the arms embargo provision of the Neutrality Act.

President Roosevelt issued a proclamation that closed all offshore United States waters and ports to submarines of belligerent nations.

Significant Events: 1940

President Roosevelt requested $1.8 billion for defense.

President Roosevelt established the Office for Emergency Management.

Congress passed the Naval Supply Act that authorized $1.5 billion for naval defense.

Congress passed the Military Supply Act to appropriate $1.8 billion for defense projects.

Congress passed the Alien Registration Act to require aliens in the United States to register, and to make it illegal for individuals and organizations to advocate the overthrow of the United States government by force.

Congress passed the Export Control Act to empower the President to stop or restrict the export of any material that is considered vital to the defense of America.

President Roosevelt submitted a request to Congress for $4.8 billion for defense.

Congress passed the Two-Ocean Navy Expansion Act, which appropriated $4 billion to provide the United States with an Atlantic and Pacific Navy.

Congress passed the Selective Training and Service Act that required men between 21 and 35 years of age to register for military training.

President Roosevelt announced an embargo on the export of scrap steel and iron outside of the Western Hemisphere to any nation, with the exception of Great Britain.

Franklin Roosevelt won the presidency by getting 449 Electoral votes. Henry Wallace was elected as Vice President/

President Roosevelt established the Office of Production Management to coordinate and expedite defense production.

Significant Events: 1941

President Roosevelt asked for $10.81 billion for defense.

President Roosevelt called for Congress to enact the Lend-Lease program that he had proposed. He also called for a formulation of social and political goals that he hoped to attain, which became known as the "Four Freedoms:" freedom of speech and expression, freedom of every person to worship God, freedom from want, and freedom from fear by a reduction in armaments.

President Roosevelt was inaugurated as President.

In the case of the *United States v. Darby Lumber Co.*, the Supreme Court ruled that the Fair Labor Standard Act was constitutional.

The United Service Organization (USO) was formed by 6 national organizations in response to a request by President Roosevelt to serve the social, educational, welfare and religious needs of those in the armed forces and defense industries.

Congress passed the Lend-Lease Act to empower the President to lend arms and other war material to any country deemed vital to the interests of the United States.

By an executive order President Roosevelt established the Office of Price Administration to control prices.

President Roosevelt issued a proclamation that declared that a state of unlimited national emergency existed.

President Roosevelt issued an executive order that established a Fair Employment Practices Commission to combat discrimination against blacks and women in defense plants.

President Roosevelt ordered the closing of German and Italian consulates in the United States. In retaliation, Germany and Italy closed down United States consulates in Europe.

President Roosevelt ordered troops to take over the North American Aviation Company in Ingleside, California to prevent striking workers from interfering with defense production.

President Roosevelt froze the assets of Germany and Italy within the United States. He also ordered the State Department to close all German consulates in the United States.

President Roosevelt established the Fair Employment Practices Committee by executive order to prevent discrimination due to race, creed or color in defense-related industries.

President Roosevelt established the Office of Scientific Research and Development (OSRD) to coordinate work related to defense, including radar, sonar and the development of the atomic bomb.

President Roosevelt froze the assets of Japan within the United States, and placed an embargo on shipments of scrap iron and gasoline to Japan.

President Roosevelt nationalized the armed forces of the Philippines and placed them under the commander of all United States forces in the Far East.

The United States landed forces in Iceland to prevent its use as a base for naval and air operations by Germany.

Congress passed the Selective Service Extension Act to extend service in the army in time of war from a period of one year to 18 months.

President Roosevelt and Prime Minister Winston Churchill of England issued the Atlantic Charter. The charter set goals for the world, including the renunciation of all aggression, the right of peoples to choose their own governments, the support of access to raw materials, guarantees of freedom from want and fear, freedom of the seas, and the disarmament of aggressor nations.

Congress passed the Revenue Act to increase taxes for money for the defense effort.

President Roosevelt commissioned Curtis Munson to investigate the Japanese population that was living in the United States. Munson reported that there was no Japanese problem.

Japanese bombers attacked the United States naval base at Pearl Harbor, Hawaii. The bombing destroyed or disabled 19 ships, destroyed 150 planes, and killed over 2,400 soldiers, sailors and civilians, while wounding almost 1,200.

Japanese bombers attacked planes and ships at United States bases in the Philippines, Guam and Midway—as well as British bases in Hong Kong and the Malay Peninsula. The Japanese invaded the Philippines, landing at Luzon. Wake Island also fell to the Japanese.

President Roosevelt asked Congress for a declaration of war against Japan, which it did. Congress also declared war against Germany and Italy. In response, Germany and Italy declared war on the United States.

Congress passed the Third Supplemental Defense Appropriation Act to appropriate $10 billion for the war effort.

President Roosevelt established the Office of Censorship by an executive order to control all matters related to information about the war effort.

Congress passed the Draft Act that called for all males who are United States citizens between the ages of 18 and 65 to register, and for all men between the ages of 20 to 44 to be liable for military duty.

British Prime Minister Winston Churchill met with President Roosevelt to discuss the war effort.

Significant Events: 1942

President Roosevelt requested $52 billion for the war effort.

President Roosevelt issued a proclamation to order all aliens in the United States to register with the government.

President Roosevelt issued an executive order to establish the War Production Board.

President Roosevelt issued an executive order to establish the Office of Civil Defense to coordinate activities, especially those of plane spotting.

Congress passed the Emergency Price Control Act to place ceilings on prices and rents, with the exception of farm products.

Daylight Savings Time was established in the United States as all clocks within the United States were turned ahead by one hour.

President Roosevelt signed an executive order that interned thousands of Japanese, Italians, German-Americans, and some emigrants from Hawaii who fled after the bombing of Pearl Harbor, for the duration of the war. 150,000 Japanese-Americans were removed from their homes, and were interned for the duration of the war in camps located in Colorado, Utah and Arkansas. 11,000 German and Italian residents of the United States were also interned.

The War Production Board stopped all construction in the United States that was deemed as not essential for the war effort.

President Roosevelt issued an executive order to establish the War Manpower Commission.

Congress passed the Women's Auxiliary Army Corps (WAAC) to establish a women's army reserve.

Gasoline rationing was initiated in 17 states along the Eastern United States, with a limit of 3 gallons per week. Price ceilings on retail products also went into effect.

President Roosevelt established the Office of War Information by an executive order.

President Roosevelt established the Office of Strategic Services (OSS) by an executive order.

Congress appropriated $42.8 billion for the armed forces.

British Prime Minister Winston Churchill met with President Roosevelt to plan the invasion of North Africa.

Congress established the women's naval reserve, which would be known as WAVES (Women Accepted for Volunteer Emergency).

The War Labor Board provided a 15% wage increase to certain steel workers.

British Prime Minister Winston Churchill met with President Roosevelt and Soviet Premier Joseph Stain to discuss the war effort.

President Roosevelt announced a plan for the creation of a United Nations Commission for the investigation of war crimes once the war was over.

Congress passed the Revenue Act to increase taxes to finance the war.

Congress changed the Selective Service Act to make males in the United States subject to active military duty at age 18. However, blacks were initially barred from frontline combat, and many of them had to perform menial tasks.

Coffee rationing was put into effect across the United States.

The Semper Paratus Always Ready Service (SPARS) was organized as a woman's branch of the United States Coast Guard.

Gasoline rationing was extended across the entire United States.

Significant Events: 1943

President Roosevelt requested $100 billion for the war effort.

British Prime Minister Winston Churchill met with President Roosevelt and other Allied representatives to discuss the invasion of Europe.

Shoe rationing began in the United States, with a limit of 3 pairs for each person per year.

The United States Marine Corps Women's Reserve was established (USMCWR).

A point-rationing system with coupon books was initiated in the United States for the purchase of processed foods.

Meats, fats and cheese were placed under rationing control.

President Roosevelt issued an executive order that froze prices, wages and salaries in order to stem inflation.

President Roosevelt issued an executive order to create the Office of War Mobilization to coordinate the war effort.

President Roosevelt issued an executive order to forbid racial discrimination in all government contracts with war industries.

British Prime Minister Winston Churchill met with President Roosevelt to further discuss the invasion of Europe.

Congress passed the Current Tax Payment Act that introduced the withholding of federal income taxes on wages and salaries before they were paid to employees.

In the case of *West Virginia Board of Education et al v. Barnette et al*, the Supreme Court ruled that it was unconstitutional for a state to have a law requiring children to salute the flag—and to be expelled from school if they didn't.

A total of 35 people were killed and more than 500 were wounded—mostly blacks—when whites protested the employment of blacks in Detroit, Michigan. Federal troops were required to quell the riot.

Congress passed the War Labor Dispute Act to require a union to give 30-days notice before calling a strike in a war plant. The act also outlawed any strike in government-operated plants. The act was passed over President Roosevelt's veto.

Eight American citizens were indicted by the government for broadcasting treasonable statements back to their native lands.

A race riot in Harlem, New York resulted in 410 people being injured and 5 killed, with $5 million in damages occurring.

President Roosevelt met with British Prime Minister Winston Churchill to work out the Pacific campaign in the war against Japan.

The House adopted the Fulbright Concurrent Resolution that called for the participation of the United States in a world organization for peace.

The Senate passed the Connally Resolution that called for the United States to support an international peace organization—and to complement the Fulbright Resolution that had been passed by the House for the same purpose.

British Prime Minister Winston Churchill met with President Roosevelt and Chiang Kai-shek to discuss the attack on Japan.

Congress repealed the Chinese Exclusion Act, which had set strict quotas on immigrants from China.

By an executive order by President Roosevelt, the federal government seized the nation's railroads, which had been threatened with a shutdown by striking workers.

British Prime Minister Winston Churchill met with President Roosevelt and Soviet Premier Joseph Stalin to discuss the invasion of Europe.

British Prime Minister Winston Churchill met with President Roosevelt and President Ismer Inonu of Turkey to discuss Turkey joining the war effort.

Significant Events: 1944

President Roosevelt requested $70 billion for the war effort.

President Roosevelt proposed a Second Bill of Rights during his State of the Union Address. He suggested that it be implemented because the political rights guaranteed by the Constitution and the original Bill of Rights had proven to be inadequate to assure the equality in the pursuit of happiness. The Economic Bill of Rights was formulated by Henry Wallace, and was his contribution towards President Roosevelt's commitment of creating 60 million jobs in the United States after the war ended. The remedy for economic security and independence would guarantee the following—regardless of station, race or creed:

- The right to a useful and remunerative job in the industries, shops, farms or mines of the nation
- The right to earn enough to provide adequate food, clothing and recreation
- The right of every farmer to raise and sell his product at a rate which will give him and his family a decent living
- The right of every businessman, large and small, to trade in an atmosphere of freedom from unfair competition and domination by monopolies at home or abroad
- The right of every family to a decent home
- The right to adequate medical care and the opportunity to achieve and enjoy good health
- The right to adequate protection from the economic fears of old age, sickness, accident, and unemployment
- The right to a good education

The railroads were returned by the federal government to their owners upon a final settlement of the wage dispute.

The United States announced that it no longer recognized the government of Argentina because of its lack of participation in the war against Germany and Italy.

The Secretary of State disclosed a 17-point program for United States foreign policy in the postwar world.

Congress approved a joint resolution that subsidized up to $1.35 billion for the United Nations Relief and Rehabilitation Agency to provide aid to people whose lives were disrupted by the war.

In the case of *Smith v. Allwright*, the Supreme Court ruled that a person cannot be denied the vote in the Democratic Party in Texas because of color.

Congress extended the provisions of the Lend-Lease Act through 1945.

The Chairman of Montgomery Ward & Company was physically removed from the company by troops for his refusal to comply with an order by the National Labor Relations Board to extend a contract with its CIO union employees.

Meat rationing was ended in the United States—except for various choice cuts of beef.

The invasion of Europe began by Allied forces.

Congress passed the Servicemen's Readjustment Act to provide financial aid to veterans—legislation that became known as the "G.I. Bill."

Delegates from 44 nations met at Brenton Woods, New Hampshire and agreed to set up the International Monetary Fund (IMF) and the International Bank for Reconstruction and Development.

French General Charles de Gaulle met with President Roosevelt and others to gain United States support for French forces that were fighting Germany.

Production for non-defense items such as electric ranges, cooking utensils and vacuum cleaners was allowed to resume by the government—although it was still subject to how the progress of the war was going.

British Prime Minister Winston Churchill met with President Roosevelt to discuss the strategies against Germany and Japan.

Congress passed the Surplus War Property Act to provide for the disposal of surplus government property after the war ended.

Congress passed the War Mobilization and Reconversion Act to provide for the removal of controls that had been imposed during the war.

Franklin Roosevelt won the presidency with 432 Electoral votes. Harry Truman was elected as Vice President.

President Roosevelt announced the 6th War Drive to borrow $14 billion through the sale of war bonds.

Congress passed an act to establish the rank of General of the Army—a 5-star general.

The Supreme Court clarified the legality of the exclusion process under President Roosevelt's executive order by handing down two decisions. In the case of *Korematsu v. United States*, the Supreme Court ruled that the exclusion process was constitutional. However, in *Ex Parte Endo*, the Supreme Court declared that loyal citizens of the United States, regardless of cultural descent, could not be detained without cause.

Significant Events: 1945

President Roosevelt was inaugurated as President.

President Roosevelt sent messages to Joseph Stalin accusing him of breaking his Yalta commitments over Poland, Germany, prisoners of war and other issues.

On April 12, 1945, President Roosevelt died.

Vice President Harry Truman was sworn in as President.

The Twenty-First Amendment

The End of Prohibition

The Twenty-First Amendment repealed the Eighteenth Amendment, which mandated nationwide Prohibition. It was ratified in 1933 by the states.

The text of the Twenty-First Amendment is as follows:

> "Section 1. The eighteenth article of amendment to the Constitution of the United States is hereby repealed.
>
> Section 2. The transportation or importation into any state, territory, or possession of the United States for delivery or use therein of intoxicating liquors, in violation of the laws thereof, is hereby prohibited.
>
> Section 3. This article shall be inoperative unless it shall have been ratified as an amendment to the Constitution by conventions in the several states, as provided in the Constitution, within seven years from the date of the submission hereof to the states by the Congress."

Proposal and Ratification

In 1932, Senator John Blaine submitted a resolution to Congress proposing the submission to the states of the Twenty-First Amendment, which would annul the Eighteenth Amendment. In 1933, the Twenty-First Amendment was sent to the state governors. Meanwhile, President Roosevelt asked Congress to modify the Volstead Act to provide for the sale of 3.2% beer. Congress complied and legalized beer. Congress proposed the Twenty-First Amendment in 1933. The proposed Twenty-First Amendment was adopted by Congress in 1933, and was then submitted to the state conventions for ratification, which happened in 1933.

Provisions

The first section of the Twenty-First Amendment ended Prohibition by repealing the Eighteenth Amendment. That meant that alcohol would once again be legal in the United States. The second section addressed the transport of alcohol between the states. It supported the individual rights of each state by making it a federal crime to import alcohol into a state if that state had laws against it. The third section stated that the people had to vote to ratify the amendment. This meant that the issue had to be placed before the citizens of the states who would go to the polls and choose between "wet" or "dry" delegates. The delegates would then meet at a statewide convention to cast their votes for or against the proposed Twenty-First Amendment.

The Twenty-First Amendment gave absolute control to the states in terms of laws about alcohol use since the government would not make any more laws concerning the issue of the legality of alcohol. Thus, many states chose to remain dry. Also, many of the states delegated the authority over alcohol granted to them by the Twenty-First Amendment to their municipalities or counties, which has led to many lawsuits over First Amendment rights when local governments have tried to revoke liquor licenses.

Section 2 has been the source of every Supreme Court ruling directly addressing Twenty-First Amendment issues. Initial rulings suggested that Section 2 enabled states to legislate with exceptionally broad constitutional powers, but later rulings clarified and limited the power of the states.

Social Security Act

Overview

The Social Security Act is a law that was enacted by Congress in 1935. The law created the Social Security program as well as insurance against unemployment. The law was part of President Franklin Roosevelt's New Deal domestic program.

President Roosevelt organized a committee led by Secretary of Labor Frances Perkins to develop a major social welfare program proposal. He presented the plan in 1935, and signed the Social Security Act into law in 1935. The act was upheld by the Supreme Court in two major cases that were decided in 1937.

The law established the Social Security program, an old-age program funded by payroll taxes. Over the ensuing decades, Social Security program contributed to a dramatic decline in poverty among the elderly, while spending on Social Security became a major part of the federal budget. The Social Security Act also established an unemployment insurance program administered by the states, as well as the Aid to Dependent Children program, which provided aid to families headed by single mothers.

History

By the 1930s, the United States was the only modern industrial country where people faced the Depression without any national system of social security, though a handful of states had poorly-funded old-age insurance programs. The federal government had provided pensions to veterans in the aftermath of the Civil War and other wars, and some states had established voluntary old-age pension systems, but otherwise the United States had little experience with social insurance programs.

For most American workers, retirement due to old age was not a realistic option. In the 1930s, Francis Townsend galvanized support for his pension proposal, which called for the federal government to issue direct $200-a-month payments to the elderly. President Roosevelt was attracted to Townsend's plan because it would provide for those no longer capable of working while at the same time stimulating demand in the economy and decreasing the supply of labor. In 1934, President Roosevelt charged the Committee on Economic Security, chaired by Secretary of Labor Frances Perkins, with developing an old-age pension program, an unemployment insurance system, and a national health care program. The proposal for a national health care system was dropped, but the committee developed an unemployment insurance program largely administered by the states. The committee also developed an old-age plan that would be funded by individual contributions from workers.

Enactment

In 1935, Roosevelt proposed the Social Security Act, which he presented as a more practical alternative to the Townsend Plan. The Social Security Act became law in 1935, with the program being expanded to provide payments to widows and dependents of Social Security recipients. Job categories that were not covered by the act included workers in agricultural labor, domestic service, government employees, and many teachers, nurses, hospital employees, librarians, and social workers. The program was funded through a payroll tax. Social Security taxes would be collected from employers by the states, with employers and employees contributing equally to the tax.

Because the Social Security tax was regressive, and Social Security benefits were based on how much each individual had paid into the system, the program would not contribute to income redistribution in the way that some reformers, including Perkins, had hoped. In addition to creating the Social Security program, the Social Security Act also established a state-administered unemployment insurance system and the Aid to Dependent Children program, which provided aid to families headed by single mothers. Compared with the social security systems in Western European countries, the Social Security Act of 1935 was rather conservative. But for the first time the federal government took responsibility for the economic security of the aged, the temporarily unemployed, dependent children and the handicapped.

Two Supreme Court rulings affirmed the constitutionality of the Social Security Act. In the case of *Steward Machine Company v. Davis* in 1937, the Supreme Court held that, given the exigencies of the Great Depression in a crisis so extreme that the use of the moneys of the nation to relieve the unemployed and their dependents is a use for any purpose narrower than the promotion of the general welfare. The arguments opposed to the Social Security Act were that the social security act went beyond the powers that were granted to the federal government in the Constitution. They argued that, by imposing a tax on employers that could be avoided only by contributing to a state unemployment-compensation fund, the federal government was essentially forcing each state to establish an unemployment-compensation fund that would meet its criteria. They argued that the federal government had no power to enact such a program.

In the case of *Helvering v. Davis* in 1937, the Supreme Court upheld the program because the proceeds of both employee and employer taxes are to be paid into the Treasury like internal-revenue taxes generally, and are not earmarked in any way, and as such, the Social Security Tax was constitutional as a mere exercise of Congress's general taxation powers.

The Manhattan Project-1

Overview

Born out of a small nuclear research program in 1939, the Manhattan Project eventually employed about 125,000 people and cost nearly $2 billion. The project resulted in the creation of multiple production and research sites that operated in secret. One of these was located in an isolated mesa top at Los Alamos near the Rio Grande River, between the Pueblo and Los Alamos Canyons near Santa Fe, New Mexico. It was here that the United States government was involved in a super-secret project to create the first atomic bomb. The government recruited some of the best scientists available in the country to work in conjunction with the military to develop a powerful bomb. The bomb was to be of a form in which a large amount of energy would be released by an atomic chain reaction of elements that would produce nuclear fission.

The three primary research and production sites of the project were the plutonium-production facility at Hanford, Washington, the uranium-enrichment facility at Oak Ridge, Tennessee, and the weapons research and design laboratory at Los Alamos, New Mexico. The essential products needed to make the bomb were produced at Hanford and at Oak Ridge for use in research and testing at Los Alamos. All three sites were code-named "W" (Hanford), "X" (Oak Ridge) and "Y" (Los Alamos) to preserve their secrecy—even though 125,000 people worked on the project during the bomb effort. Project research also took place at over 30 sites across the United States, Canada, and Britain.

By 1945, Oak Ridge and Hanford had produced enough uranium and plutonium for at least one bomb of each type. The first test explosion of an atomic bomb took place on July 16, 1945, at the Trinity test site near Alamogordo, New Mexico in the early morning. The creation of this new military weapon changed the world forever, especially after two of these bombs were dropped over the Japanese cities of Hiroshima and Nagasaki in August 1945. The dropping of the two atomic bombs ended the war against Japan through their subsequent surrender, but in the process raised questions about the purpose of war and its extreme destructive capability—as well as its inhumane results. The total physical destruction and the horrific killing of human life altered human consciousness as the facts, pictures and survivor accounts from Japan began to be known in their entirety.

The test explosion in the New Mexico desert and the subsequent dropping of the two atomic bombs over Japan at the end of WWII ushered in the atomic age, which was made possible by the Manhattan Project. The Manhattan Project developed the first nuclear weapon in a joint effort by the United States, Great Britain and Canada. Formally designated as the Manhattan Engineer District, the project covered a period from 1941 to 1946 under the control of the United States Army Corps of Engineers. The military control was administered by General Leslie R. Groves, and the scientific research was under civilian control and directed by J. Robert Oppenheimer.

The Beginning of the Project

Adolf Hitler had been appointed chancellor of Germany in 1933, and his anti-Semitic ideology caused many Jewish physicists to be fired from their government posts. Consequently, many of these physicists went into exile in the United Kingdom and the United States. After Nazi Germany invaded Poland in 1939, which marked the start of WWII, many scientists in the United States and the United Kingdom became concerned about what Germany might do with nuclear technology—especially if it were to be applied to weapons. Thus, in August 1939, Albert Einstein, who was living in New Jersey, wrote a letter to President Franklin Roosevelt urging him to establish a military application of this nuclear capability before the Germans did. However, the letter was not received by President Roosevelt until October 1939.

In October 1939, Dr. Alexander Sachs, who was an unofficial Wall Street advisor to President Roosevelt, met with him to discuss Einstein's letter concerning nuclear fission chain reactions to create very powerful bombs. President Roosevelt responded to the letter by appointing Lyman J. Briggs, who was the director of the National Bureau of Standards, to head an advisory committee to coordinate and provide funding for uranium research. This committee coordinated its activities with Sachs to recommend an appropriate role for the government to undertake in this endeavor. In 1940, the uranium committee recommended research on isotope separation, and on fission chain reactions— in particular, the work by Enrico Fermi and Leo Szilard at Columbia University in New York City, New York. The design of an atomic pile was considered to be the crucial part that was needed to create the methodology for atomic energy to be used to make an atomic bomb. But, only $6,000 was appropriated to the committee—primarily to fund nuclear pile experiments at Columbia University—and as a consequence not much else was done.

In 1940, President Roosevelt transferred the uranium committee to the National Defense Research Committee (NDRC), and appointed Vannevar Bush to head the NDRC. Bush recommended further research into the most promising methods of isotope separation, and on chain reaction work. In 1941, experiments conducted at the University of California at Berkeley by Edwin McMillan and Philip Abelson indicated that a graphite uranium pile to produce plutonium was the most feasible approach to isotope separation. Ernest D. Lawrence, director of the Radiation Laboratory at Berkeley, met with Bush, and recommended a quick mobilization of all scientific endeavors by the government. Bush appointed Lawrence as an advisor to Briggs of the NDRC to help with this effort.

In 1941, the MAUD Committee in Britain produced a report that was submitted to Bush. Its primary recommendation was to pursue research in creating a critical mass of uranium-235 to produce a powerful atomic explosion. It also alerted the United States to the fact that nuclear fission had been discovered in Nazi Germany in 1938, and that since 1940, the Kaiser Wilhelm Institute in Berlin had been devoted to uranium research. As a result, Bush asked the National Academy of Sciences to review the uranium research program and selected Arthur Compton of the University of Chicago at Illinois to create a report on its findings. In 1941, the Compton Report was submitted to Bush with the following recommendations:

- Increased uranium funding to produce radioactive material
- Nuclear pile research that could be used to power naval vessels
- The development of a nuclear bomb by 1945

In 1941, Bush was appointed as head of the Office of Scientific Research and Development (OSRD) that was formed with a purpose of gathering all uranium and fission projects that could lead to the achievement of a contained nuclear chain reaction. The uranium committee was made a part of OSRD, being designated as the S-1 committee that would be responsible for the organization, research and implementation of the objective of creating an atomic weapon. James Conant, President of Harvard University who replaced Bush as head of the NDRC, was named as an advisor to the OSRD. In 1941, Bush met with President Roosevelt and Vice President Henry Wallace to explore further work on uranium research. President Roosevelt wrote to Prime Minister Winston Churchill of England to propose a joint effort by both countries to develop the bomb. In 1941, the Committee of the National Academy of Science agreed with the findings of the MAUD report.

Acceleration of the Project

Many scientists had argued for the acceleration of atomic research if a bomb was going to be produced in a timely fashion to affect the outcome of the war. But, it was not until Japanese forces attacked the United States at Pearl Harbor in Hawaii in 1941, that President Roosevelt decided to act by giving the approval to proceed with the development of an atomic bomb. In 1942, President Roosevelt authorized the full-scale funding for the project. Bush removed all uranium work from the NDRC, and obtained $400,000 from the S-1 Committee for isotope research to be conducted by Lawrence. In 1942, Bush sent a progress report to President Roosevelt that indicated that a small critical mass was achievable that could detonate a powerful atomic weapon. Bush also stated that if the program were to be expedited, then a bomb might be possible by 1944. In 1942, a program review published as the Conant Report recommended that the isotope separation and nuclear pile research be accelerated.

In 1942, Compton, who was the director of the Metallurgical Laboratory (Met Lab) at the University of Chicago, decided to centralize the research effort and to concentrate it on developing plutonium and fission piles. Under his direction Samuel Allison began building the graphite and uranium pile. He also chose Robert Oppenheimer to be in charge of this team doing research on fast neutron calculations—the key to critical mass and weapon detonation and informed Oppenheimer of the work that Fermi was doing with nuclear piles. He assigned John Manley to help Oppenheimer find answers by coordinating and contacting several experimental physics groups scattered across the country.

In 1942, Oppenheimer gathered the top theoretical physicists in the United States to meet regularly at Le Conte Hall at the University of Berkeley. Their progress indicated that the goal of developing a fission bomb was feasible. A number of the different fission bomb assembly methods were also explored, with the gun method and an implosion design, being chosen as the methods that would be used to create a critical mass to detonate the bomb. However, there were still many unknown factors in the development of a nuclear bomb even though it was considered to be theoretically possible—especially since no functioning nuclear reactor had been built yet.

Considering the idea of the fission bomb theoretically settled until more experimental data were available, Edward Teller pushed for research to be done on an even more powerful bomb that would use nuclear fusion. This hydrogen bomb was a thermonuclear device that required an atomic fission bomb as a detonator, and hence was more complex in its design. Although Teller pushed hard for his hydrogen bomb—proposing scheme after scheme—they were all refuted, and the fusion concept was put aside to concentrate on the development of a fission bomb. Oppenheimer assigned the fusion bomb task to Teller who spent the rest of his time on the Manhattan Project working on his idea of developing a super bomb—something that he eventually brought into fruition.

The difficulties in conducting studies on nuclear weapons at universities scattered throughout the country indicated the coordination need for a laboratory site that was dedicated solely to that purpose. An even greater need was for the construction of industrial plants to produce uranium-235 and plutonium—the fissionable materials that were to be used to make the atomic weapons. Bush asked President Roosevelt to assign the operations connected with the nuclear weapons project to the military. President Roosevelt chose the United States Army to work with the OSRD in building the production plants, and in overseeing the project.

The Quest for the Bomb

Working with the OSRD and the United States Army, Bush earmarked $54 million for the 1943 budget to be used for process development, materials procurement, engineering design and site selection. The S-1 Executive Committee was allocated $30 million to fund university research and pilot plant studies. One of these was the effort by Glenn Seaborg on transuranium chemistry to ensure that plutonium could be chemically separated from the uranium, which was to be produced and irradiated in a production reactor.

The Manhattan program was placed under the control of the Army Corps of Engineers with headquarters in the Manhattan District of New York City. In 1942, Colonel James Marshall was appointed to direct the "Laboratory for the Development of Substitute Metals" (DSM), and to oversee the construction of the factories to separate uranium isotopes and manufacture plutonium for the bomb. Colonel James Marshall, and his deputy, Colonel Kenneth Nichols, struggled to understand the proposed processes and the scientists with whom they had to work. They acted cautiously, delayed things, and did not coordinate the project very well between the S-1 Executive Committee and the Army.

Thrust into the new field of nuclear physics, they were unable to differentiate between technical and personal preferences. Thus, the scientists' work and production plant construction were often delayed by Colonel Marshall's inability to obtain critical materials, such as steel, that were needed for the experimental project, but which had higher priority for use by other ongoing military projects. Although they decided that a site near Knoxville, Tennessee, would be suitable for the first production plant, they did not know how large a site would be required, and thus they delayed its acquisition.

Bush became dissatisfied with Colonel Marshall's inadequacy to get the project moving forward quickly and expeditiously, and he conferred with Secretary of War Henry Stimson and Army Chief of Staff General George Marshall on what to do. In 1942, General George Marshall directed General Somervell to replace Colonel Marshall, and Colonel Leslie Groves was chosen for the task instead. Colonel Groves was hoping for an overseas command, and he objected when he was appointed to head the weapon project—something that he thought had very little chance of success. Colonel Groves renamed the project to "The Manhattan Engineer District" (MED) to divert attention away from it. He was also promoted to brigadier general, giving him the rank that was necessary to deal with the senior scientists on the project. General Groves moved the headquarters of the project to Washington, D.C. The S-1 Committee delegated the entire atomic bomb project to General Groves as director acting under the Military Policy Committee that Bush had created to coordinate the various efforts, and which included Conant as a member.

General Groves first met Robert Oppenheimer in 1942, and shortly thereafter appointed him as the scientific director of the project to head the bomb research and design effort. He did so because he was convinced that Oppenheimer was a genius who could talk about and understand nearly anything, and because he was convinced that such an individual was needed for this proposed project. Oppenheimer perceived the benefits of having a single centralized laboratory to manage the research for the bomb project, rather than having specialists spread out at different sites across the United States. In a meeting with General Groves, Oppenheimer suggested that a single research laboratory be located in an isolated region that was far away from any large population center. General Groves ordered Lieutenant Colonel John Dudley to find a possible site for the central facility.

Colonel Dudley surveyed California, Nevada, Utah, Arizona and New Mexico, and then narrowed the search to five sites in New Mexico only: Gallup, Las Vegas, La Ventana, Otawi and Jemez Springs. In 1942, Colonel Dudley took Oppenheimer to Jemez Springs, which was in a deep canyon in the Jemez Mountains. When General Groves arrived he vetoed the site whereupon Oppenheimer suggested the high mesa nearby where the Los Alamos School Ranch—a private school for boys—was located. This site was bounded on the North and South sides by steep rock canyons, which offered the necessary protection to maintain security. General Groves approved of this site that was located 35 miles West of Santa Fe, New Mexico near the Sangre de Cristo Mountain. He considered it an ideal site because it offered isolation for safety and security, it had access to both rail and road, possessed a mild climate that would permit work throughout the whole year, contained a large enough area for testing grounds, and was located in a sparsely populated area. The property was obtained by the use of eminent domain by the United States government who purchased it for $440,000. The school received a letter of eviction from Secretary of War Henry Stimson and was closed in 1943.

In 1942, General Groves met with the S-1 Executive Committee and the Military Policy Committee to accelerate the isotope isolation effort. In 1942, the Chicago Pile Number One (CP-1) research being conducted by Fermi and other scientists achieved critical mass and produced the first self-sustaining nuclear reaction. This event meant that the release of energy on a large scale was now only a matter of time. President Roosevelt gave the authorization to proceed with the construction of the atom bomb. He approved the full-scale effort to build diffusion and plutonium plants to develop an atomic bomb, with an initial outlay of $500 million.

General Groves obtained the Oak Ridge, Tennessee site for the construction of the isotope separation plant. He chose the location of the plants away from Knoxville to prevent a catastrophe from affecting the population who lived there. An area of 225 square miles was chosen that was away from all major towns, highways, rail lines and nearby laboratories. The location of the diffusion plants was also placed far enough away from the location of where the plutonium producing plant was going to be placed to minimize the hazards. The Oak Ridge site included 60,000 acres of farm communities in the eastern Tennessee Valley area. The government used eminent domain again, with some of the Tennessee families being given only two weeks' notice to vacate family farms, many of which had been their homes for generations.

In 1942, General Groves, Colonel Franklin Mathias and two DuPont engineers investigated possible sites in the Northwestern and Western parts of the United States. After viewing six locations in California, Oregon and Washington, two rivers were found to be ideal for hydroelectric power: the Columbia River and the Colorado River. They chose the area near Richland, Washington for the establishment of the Hanford Engineer Works. It was considered an ideal site, and a total of 500,000 acres were set aside for the plant site. In 1943, the Hanford site was taken by eminent domain once more by the government, which began acquiring property that contained irrigated farm land, fruit orchards, a railroad, and two farming communities in a sparsely populated area adjacent to the Columbia River.

The Manhattan Project-2

Project Sites

Although the project involved over 30 different research and production sites, including some in Canada and Britain, the Manhattan Project was largely carried out at three secret sites: Los Alamos, New Mexico; Oak Ridge, Tennessee; and Hanford, Washington. The Oak Ridge site was chosen for the vast quantities of hydroelectric power already available there that would be necessary to produce uranium-235 by using huge magnets. The Hanford Site was chosen for its location near the Columbia River that could supply sufficient water to cool the reactors that would produce the plutonium. The Los Alamos site was chosen because of its isolated location that would provide security and protection. A fourth and very crucial site was located at Dayton, Ohio where the bomb trigger mechanism was developed. Two other important sites were the University of Chicago in Illinois where the first nuclear reactor was developed, and the University of California at Berkeley where a separation method was developed with the use of a cyclotron device.

Los Alamos

The Los Alamos site was located on a mesa high in the Jemez Mountains of New Mexico, and was selected as the location for the secret bomb development site. The school buildings that were there served as housing for the first scientists that arrived in 1943. The 54,000 acres of land surrounding the site were closed off and made into a military reservation by miles of steel fence and barbed wire. A large military force constantly patrolled the fenced perimeter round-the-clock, and used K9 Corps dogs to guard the base of the cliffs. 3,000 Army engineers were employed to build the Los Alamos site.

Basic research on theoretical issues was done here, including the implosion type design that was deemed as the most feasible method of detonation. In addition to being the main "think-tank", the Los Alamos site was responsible for the final assembly of the bombs from materials and components produced by other sites. Manufacturing at Los Alamos included casings, explosive lenses, and fabrication of fissile materials into bomb cores.

The Oak Ridge Facility

The Oak Ridge facility, consisting of 59,000 acres of Appalachian wilderness extending from the Cumberland foothills, was located along the Clinch River in eastern Tennessee about 20 miles from Knoxville. It was known as the Clinton Engineer Works, and its purpose was to produce the uranium isotope U-235 for the fuel needed to make an atomic bomb. It was operated by the Tennessee Eastman Corporation, and a total of 22,000 employees worked there during WWII. Two primary plants were created—Y-12 and K-25—each of which used a different method to separate the isotopes.

The Y-12 plant to produce enriched uranium was built by Stone & Webster of Boston, Massachusetts, and employed about 22,000 workers. The company designed and constructed a 500-tank facility starting in 1943. The construction of the massive structure required 38 million board feet of lumber, 15,000 tons of silver for coils, plus countless tubes, generators, regulators and other equipment. Because of various problems that were encountered, the full operation of the plant was not achieved until 1944.

The K-25 plant to produce plutonium was built by the DuPont Corporation, which began construction in 1943. DuPont used the CP-1 model to design a water-cooled, graphite production reactor, which would be known as X-10. The first pile known as the B-reactor became operational in 1944. The K-25 process used more than 3,000 repetitive diffusion steps to separate U-235 atoms from U-238 atoms to create the uranium enrichment process that was necessary to make a nuclear weapon. The K-25 plant was built on 44 acres in a mile-long U-shaped building that was 4 stories high and 440 feet wide. It used hundreds of miles of piping, all with nickel plating to prevent pinholes. This plant supplied the first plutonium material to Los Alamos in 1945, and became the base for expansion of U-235 production.

The Hanford Facility

The Hanford plant was located in a remote area in a desert plateau in eastern Washington by the Columbia River near the tri-cities of Pasco, Richland and Kennewick. The site, known as the Hanford Engineer Works, was 780 square miles in size—although only about 5% of the area was actually used. The whole area was fenced off by the Army to provide maximum security. From the beginning work force of 300 people in Hanford in 1943, the site grew until 51,000 workers were involved, with DuPont being the primary employer.

The purpose of the site was for a fuel fabrication plant that was used to make 22 million metal pieces of uranium fuel shaped into cylindrical slugs that would in turn be used to make an atom bomb. These slugs were inserted as rows into horizontal holes of water-cooled and graphite-lined reactors—of which there were three—to physically separate the plutonium, of which only .05% was useable. The Hanford plant was designed from the work by Enrico Fermi, and was used to convert uranium-238 into plutonium-239. The DuPont Corporation was chosen as the primary contractor, with Crawford Greenewalt being the director and liaison for the project. Colonel Matthias was assigned to oversee the construction of the three nuclear reactors as well as the building of the 4 chemical separation plants.

Construction for the B-Reactor was started in 1943 and was completed in 1944. The building of the reactor required 390 tons of steel, 17,000 cubic yards of concrete, 50,000 concrete blocks for the foundation, and 71,000 concrete blocks to create the nuclear pile. The largest atomic pile ever assembled on earth for the B-reactor went critical in 1944, and the D-reactor went critical later in 1944. The first irradiated slugs were produced in 1944, with a highly purified form of plutonium being available in 1945. This material was shipped to Los Alamos in 1945.

Dayton Site

Dayton, Ohio was another Manhattan Project site that was so secret it was never publicized, and hence is often overlooked in the historical accounts of the program. In 1943, Oppenheimer assigned the separation of polonium—the critical element that was needed as a trigger device to ignite the bomb—to Charles Allen Thomas. As director of the Monsanto Chemical Company's research department, Thomas convinced the company to undertake the work of extracting the polonium. He also persuaded his mother-in-law to let them use the Runnymede Playhouse and its facilities that were part of the Talbott estate in nearby Oakwood.

The scientists and engineers at this site produced the polonium triggers, which were used to start the chain reaction that was necessary to explode the atomic bombs. They worked out the methodology for separating the highly radioactive polonium from irradiated bismuth slugs, and then purifying them to form the atomic trigger, the key device to producing the bomb.

University of Chicago

The Metallurgical Laboratory at the University of Chicago was created by the United States to develop an atomic bomb. Immediately after the Japanese attack on Pearl Harbor in 1941, Arthur Compton gained support for consolidating plutonium research at the University of Chicago. The objectives were to produce chain-reacting piles of uranium to convert to plutonium, to find ways to separate the plutonium from the uranium, and to design a bomb.

A group headed by Thomas Moore began designing the production pile in 1942. Moore's first goals were to find the best methods of extracting plutonium from the irradiated uranium, and for cooling the pile. In 1942, a team of scientists under Glenn Seaborg isolated the first weighable amount of plutonium from uranium irradiated in cyclotrons. Meanwhile, work continued under Enrico Fermi to build uranium and graphite piles that could be brought to critical mass in a controlled, self-sustaining nuclear reaction.

Fermi and his associates built the piles (the nuclear reactor) in a racquets court under the abandoned west stands of the Chicago University's Alonzo Stagg Field. The piles consisted of uranium pellets as a neutron–producing core that was separated from one another by graphite blocks to slow the neutrons. The controls consisted of cadmium-coated rods that absorbed neutrons. Withdrawing the rods would increase neutron activity in the pile to lead to a self-sustaining chain reaction, while re-inserting the rods would dampen the reaction. In 1942, Fermi was able to conduct the experiment that created the first critical mass of fissile matter, which produced the world's first self-sustaining nuclear chain reaction in the Chicago Pile (CP-1).

The CP-1 provided little technical guidance other than to suggest a lattice arrangement of graphite and uranium. Any pile producing more power than the few watts generated by Fermi's experiment with the CP-1 would require elaborate controls, radiation shielding, and a cooling system. These engineering features would all contribute to a reduction in neutron multiplication so it was imperative to determine which pile design would be safe and controllable, and still sustain a chain reaction. The information gathered from the Metallurgical Laboratory would eventually be used by Crawford Greenwalt of the DuPont Corporation to establish the specifications for building the separation plants at Oak Ridge and Hanford.

Operation of CP-1 was terminated in 1943. The reactor was dismantled and moved to Red Gate Woods, the former site of the Argonne National Laboratory, where it was reconstructed using the original materials—plus an enlarged radiation shield—and was renamed as the Chicago Pile-2 (CP-2). CP-2 began operation in 1943 and was later buried at the same site.

<u>University of Berkeley</u>

The Radiation Laboratory at the University of Berkeley concentrated on the production of radionuclides. In 1931, Ernest Lawrence acquired a disused civil engineering laboratory on the Berkeley campus of the University of California to house his first large cyclotron. From 1934 until the Radiation Laboratory became part of the WWII effort, the investigation and production of artificial isotopes by neutron, proton, deuteron, and alpha-particle beams dominated its research program. Accelerated by the Manhattan Project, a crash program was initiated in 1939 to build a very powerful cyclotron of 100 Mev energy for research into making the first nuclear explosives.

The device, which was called a calutron, was funded by the OSRD in 1942. The research with the use of the calutron produced groundbreaking work into knowledge of chain reactions and the release of vast amounts of nuclear energy. A huge mass spectrograph was also built to test the feasibility of separating the fissile part of natural uranium, U-235, from its much more plentiful companion isotope, U-238. The information derived by the research at the Radiation Laboratory, including the fissionability of plutonium, was utilized in the construction of the separation plants at Oak Ridge.

Aspects of the Project

<u>Organization</u>

Oppenheimer began to recruit the very best scientists for the Los Alamos Laboratory by visiting the various universities that were engaged in nuclear research, and he enlisted James Conant to assist him in getting the most qualified talent that was available. A contingent of British scientists also arrived in 1943. The initial staffing plan provided for 100 scientists to be grouped into 4 major divisions, each of which would have subgroups with special assignments. Hans Bethe was chosen as head of the Theoretical Division, Robert Bacher was selected as leader of the Experimental Physics Division, Joe Kennedy was put in charge of the Chemical Division, and Navy Captain William Parson was places as leader of the Ordnance Division. A Special Engineer Detachment (SED) of the Army consisting of soldiers with backgrounds as mechanics, machinists and electronics technicians was also assigned to act as assistants to the senior scientists.

Initial Work

The initial work at Los Alamos was concerned with briefings on nuclear physics. Oppenheimer nominated Robert Serber to give a series of lectures to the scientists, and Edward Condon compiled these tutorials and mimeographed them as copies of the *Los Alamos Report Number 1: The Los Alamos Primer*. This document contained a summary of all of the research that had been done, and became required reading for every new scientist who joined the project. For the planning research, Oppenheimer established weekly colloquiums where division and group leaders could report on the progress that had been achieved and on all the problems that had been encountered. A governing board consisting of 8 leaders, a governing council of 50 members, and a review committee consisting of 5 scientists were also established to discuss the progress and problems.

Firing Mechanism

Captain Parsons directed the effort for the firing mechanism of the bomb, which involved having 2 sub-critical masses of fissionable material come together to form a supercritical mass for an explosion. This process also had to ensure that the explosion would occur in a precise manner and at a high speed such that the highly unstable sub-critical masses did not pre-detonate. A conventional artillery method of firing one sub-critical mass into the other was under consideration for uranium-235, but this method would work for plutonium only if absolute purification of the plutonium could be achieved. The gun-type design was designed for uranium because of the inability to solve the purification problem for plutonium.

The primary approach was directed towards the development of a gun-type design, but complications, especially about the size required, eventually forced the project to stop the gun approach in 1944. The bomb designers turned instead to the implosion method for plutonium as the trigger mechanism for the detonation of the bomb. John Von Neumann's theoretical work proved that an implosion technique would work, and Oppenheimer assigned George Kistiakowsky, Captain Parson's deputy, Samuel Allison and Robert Bacher to work on this device. But, it was primarily Kistiakowsky who worked with the scientists to develop the mechanism and explosive components that would ultimately be used to detonate the bomb. Oppenheimer reorganized the group to pursue the implosion technique and Robert Bacher was assigned to head the development of the bomb that would work with the implosion method. James Tuck also developed the shaped charge cone method to converge the shock waves into a high-speed jet for the implosion to occur. The implosion device delayed the project to the extent that a bomb would not be available until 1945.

Bomb Design

Captain William Parsons directed his efforts at working towards the development of the bomb hardware. Two models were developed by 1944: a "Thin Man" type, which utilized the gun device, and a "Fat Man" type, which utilized the implosion design. The bomb design proved to be very complicated and was affected by personnel shortages and supply difficulties. James Conant sent as many scientists as could be spared from the Metallurgical Laboratory and Oak Ridge to Los Alamos as well as civilian machinists and SED soldiers. General Groves made changes to the procurement system to ensure the timely shipment of supplies.

Early work on the design of the atomic bomb began in earnest, with the properties of uranium being reasonably well understood, those of plutonium less so, and the knowledge of fission explosions being entirely theoretical. That neutrons were produced when uranium-235 fission was achieved, but it was not yet known if plutonium would release neutrons during bombardment. Further, the exact sizes of the cross sections (the probability of capturing neutrons) of fissionable substances had yet to be determined in experiments, and the theoretical consensus was that fission chain reactions did take place with sufficient speed to produce powerful releases of energy—but only experiments could test this theory. The optimum size of the critical mass still remained to be established—as did the optimum shape. Even when enough data were gathered to establish the optimum critical mass, the optimum effective mass still had to be determined. It was not just a matter of starting a chain reaction in a critical mass; it was also necessary to start one in a mass that would release the greatest possible amount of energy before it was destroyed in the explosion.

Extraction of Weapon Fuel

Work continued at the Oak Ridge and Hanford facilities to extract uranium-235 and plutonium. The required supplies of uranium ore were obtained from stored amounts at Staten Island, New York, and later from sources in Canada and Colorado. Uranium in the form of hexafluoride as feed material for diffusion processes in isotope separation were obtained from the E. I. DuPont de Neumann and Company, and from the Harshaw Chemical Company in Cleveland, Ohio. Despite operational problems, the Oak Ridge uranium enrichment process made considerable progress to meet the experimental needs at Los Alamos. At Hanford, unexpected problems were solved and enough plutonium was also produced to meet the needs of the research at Los Alamos.

The Trinity Test

Because of the complexity of an implosion-style weapon, it was decided that, despite the waste of fissile material, an initial test would be required. The atomic test posed a significant safety hazard so planners chose a flat, desert scrub region in the Northwest corner of the isolated Alamogordo Bombing Range in south central New Mexico known as the "Jornada del Muerto," ("Journey of Death") that was 210 miles south of Los Alamos for the explosion site, but still only 20 miles from the nearest offsite habitation. A pre-test explosion was done in 1945 by using 100 tons of TNT to simulate the bomb's effect. The detonation of the TNT took place at Trinity and created a fireball that was seen as far away as 60 miles.

Dangers from blast, fragments, heat, and light would be minimal if personnel were sufficiently removed from ground zero, but the real concern was with radiation. The plutonium explosion would fission into other radionuclides. Neutrons would also strike various elements on the ground and turn some into radioactive isotopes. This radioactive debris would be swept with fission products into a growing fireball and lifted high into the air. Once in the atmosphere, a cloud of intense radioactivity would form, and the radioactive fallout over local towns posed a potential hazard.

On July 16, 1945, inside the shelter at Trinity site near Alamogordo, New Mexico, Oppenheimer, Charles Thomas, General Farrell, General Groves and others gathered to watch the first test of the weapon. A great variety of instruments were inside the shelter to collect as much data as possible. Three observation bunkers that were located 10,000 yards to the North, West, and South of the firing tower at ground zero would measure key aspects of the reaction such as the symmetry of the implosion and the amount of energy released. Additional measurements would be taken to determine the behavior of the fireball, and to measure the radioactivity that the test device would release. With just 20 minutes to zero hour, General Groves left the shelter to go to the base camp where a better observation point was located—and to guard against both principals (he and Oppenheimer) being in the same location in case something went wrong. General Farrell also left at the same time to go to the main observation point located about 10 miles from ground zero.

At 5:29:45 AM, the first atomic bomb called "Fat Man," which was made from plutonium-239 that was supplied by the Hanford site, was detonated with a yield of 18,600 tons of TNT. As the device exploded, it vaporized the tower on which it had been mounted, and it turned the asphalt around the base of the tower to green fused sand. Scientists stationed 6 miles away witnessed the test shot which resulted in a tremendous burst of white light followed by the formation of a mushroom-shaped cloud that rose to 36,000 feet high. A thunderous roar occurred with an accompanying shock wave that knocked several of the observers in the shelter to the ground. The light from the blast was visible from 250 miles away and many people watched the phenomena although they had no idea what it was. The noise of the explosion was heard as far away as 50 miles from the detonation site, and some glass was reported to have shattered at a distance of 125 miles away. The crater that was created by the atomic bomb blast at its detonation point was more than 1,000 feet in diameter.

The success of the Trinity test meant that both types of bombs—the uranium and plutonium ones—were now available for use against Japan. On Saturday morning, trucks from Los Alamos left with the bomb cargo to Albuquerque, New Mexico. Two DC-3s flew from the Kirtland Base in Albuquerque to San Francisco, California with the parts for the atom bomb. Four hours after the blast had occurred at Trinity site, the cruiser USS Indianapolis sailed from San Francisco to Tinian in the Mariana Islands close to Guam with an assembled uranium bomb named "Little Boy." Oak Ridge provided the uranium fuel for "Little Boy" that would be destined for Hiroshima. A second assembled plutonium bomb shipment called "Fat Man" was sent to Tinian by air for a second target. Made from fuel supplied from Hanford, destiny influenced by weather picked the target to be Nagasaki.

The Manhattan Project-3

Ending the War with Japan

<u>Decision to Use the Bomb</u>

When President Harry Truman assumed the office upon President Roosevelt's death in 1945, Japan was close to being defeated. Since Germany and Italy had both surrendered, Japan had no allies to come to her aid. Also, her navy was nearly destroyed, and thus could not counter any blockade that might be imposed to deprive her of food and supplies. With very little air force left, Japan could not defend herself against concentrated air attacks. Moreover, Japan had the imminent threat of both Chinese and Soviet Union forces who were ready to attack the homeland. In spite of this, Japan's resistance was manifested by sacrifices of its population—especially as American losses grew. Japan seemed willing to fight to the end with a population of 100,000,000 to defend its homeland—especially since they had never experienced being conquered.

This was very evident from the fact that American bombers had already burned 66 Japanese cities, killing almost 300,000 Japanese, injuring 1.3 million others and leaving 8 million without homes. Yet, Japan remained adamant in fighting the war, and quadrupled their forces on Kyushu to 545,000 men, doubled the size of their homeland army to 2 million soldiers, and readied 5,350 planes and 6,200 boats for suicide attacks against a United States invasion.

Because an invasion of Japan would be a very costly endeavor in terms of lives, the American policy shifted towards the dropping of atomic bombs to hasten the end of the war. It was thought that through such devastation Japan would be convinced that further resistance on their part would be futile. In 1945, the Secretary of War set up the Interim Committee to advise President Truman as to the possible use and implications of the atomic bomb. A scientific panel was also formed to provide advice to President Truman. After much discussion, the committee and panel reached 3 unanimous decisions:

- The atomic bomb should be used against Japan as soon as possible
- The atomic bomb should be used against war plants that were surrounded by workers' homes and other buildings susceptible to damage in order to inflict the greatest and most profound psychological impact on as many inhabitants as possible—especially with regard to the visual effects
- The atomic bomb should be used without any warning

The military advisers all stressed that it would be the shock value of the weapon that would make Japan surrender and stop the war. Nevertheless, the Joint Chiefs of Staff still continued with their plan of a ground invasion that was to occur in 1945. The plan included an intensified air and sea blockade, a greatly intensified air bombing, and an invasion of the island of Kyushu. This would then be followed by an invasion of the island of Hunshu in 1946, with a total of 5 million American men involved in the fighting—with estimates of as high as 1 million American soldiers being killed in the invasion of the mainland of Japan, as well as probably 5 million Japanese deaths.

In July 1945, the official orders were issued to the 509th Composite Group of the Army Air Force to deliver the first bomb in August 1945. The Potsdam Declaration was issued by President Harry Truman, by Prime Minister Winston Churchill of Great Britain and by President Chiang Kai Shek of Nationalist China in July 1945. The declaration called for the immediate and unconditional surrender of all Japanese armed forces—or else face the alternative of prompt and utter destruction. Japan rejected the ultimatum, thus setting the stage for the dropping of the bombs.

Selection of Targets

A Target Committee, chaired by General Groves, was created in April 1945 to select a list of Japanese cities as candidates. A broad list of 16 initial targets was considered, with the aim being to determine the best techniques and the most effective destruction to produce the desired psychological effect on the Japanese Empire and its leaders. By the July 1945, the list had been shortened to 4 cities: Hiroshima, Kokura, Niagara and Nagasaki. Hiroshima was considered as the top choice because it contained an important army depot, an important port, had a large industrial area and presented a very good radar target.

Testing the Drop

In 1943, physicist Norman Ramsey organized the dropping of a scale model of the atomic bomb at the Dahlgren Naval Proving Grounds in Virginia. The "Sewer Pipe Bomb" test proved to be a failure, but it did lead to the problem of stability for the bomb while in descent being mastered. In 1944, another dummy test bomb simulating the atomic bomb was dropped at Muroc Army Air Force Base in California.

In December 1944, Lieutenant Paul Tibbets was placed by General Henry Arnold to be in command of the 393rd Bombardment Squadron of the 509th Composite Group of the Army Air Force with a top-secret mission to drop the first atomic bombs on Japan. To test for the mission, his crew dropped pumpkin bombs that were filled with 5,000 pounds of conventional explosives to simulate the weight of the atomic weapons from specially modified B-29 planes that had been built by the Boeing Company. The training took place in 1945 at a base located in Wendover, Utah. The training resumed at Batista Field in Cuba, and was finally concluded at Tinian Island in the Marianas in 1945.

Dropping the First Bomb

On August 6, 1945, Colonel Tibbets and his crew took off from Tinian Island aboard the *Enola Gay* B-29 bomber, heading towards Hiroshima, Japan, with a bomb that weighed 9,700 pounds, and which had a length of 10½ feet—with the plane having 65 tons of weight altogether, including the 7,000 gallons of fuel. Two other aircraft accompanied the *Enola Gay*: the *Great Artiste*, which was an instrument aircraft piloted by Major

Charles Sweeney, and another B-29 aircraft, the *Necessary Evil* commanded by Major George Marquadt, which was equipped with photographic equipment.

At 8:16:02 AM local Japanese time, the *Little Boy* uranium bomb detonated above the courtyard of Shima Surgical Hospital of Hiroshima, missing the aim point of the Aioi Bridge by 800 feet. After having been released from the *Enola Gay* at a height of 31,000 feet, the atomic bomb exploded at an altitude of 1,800 feet with a force of 12,500 tons of TNT, and it generated a fireball whose temperature reached 300,000 degrees Fahrenheit. The temperature on the ground reached an estimated 9,752 degrees Fahrenheit as a fireball cloud that was one-half mile wide reached a height of 2 miles. Three shock waves with a force of twice that of earth's gravity were also generated—two of which shook the *Enola Gay* violently, even though the plane was 11½ miles away by that time.

A total of 80,000 people were instantly killed, and all buildings within a 2-mile radius were completely destroyed. The resulting firestorm covered about 4½ square miles of the city, and killed anyone who had not escaped in the first minutes after the attack. All major facilities and organizations were destroyed, including government offices, fire departments, police stations, hospitals, first-aid clinics, broadcasting stations, sewage systems, and telephone systems, as well as electricity, gas and water utilities. 90% of medical personnel were either killed or disabled, and only 3 out of 45 hospitals were left standing. The blast wave shattered glass in suburbs that were 12 miles away from the center of the explosion. All forms of human organization vanished, including those of family, relatives, neighbors and friends. All traces of the traditional community life also disappeared such as restaurants, theaters, schools, inns, sporting activities, laundries, temples, shrines, gardens, cemeteries, markets, automobiles, horses, sidewalks, roads and public transportation systems.

Dropping the Second Bomb

The incineration of Hiroshima did not bring an end to the war as the Japanese generals and admirals still refused to surrender, and so another bombing mission was initiated. On August 9, 1945, five specially designed B-29 Superfortress planes took off towards the mainland of Japan. The lead plane, *Bock's Car*, piloted by Major Sweeney carried the atomic bomb, two were weather scout planes, and the other two planes carried instrumentation and photographic equipment. Kokura was the primary target, but the weather obscured the target with a dense cloud layer, and so a decision was made by the weapons officer, Commander Frederick Ashworth, to drop the atomic bomb over the secondary target, Nagasaki, which had several wartime industrial plants and a large seaport.

The plutonium bomb named *Fat Man* was dropped from *Bock's Car*, and detonated at 11:02:00 AM local time at an altitude of 1,650 feet above the Urakami Valley in Nagasaki over the Urakami Tenshudo Roman Catholic Church. The atomic bomb exploded with a blast equivalent of 22,000 tons of TNT, generated a heat of 7,000 degrees Fahrenheit and created winds with a velocity of 625 miles per hour. A giant pillar of purple fire rose to a height of 2 miles, with an accompanying mushroom cloud that rose to a height of 12 miles.

Although the bomb missed its intended target by 2 miles, it still did extensive damage, especially to the Mitsubishi Steel and Arms Works, the Mitsubishi-Urakami Ordnance Works, and all of the factories and industrial plants along 3 miles of the Urakami River. The steep hills confined the blast, heat, and radiation effects of the explosion, but it still obliterated one-third of the city and one-half of the population, with a total of 40,000 people being killed outright. Almost everything up to ½ mile from ground zero was completely destroyed, and almost all homes within 1½ miles were destroyed. Dry, combustible materials instantly burst into flames as far away as 2 miles from ground zero. Despite the absence of a firestorm, secondary fires erupted throughout the city, which firemen could not put out because of breaks in the water system. Although the damage was not as great as in Hiroshima, 14,000 homes were destroyed and 5,400 more were damaged.

Interim Activity

Even after 2 atomic bombs had been dropped, Japan still did not surrender. Since there was no atomic bomb available for use immediately, one more conventional bombing run was scheduled on August 14, 1945, with 800 B-29 airplanes in the 509th Group being involved in the strike. The planes flew from Guam, Saipan and Tinian loaded with pumpkin bombs. Each of these bombs was filled with 10,000 pounds of Torpex, and were flown to drop them over the cities of Koromo, Kumagaya and Izesaki.

A third atomic bomb became available, and the Strategic Air Forces Commander Carl Spaatz proposed dropping it over Tokyo to enable a devastating psychological effect on Japanese government officials. Plans for more atomic bomb attacks on Japan were also made, which were to be carried out in August, September and October of 1945. General Groves sent a memo to General George Marshall to have more atomic bombs ready, with a fourth one to be made available during August 1945, for dropping over either the Kokura Arsenal or the city of Niigata. Three more bombs were to be made ready in September 1945, and an additional three more bombs in October 1945—with all of them to be dropped before the planned ground invasion of Japan in November 1945. In addition, seven more bombs were to be available by December 1945, after the invasion had begun. However, President Truman ordered a halt to atomic attacks while surrender negotiations were ongoing.

The Surrender of Japan

On August 10, 1945, Emperor Hirohito broke the 3 to 3 deadlock in the Japanese Cabinet, and made the initial effort to surrender. The allied powers replied, and on August 14, 1945, Japan unconditionally surrendered. President Truman announced it to the world, and on August 15, 1945, Emperor Hirohito capitulated in a recorded radio address that was broadcast to the Japanese people, citing the cruel weapon as the reason to do so. On September 2, 1945, the surrender signing was held aboard the *Missouri* in Tokyo Bay.

The Manhattan Project-4

The Aftermath

Unveiling the Project

In 1945, after the two atomic bombs had been dropped over Japan, the United States government unveiled the Manhattan Project to the American people. The United States Army released the report entitled *Atomic Energy for Military Purposes* written by Henry DeWolf Smyth, the Chairman of the Princeton Physics Department. It was a comprehensive review of the undertaking, and although it did not contain the secret technical details, the report described the endeavor of building the atomic bomb. The full effects of the bomb on the populace of Japan, however, were not disclosed until John Hersey published a series of articles in the *New Yorker* in 1946, which later became a book that was entitled *Hiroshima*. The book detailed the horrific effects and complete destruction by telling the stories of 6 survivors of the initial atomic bomb blast.

As support for the use of the atomic bomb against Japan waned, the Secretary of War Stimson wrote an article in *Harper's Magazine* entitled "The Decision to Use the Atomic Bomb" that explained the rationale for the decision. Another supportive article was written by Paul Russell that was entitled "Thank God for the Bomb." Karl Compton also wrote an article entitled "If the Atomic Bomb Had Not Been Used" that justified the use of the weapon.

An alternative view of the motives behind the use of the bomb was published by Patrick Blackett. He argued that the weapons that were dropped on Japan were done so with an aim of achieving a defense policy against the Soviet Union. Another opposite and negative view was published by Felix Morley in his article "Return to Nothingness." After the war, military officers such as General Dwight Eisenhower, General Curtis Lemay and Admiral William Leahy publicly stated that they had been against the use of the atomic bombs. Even conservative publications such as *Human Events* and *National Review* criticized the decision to use the bomb—as did former President Herbert Hoover.

Efforts at International Control

In the aftermath of the atomic bombings of Hiroshima and Nagasaki, President Harry Truman and his top officials viewed the Soviet Union as the primary opponent in the move toward international control of the atomic bomb. Despite his misgivings concerning the Soviets, Secretary of War Stimson determined that unless the United States offered full partnership in the development of atomic energy, the Soviet Union would begin an armament race. However, Secretary of State Byrnes remained opposed to any attempt to cooperate with the Soviets on atomic energy, and viewed the possession of the atomic bomb as a diplomatic asset that would make the Soviets more amenable to negotiations.

Secretary of War Stimson approached President Truman about a direct offer to the Soviets on controlling the atomic bomb rather than reverting to power politics. The United States would propose to stop all atomic weapons work if the Soviets did likewise, with the current nuclear stockpile being impounded if an agreement could be reached on banning the atomic bomb as a weapon of war. Inducements would include exchanging information on commercial and humanitarian applications of atomic energy. However, President Truman's Cabinet was unenthusiastic about this proposal and focused instead on sharing information about the atomic bomb. Secretary of the Navy James Forrestal saw the atomic bomb as the property of the American people, which was not to be given away without public approval. 70% of the American populace and over 90% of the United States Congressmen objected to sharing atomic secrets with other nations.

President Truman did not commit to Secretary of War Stimson's proposal, and in 1945, he called for international arrangements for the renunciation of the use and development of the atomic bomb, singling out Britain and Canada for initial discussions — but not the Soviet Union. Later, President Truman downgraded the significance of international control, noting that the engineering and technical details on the bomb could not be shared with other nations. Nevertheless, the Soviets refused to be cowed by the American monopoly on the atomic bomb and they rejected all attempts at negotiations on international control.

In 1945, Vannevar Bush proposed a 3-stage approach to international technical cooperation on atomic energy. In the first stage, all nations would open their research laboratories to foreign scientists. A second stage would involve a free exchange of information on practical aspects of atomic energy such as industrial uses. In the third stage, all nations would agree to use atomic energy only for peaceful purposes. An inspection system would also safeguard against cheating by diverting fissionable materials to make atomic bombs. Bush suggested that the Soviet Union be asked to join with the United States and Britain in proposing that the United Nations create a scientific agency to implement a program of international cooperation and control.

Both Bush and General Groves favored the manufacture of fissionable material to be continued until negotiations reached a suitable point, at which time the President would announce that no more atomic bombs would be produced. The fissionable material would be stored for later use in atomic power plants, with an international inspection system verifying that the fissionable material was not being diverted for military purposes. Britain and Canada agreed to the Bush plan, and proposed the establishment of an atomic energy commission under the United Nations. This commission would prepare recommendations for the United Nations on international control that would include information exchange, safeguards, and the elimination of atomic weapons.

Failure of the Negotiations

Secretary of State James Byrnes arranged for foreign ministers from the United States, Britain and Canada to meet in Moscow in 1945 to discuss atomic energy in terms of the United Nations proposal. The Soviets acquiesced to the American proposal, but with one exception: that the United Nations commission report to and be accountable to the Security Council. The reason was that in the Security Council, the Soviet Union possessed a veto, and could halt any commission actions that it found to be objectionable.

Byrnes named Under Secretary of State Dean Acheson to chair a committee to formulate policy on international control. Other members of this committee were Vannevar Bush, General Groves, James Conant, and John McCloy. The committee also set up a board of consultants headed by Tennessee Valley Authority Chairman David Lilienthal, with Robert Oppenheimer as the panel's resident physics expert. They followed Oppenheimer's lead in recommending that an Atomic Development Authority be the centerpiece for controlling the atom. The proposed international authority would have a worldwide monopoly in the major areas of atomic energy, with the control relying on the dynamic international organization of scientists and administrators who were committed to developing atomic energy for peaceful purposes. The scientists would exercise proprietary authority over facilities, materials, and processes required for making atomic weapons.

Acheson's committee embraced the proposal and in 1946, issued the Acheson-Lilienthal report. President Truman asked Bernard Baruch to be the lead United States negotiator at the United Nations. Baruch inclined toward drafting his own proposal and did not want to be constrained by the parameters set by the Acheson-Lilienthal report. Although he accepted the Acheson-Lilienthal plan, Baruch's major change was on the issue of enforcement in which he insisted on specific penalties. Violations would be met with immediate and certain punishment that would not be subject to a Security Council veto. In 1946, Baruch unveiled the proposal to the United Nations Atomic Energy Commission.

Andrei Gromyko, the Soviet delegate, proposed an international convention prohibiting the possession, production, and use of nuclear weapons. Only after the convention was implemented, would measures be considered to ensure the strict observance of the terms and obligations. Gromyko rejected any attempts to negate the veto, and added that the Baruch proposals could not be accepted.

During the debate in the United Nations in the following 6 months, neither side demonstrated an inclination to alter its position. The Soviets never expressed any intent either to negotiate seriously, nor to abandon their own atomic research project. The Soviet Union declared that it was not interested in the Baruch proposals, but instead sought to pursue its own policies in complete freedom and without any interference or control from the outside. The United States concluded that stopping bomb production would in no way induce the Russians to accept any form of international inspection and control. The conclusion arrived at was that no general understanding based on mutual trust and cooperation would be possible between the two systems of government.

In 1946, the United Nations General Assembly voted to exchange atomic information and established the United Nations Atomic Energy Commission (UNAEC). But, the United States, believing that Soviet troops posed a threat in Europe with the rapid demobilization of American conventional forces, refused to surrender its atomic deterrent without adequate international controls. Unwilling to surrender its veto power, the Soviet Union abstained from the 1946 vote on Baruch's proposal to the United Nations on the grounds that it did not prohibit the bomb. The Soviet Union continued its research effort to develop its own atomic bomb while the United States continued to develop and expand its own nuclear arsenal, especially with further testing by detonating 2 atomic bombs at the Bikini Atoll in 1946. The United States conducted another test in 1948 in the Marshall Islands, and the first test of a precursor hydrogen bomb in 1951—followed by an actual hydrogen bomb test in 1952.

Thus, in an atmosphere of mutual suspicion, the Cold War began. It eventually cost the United States $4 trillion to develop these atomic weapons and their delivery systems. The expense of the arms race resulted in a huge national debt, in a decaying infrastructure of roads, railways and bridges, a severe social and educational neglect, and a decline in the living standards of the United States—especially since huge defense spending limited both civilian investments and public consumption. It also brought about the increased risk of suicidal war with the other superpowers such as Russia and China.

The Soviet Union pursued the acquisition of the atom bomb with the work headed by Igor Kurchatov at a research facility located in Sarov in an old abandoned monastery located 250 miles east of Moscow—and by an active espionage effort of the research conducted at Los Alamos. In 1949, the Soviet Union exploded its first atomic bomb.

In 1953, President Dwight Eisenhower addressed the United Nations, calling for an "Atoms for Peace," endeavor that was aimed at the reduction of the threat from nuclear weapons, and the development of peaceful applications of atomic energy. However, other countries joined the nuclear weapons club, thus ending the United States monopoly on atomic weapons. Since the 1950s, the threat of a nuclear war has escalated.

WWII—1939

The Beginning of the War

The Fall of Poland

To create an incident of Polish aggression, a prisoner from one of the German concentration camps was dressed in a Polish military uniform. He was taken to Gleiwitz, Germany, and was shot there by the Gestapo—the German secret police. He was accused of allegedly conducting an attack on a local German radio station transmitter—an event that Hitler used to invade Poland to regain the territories that were lost by Germany after WWI ended.

The Blitzkrieg

When Germany attacked Poland, it did so with a blitzkrieg—a fast-moving and mechanized push of an army of 1.5 million men using tanks, Luftwaffe fighter planes and bombers, and motorized rolling guns of Panzer units. The Germans conducted air attacks on the Polish air force, and bombers dropped bombs on roads, rails, ammunition dumps, communication installations and civilian centers. Dive bombers also strafed marching columns of soldiers and machine-gunned civilians. On land, waves of motorized infantry, tanks, artillery and foot soldiers pushed into the countryside to join the initial strike force.

The Germans used radio, telephone and telegraphic communications to coordinate the lightning attack. Within one week the Polish Air Force was destroyed, the Polish Army was vanquished, and the Polish government was forced to flee from Warsaw to Lublin. Russia then attacked Poland from the East, and after 2½ weeks, the Polish government ceased to exist. Soviet troops occupied Eastern Poland—as well as Lithuania—and the German forces withdrew, giving up the captured Polish soldiers to the Soviets. The Soviet Union then negotiated a treaty with Estonia.

Four weeks after the initial invasion, the German air attack of Warsaw, Poland began with 480 bombers and other Luftwaffe aircraft. Incendiary bombs caused widespread destruction with intense fires killing or wounding 10,000 civilians. The Polish army at Warsaw surrendered and 170,000 Polish soldiers were taken as prisoners. However, even though the defeat for Poland was total—with over 66,000 soldiers and 25,000 civilians being killed—Polish soldiers still managed to inflict about 14,000 casualties and over 30,000 wounded to the German Army. But, 27 million Poles came under German rule, including 700,000 captured Polish soldiers. Hitler then issued a decree that annexed Silesia and eastern Prussia.

As a result of the invasion of Poland, Britain and France declared war on Germany. Winston Churchill, the First Lord of the Admiralty, proposed the creation of 20 army divisions, with 35 more divisions to be ready by 1941. President Roosevelt clandestinely helped the British, but chose to maintain a policy of neutrality for the United States.

Naval Actions

The German Navy sank 11 British ships, most of them by U-boats. Since the German navy maintained radio silence, Britain was only able to sink 2 of these U-boats during the first month of war. German U-boat attacks on passenger ships were authorized by the high command. A German U-boat torpedoed the ocean liner S. S. *Athenia*, resulting in 112 deaths—including 28 American citizens. A German U-boat torpedoed the British aircraft carrier *Courageous*, and another U-boat sank the British battleship *Royal Oak* with a loss of 800 men. Two German battleships sank 7 British merchant ships, and also captured an American ship, the *City of Flint*. A British minelayer, the HMS *Adventure*, struck a mine in which 12 sailors were killed. In response, the British instituted a blockade in the North Sea of all German export shipments.

The War in Europe

Germany's Next Attacks

The German Fuhrer Hitler extended a message of peace to France and Britain. Britain and France turned down Hitler's offer. Hitler then began his offensive, with the immediate targets being Luxembourg, Belgium and Holland.

Spanish Civil War

When the Spanish Civil War broke out in 1936, Adolph Hitler and Benito Mussolini supported Generalisimo Francisco Franco's nationalist forces in his civil war against the Soviet-supported Spanish Republic. The nationalists under Franco were victorious, and Spain became a fascist regime.

Finland

The Soviet Union attacked Finland with 26 divisions totaling 465,000 men, and bombed its capital, Helsinki.

Albania

Italian troops invaded Albania. Previously, Italy had invaded Ethiopia in 1935.

Conflicts in the Far East

Chinese Civil War

The Kuomintang Party in China launched a unification campaign against regional warlords and unified China in the mid-1920s. However, the country became embroiled in a civil war against its former Chinese communist allies.

The Rise of the Japanese Empire

In 1931, the Japanese Empire invaded Manchuria. Japan and China fought several small conflicts, in Shanghai, Rehe and Hebei until they agreed to the Tanggu Truce in 1933. In 1937, Japan invaded China, and in 1938, Japan entered territory that was claimed by Russia. Japanese troops occupied Hainan Island. Japan and the Soviet Union fought an undeclared war on the Mongolian plains that ended with a Soviet victory. At the Battle of Khalkin Gol, the Russians defeated the Japanese Kwangtung Army on the border of Manchuria and Mongolia.

WWII—1940

More German Invasions

German armies attacked Denmark and Norway. The Danes had no option except to capitulate after a brief defensive response, but the Norwegians resisted with aid from the British navy. German forces captured Oslo, Norway. Still, the British navy inflicted heavy losses, including all German war vessels that were near Narvik, Norway in the Battle of Narvik. But, the German Luftwaffe air force bombed the British and Norwegian forces at Lillehausner and forced them to retreat. In spite of this, allied forces of 25,000 troops succeeded in driving the German forces out of Narvik.

With the Belgian army retreating in collapse near Dunkirk, British and French forces evacuated over 338,000 men from the Dunkirk, Belgium harbor in a dramatic escape by sea. After the fall of Dunkirk, France collapsed under a massive German assault. The German forces occupied Paris, France where France was forced to sign an armistice treaty. Germany defeated Luxembourg, Belgium and Holland with an advance of 136 divisions. Germany then invaded the English Channel Islands.

Germany prepared for an invasion of England—but only with the use of the Luftwaffe and the navy. The first objective was to land 13 divisions of the German army on the south coast of England. Germany began the first massive bombing of London, England with 625 bombers and 645 fighter planes. In response, the British Royal Air Force (RAF) and the British navy began shelling harbors at Octeal, Dunkirk, Antwerp, Cherbourg, Calais and Boulogne. The Battle of Britain raged as the German Luftwaffe battled the RAF in the skies, with the British having the advantage of radar that accurately plotted the course of incoming German airplanes. The Germans sent over 1,000 planes a day while Britain sent bombers into Berlin, Germany. In spite of bombings conducted by German planes for a period of 2 consecutive months, plans for an invasion of Britain were thwarted by British air and sea forces, which inflicted heavy losses on German forces. The campaign failed, and the invasion plans by Germany against England were cancelled by Adolph Hitler. Instead, Germany diverted its army and air forces to Romania to capture and defend the oil fields.

Other Actions

Finland sued for peace with the Soviet Union.

The Soviet Armed Forces occupied the Baltic States, including Estonia, Latvia and Lithuania and achieved their surrender. Russia also occupied parts of Romania. However, the Russian offensive in Finland was halted by several Finnish victories. Nevertheless, the Russians extracted a treaty from Finland by which Finland gave up its territory along the Baltic coast in exchange for its independence.

Italy declared war on France and Britain. Italian forces attacked Albania., and then invaded Greece. but were repulsed and pushed back into Albania, where a stalemate occurred. Italy also began operations in the Mediterranean, initiating a siege of Malta in J1940, conquering British Somaliland, and making an incursion into British-held Egypt. But, the Italian forces were halted at Sidi Barrani by the British army. Italy invaded Greece, but was repelled. Greece invaded Albania, which was held by Italy.

Naval Actions

By using the captured French ports as bases, the German Navy used U-boats against British shipping in the Atlantic, causing the Allies to lose 440,000 tons of shipping. A U-boat sank the British destroyer HMS *Exmouth*, with a crew of 135 being lost.

The Italian Navy suffered significant defeats, with the British Royal Navy putting 3 Italian battleships out of commission via a carrier attack at Taranto, and several more Italian warships neutralized at Cape Matapan.

A British minesweeper, the HMS *Gleaner*, sank a German submarine. From this submarine were recovered three Enigma rotors, one of Germany's most secret wartime communications systems. Although only one of the keys was deciphered, they did provide Britain with an insight into German operating procedures. British decrypters broke the Enigma key most used by the German Luftwaffe, allowing them to intercept messages from the field to headquarters.

The United States supported Britain by creating a security zone spanning one-half of the Atlantic Ocean where the American Navy protected British convoys.

British bombers struck the Italian fleet at the port of Taranto, and sunk the battleship *Duilio* plus 2 other battleships and 2 cruisers.

The British steamer *Automedon* was attacked by the German raider *Atlantis*. The Germans were able to board and extract secret documents as well as a British Merchant Navy code book that contained vital information about their Far East operations.

Far East Activities

Japan blockaded China by seizing several bases in the northern part of Indochina. But, the war between China and Japan stalemated when China—with help from the Soviet Union—launched an offensive against Japan.

WWII—1941

War in Europe

The Germans intervened in the Balkans, invading Greece and Yugoslavia, and conquering the Greek island of Crete by defeating the British. Germany then occupied Estonia.

Invasion of the Soviet Union

Germany invaded the Soviet Union. German forces made significant gains into Soviet territory, inflicting immense losses in personnel and materiel., German forces advanced to Smolensk and marched towards Leningrad and Moscow. However, despite heavy losses experienced by Russian forces, their resistance prevented Germany from capturing both cities. Germany decided to suspend the offensive of a considerably depleted Army Group Center, and chose to divert a part of its armored force to reinforce troops that were advancing toward central Ukraine and Leningrad. The Kiev offensive was successful, and resulted in the elimination of 4 Soviet armies. Germany then advanced into Crimea and the industrially developed Eastern Ukraine.

When German operational objectives in the Ukraine and the Baltic region were achieved, and with only Leningrad and Sevastopol resisting the sieges, a major offensive against Moscow was renewed. The German army was within 20 miles of Moscow, and were at Khimki, a suburb of Moscow. However, ice began causing problems for the German army, especially in starting engines of tanks, making machine guns ineffective and telescopic sights useless. Frostbite also began to take its toll among the soldiers due to lack of shelter and shortage of warm clothing to combat the bitter cold.

The German advance was halted by fierce Russian resistance led by its infantry, with support from artillery, tanks, cavalry and planes. The exhausted German troops were forced to suspend their offensive. Despite the territorial gains, the 2 major Soviet cities of Moscow and Leningrad were not captured, the Soviet Army's capability to resist was not diminished, and the Soviet Union retained a considerable part of its military potential.

Soviet reserves allowed them to achieve numerical parity with the German troops. Since a minimal amount of Soviet troops in the East were sufficient to prevent the Japanese Army from any attack, the Soviets deployed most of their troops and mounted a massive counter-offensive along 600-mile front to push the German forces back towards the West.

The Far East

The Soviet Union and Japan signed a neutrality pact. Japan seized control of southern Indochina. The United States, United Kingdom and other western governments reacted to the seizure of Indochina with a freeze on Japanese assets, while the United States, which supplied 80% of Japan's oil, responded by placing a complete oil embargo, which the Japanese military considered as a declaration of war.

Naval Actions

A German U-boat sank the American freighter *Robin Moor* that was en route to South Africa. In the Atlantic Ocean, the British Navy sank the German flagship *Bismarck*. A German submarine fired torpedoes at the American destroyer *Greer* off the coast of Iceland, prompting President Roosevelt to order the Navy to shoot any German or Italian vessels on sight. A United States merchant ship, the *Steel Seafarer*, was sunk by German aircraft in the Red Sea.

The United States destroyer *Kearney* dropped depth charges on a German U-boat, which then retaliated by torpedoing it off the coast of Iceland. Eleven of the crew were killed, the first American casualties in the undeclared war between Germany and the United States. A United States destroyer, the *Reuben James*, was sunk off the coast of Iceland by a German U-boat, resulting in the loss of 115 American lives.

Japan attacked British, Dutch and American bases along with simultaneous offensives against Southeast Asia and the Central Pacific. These included an attack on the American fleet stationed at the naval base in Pearl Harbor, Hawaii, and landings in Thailand and Malaya. The Japanese also attacked Guam, Wake and the Midway Islands as well as Hong Kong and Singapore. Japan achieved naval victories in the South China Sea, Java Sea and Indian Ocean, and bombed the Allied naval base at Darwin, Australia and the United States air base at Luzon in the Philippines. Japanese troops seized the American garrisons at Shanghai and Tientsin, China—and captured the American gunboat *Wake*. They also sank 2 British battleships: the *Repulse* and *Prince of Wales*. These attacks prompted the United States, Britain, China and other Western Allies—except the Soviet Union—to declare war against Japan. Germany and Italy responded by declaring war on the United States.

The Middle East

The diversion of Axis troops and the majority of air forces from France to the Soviet Union front prompted Britain to form a military alliance with the Soviet Union against Germany. They jointly invaded Iran to secure the Persian Corridor and Iran's oilfields. British Commonwealth forces launched a counter-offensive in the North African desert, reclaiming all gains that the Germans and the Italian forces had previously made. The British quashed a coup in Baghdad, Iraq, which had been supported by German aircraft from bases within Syria. Britain invaded Syria and Lebanon to prevent any further occurrences.

Africa

Hitler sent German forces to Libya to launch an offensive against Britain, and pushed British forces back to Egypt. The British attacked Italian forces in Eritrea, Somaliland and Ethiopia. British forces advanced to the capital city Addis Ababa in Ethiopia. British and Australian forces captured parts of Libya, and Britain captured Mogadishu in Somalia.

The Attack on Pearl Harbor

Overview

The Japanese naval and air forces carried out a surprise military strike against the United States naval base at Pearl Harbor, Hawaii on December 7, 1941, which resulted in the entry of the United States into WWII. The naval base was attacked by 353 Japanese aircraft in 2 waves that were launched from 6 Japanese aircraft carriers. 4 American battleships were sunk and 4 other American battleships were damaged. The Japanese also sank or damaged 3 American cruisers, 3 destroyers, an anti-aircraft training ship and one minelayer. 347 American aircraft were damaged or destroyed, 2,400 personnel were killed and 1,200 were wounded. However, the power station, shipyard, maintenance, fuel and torpedo storage facilities, as well as the submarine piers and headquarters building were not attacked because a third Japanese wave of attack was canceled. Japanese losses were 29 aircraft, 5 small submarines lost, and 55 airmen and 9 submariners killed, with one Japanese sailor from a downed submarine being captured.

Prelude to the Attack

In 1937, Japanese planes bombed, strafed and sank the United States gunboat *Panay* in the Yangtze River in China. Two American sailors and an Italian journalist were killed, with 40 other sailors and civilian passengers being wounded. A formal protest against Japan was lodged by the American ambassador. The Japanese government accepted responsibility, apologized for the incident, and agreed to pay an indemnity of $2 million.

In 1940, following Japan's invasion of Indochina, the United States halted shipments of airplanes, parts, machine tools, and aviation gasoline, which was perceived by Japan as an unfriendly act. However, the United States did not stop oil exports to Japan because the United States deemed that such an action—given Japanese dependence on United States oil—would likely be considered a provocation by Japan.

The United States froze all Japanese assets in America and ceased oil exports to Japan in 1941, in the hope of discouraging further Japanese aggression in the Far East. The Flying Tigers, airmen officers of the United States, were secretly furnished to China for combat duty against Japan prior to the attack on Pearl Harbor. Because the Japanese high command was certain that any attack on the British Southeast Asian colonies would bring the United States into the war, a devastating preventive strike appeared to be the only way to avoid naval interference by the United States. An invasion of the Philippines was also considered to be necessary by Japanese war planners.

The transfer of the United States Pacific Fleet from its previous base in San Diego, California to its base in Pearl Harbor, Hawaii by President Roosevelt in 1940 was seen by the Japanese military as a preparation for conflict. Preliminary planning for an attack on Pearl Harbor began under Admiral Isoroku Yamamoto, the Commander in Chief of Japan's Fleet. He planned and trained for an attack in 1941, assisted by Captain Minoru

Genda. Pilots trained, equipment was adapted, and intelligence was collected, but the attack plan was not approved by Japanese Emperor Hirohito until November 1941, and final authorization was not given until December 1941.

The attack had several major aims. It intended to destroy important American fleet units, thereby preventing the Pacific Fleet from interfering with Japanese conquests of the Dutch East Indies and Malaya. It was also hoped to buy time for Japan to consolidate its position and increase its naval strength before shipbuilding started in the United States. Moreover, it was meant to deliver a severe blow to American morale, which would discourage Americans from committing to a war extending into the western Pacific Ocean and Dutch East Indies. To maximize the effect of the attack, battleships were chosen as the main targets since they were the prestige ships of the United States Navy.

The Approach

The Japanese Fleet

In November 1941, a Japanese task force consisting of 6 aircraft carriers, 2 battleships, 3 cruisers, 11 destroyers, 3 submarines, 3 oilers and 8 supply ships departed from Japan en route to Hawaii The Japanese intended to launch aircraft to attack the United States Naval Forces stationed at Pearl Harbor in Oahu, Hawaii in a surprise operation. In all, 408 aircraft were to be used: 360 for the attack waves, and 48 for defensive combat air patrols. The fleet traveled under a strict blackout with radio silence. There were 12 submarines positioned off the coast of the United States, from Cape Flattery near the Strait of Juan de Fuca off the Washington state coast to Guadalupe Island off the coast of Baja California near San Diego, California. The task force was under the command of Admiral Chuichi Nagumo who was aboard his flagship destroyer, the *Akigumo*.

The Attack

First Wave

The first wave consisting of 183 planes formed the primary attack, and contained the bulk of the weapons such as aerial torpedoes. 10 formation triangles consisting of 5 high level bombers each flew toward the target at a height of 10,000 feet. Accompanying them were 2 groups of dive bombers flying at 11,000 feet, 4 groups of torpedo planes flying at 9,000 feet, and fighter planes at 14,000 feet—the different altitudes being for the sake of avoiding collisions with each other. All of the planes were launched when the carriers reached a point that was 230 miles North of the island of Oahu.

The aircrews were ordered to select the highest value targets like battleships and aircraft carriers, or any other high value ships such as cruisers and destroyers. Dive bombers were to attack ground targets while fighter planes were ordered to strafe and destroy parked aircraft to ensure that they did not get into the air to counterattack the Japanese bombers. When the fighters' fuel got low they were instructed to refuel at the aircraft carriers and then return to combat.

Before the attack started, 2 reconnaissance aircraft were launched from cruisers to scout over Oahu and report on enemy fleet composition and location. Another 4 scout planes patrolled the area between the fleet and Niihau to prevent the Japanese task force from being caught by a surprise counterattack by American planes. Tuning in to the Hawaiian radio station KGMB to direct his lead plane to the target area was Commander Mitsuo Fuchida. He fired a rocket pistol twice and shortly thereafter sounded out the code words (Tiger! Tiger! Tiger!), which indicated that the American Navy had been caught unaware. He then signaled for the general attack to begin.

The first wave inflicted massive damage, with the loss of only 9 Japanese planes. The targets that were attacked by dive bombers were Kaneohe, Wheeler Field, Ford Island and Hickam Field. Torpedo bombers attacked the 8 battleships that were present: the *California, Maryland, Oklahoma, Tennessee, West Virginia, Arizona, Nevada* and *Pennsylvania*. Several United States aircraft were shot down as the first wave approached land.

Second Wave

The second wave of the attack consisting of 171 planes was for the purpose of finishing whatever else remained to be bombed, with the planes being launched when the carriers were 200 miles North of Oahu. The planes, again flying at staggered altitudes to avoid collisions, were led by Lieutenant Commander Shigekazu Shimazaki. The attack centered on the hangars and aircraft on Hickam Field, Kaneohe, Wheeler Field, Ford Island, and Barbers Point—as well as the cruisers and destroyers. They also strafed homes, cars, pedestrians and firemen who were fighting the blazes. 9 more ships were damaged: the cruisers *Helena, Raleigh* and *Honolulu*; the destroyers *Cassin, Downes* and *Shaw*; the repair ship *Vestal*; the seaplane tender *Curtiss*; and the minelayer *Ogala*. Although the second wave inflicted further damage, it cost the Japanese 20 of their planes due to American anti-aircraft fire.

Submarines

Small submarines left Japan in November 1941, and came within 12 miles of Pearl Harbor from where they launched their charges. The American minesweeper *Condor* spotted a midget submarine periscope Southwest of the Pearl Harbor entrance buoy and alerted the destroyer *Ward*. That midget submarine entered Pearl Harbor, but the *Ward* sank another one. A midget submarine on the North side of Ford Island missed the seaplane tender *Curtiss* with her first torpedo and missed the attacking destroyer *Monaghan* with her other torpedo before being sunk by the *Monaghan*. A third midget submarine grounded twice, once outside the harbor entrance and again on the East side of Oahu, where it was captured. A fourth submarine was damaged by a depth charge and was abandoned by its crew before it could fire its torpedoes. Japanese forces received a radio message from a fifth midget submarine claiming damage to one or more large war vessels inside Pearl Harbor.

Aborted Third Wave

Several Japanese officers urged Admiral Nagumo to carry out a third wave of attack to destroy the torpedo storage areas, oil storage tanks, maintenance hangars, the navy yard and dry dock facilities as well as the submarine base and central intelligence headquarters. However, Admiral Nagumo decided to withdraw because of the following reasons:

- American anti-aircraft performance had improved considerably during the second wave, and two thirds of Japan's losses were incurred during the second wave. With 29 planes being shot down, with 74 additional planes being damaged, and 6 submarines being lost, Nagumo reasoned that if he launched a third wave, he would be risking three quarters of the Combined Fleet's strength to wipe out the remaining targets while suffering higher aircraft losses.
- The location of the American aircraft carriers remained unknown. Admiral Nagumo was concerned that his force was now within range of American land-based bombers. He was also uncertain whether the United States had enough surviving planes remaining on Hawaii to launch an attack against his carriers.
- A third wave of attack would have required substantial preparation and turnaround time, and would have meant that returning planes would have had to land at night. Only the British Royal Navy had developed night carrier techniques, so this was a substantial risk.
- The task force's fuel situation did not permit him to remain in waters off Pearl Harbor much longer, since he was at the very limits of logistical support. To do so risked running unacceptably low on fuel, perhaps even having to abandon destroyers en route home.
- He believed the second wave had satisfied the main objective of his mission—the neutralization of the United States Pacific Fleet—and thus, he did not wish to risk further losses. It was Japanese Navy procedure to prefer the conservation of strength instead of the total destruction of the enemy.

Admiral Nagumo did not send out patrols to find the American aircraft carriers, nor did he request that submarines to check out the area around Oahu. Having made the decision not to attack again, the Japanese fleet headed for home. But, they got an order to attack Midway and Wake Islands on the way back. He ordered the cruisers *Tone* and *Chikuma,* the aircraft carriers *Soryu* and *Hiryu,* and the destroyers *Tanikaze* and *Urakaze* to attack Wake Island. After a fierce battle, the Japanese captured the island, which they held until 1945. About 100 Marines were also captured and were later executed.

Ultimately, the targets that were not attacked at Pearl Harbor by the Japanese because of the failure to launch a third wave—such as the submarine base and the old headquarters building—proved to be more important in the long run. It was the American submarines that crippled the Japanese Navy's heavy ships and brought Japan's economy to a standstill by disrupting the transportation of oil and raw materials. Also, the basement of the old administration building was the home of the cryptanalytic unit, which contributed significantly to the American Midway Battle victory and the American submarine force's success by intercepting and decoding secret Japanese military transmissions.

United States Response

United States Admiral Kimmel's headquarters transmitted a message to Washington, D.C. that the air raid on Pearl Harbor was not a drill. The message was transmitted to Admiral Stark who then informed Secretary of the Navy Frank Knox. Knox then telephoned President Roosevelt. President Roosevelt called Secretary of State Cordell Hull who was about to receive the Japanese diplomats. President Roosevelt also called Secretary of War Henry Stimson to inform him of the attack on Pearl Harbor.

Initial Actions

Admiral William Furlong, who was aboard the minelayer *Ogala*, saw the Japanese insignia on a passing plane and alerted the ship's crew to man their stations. The *Ogala* also flashed the alarm to all ships in the harbor. On the *West Virginia*, Ensign Roland Brooks saw an explosion and sounded the alarm, which brought officers and men topside, thereby saving their lives. The officer of the deck on the *Raleigh* called the antiaircraft men to their guns, but the electricity went out as a torpedo struck the cruiser. Nevertheless, Ensign John Beardall, Jr. put the antiaircraft battery into action. Ensign Nathan Asher on the bridge of the destroyer *Blue* got his men to man the antiaircraft guns. The officer of the deck on the *Vestal*, Chief Warrant Officer Fred Hall, sounded general quarters. The *Nevada* opened fire with her machine guns, and with antiaircraft fire directed by Ensign Joseph Taussig.

Admiral Kimmel figured out that the Japanese attack ships lay Northward of Oahu. He advised his forces at sea to search the waters. A Japanese submarine intercepted the message and relayed it to Lieutenant Commander Sadao Chigusa who was aboard the *Akigumo*. However, the American forces did not pursue and scouted mostly in the Southwest area.

Major Truman Landon, who was flying one of the B-17 planes, noticed some of the Japanese planes heading away in a Northward direction. He reported this to the Hawaiian Air Force Headquarters, but everyone was more preoccupied with saving their own lives than they were in locating the Japanese task force.

The Opana radar station plotted a Northbound track of the Japanese planes, which the Army radar control center at Fort Shafter recorded, but they did not inform the Navy of this intelligence.

General Frederick L. Martin, Commander of the Hawaiian Air Force, had 4 A-20 bombers take off from Hickam Field, but gave them a mission to find a Japanese carrier that he surmised was South of Barber's Point. They intercepted the cruiser *Minneapolis* instead.

Admiral Wilson Brown, who was aboard the United States cruiser *Portland*, reported the sighting of a Japanese carrier South of Pearl Harbor.

Captain Brooke Allen flew his B-17 off the Hickam Field runway, but followed the official intelligence and headed South—locating the aircraft carrier *Enterprise* instead. When he flew in a Northward direction, the Japanese carrier force had already sailed out of range.

The Hawaiian Air Force received a map recovered from a Japanese pilot that had been shot down near Fort Kamehameha, which had 10 courses laid out from a Northwest point. General Martin dispatched planes Northward in the afternoon, but they found nothing.

Damage Assessment

Within 1½ hours, the United States Navy had suffered extensive damage to 8 battleships, 3 cruisers, 4 destroyers, 1 minelayer, 4 auxiliary vessels and 123 planes. The United States Army suffered damage to 205 planes and extensive damage to its installations at Hickam, Wheeler, Ford Island, Kaneohe and Ewa. Another 25 planes were lost by friendly fire. The human toll was 2,400 casualties and 1,200 wounded.

Decision to Declare War

On December 7, 1941, the Cabinet met at the Oval Office with President Roosevelt. Henry Morgenthau reported to President Roosevelt that they were seizing all Japanese funds. He also stated that they were putting government people in all of the Japanese banks and businesses, and that they were not going to let the Japanese get into them at all.

Following meetings with his military advisers, President Roosevelt dictated to his secretary a request to Congress for a declaration of war. He composed the speech as a brief, uncomplicated appeal to the people of the United States rather than as a recitation of Japanese treachery—as Secretary of State Cordell Hull had urged. On December 8, 1941, Roosevelt addressed a joint session of Congress and, via radio, the nation. The Senate responded with a unanimous vote in support of war, with only Representative Jeanette Rankin dissenting in the House. President Roosevelt then signed the declaration of war against Japan.

Change in Command Structure

For the Navy, Admiral William Pye relieved Admiral Kimmel after Kimmel and General Walter Short were made the responsible persons for the Pearl Harbor disaster. Admiral Pye launched an attempt to relieve Wake Island with a force led by the carrier Saratoga, which would have evacuated the wounded and civilians and placed 400 more Marines on the island. When the force was 800 miles away from the island, the attempt was aborted by Admiral Pye because he believed that Wake was already lost and he did not want to lose the relief force. Admiral Pye was then replaced by Admiral Charles Nimitz as the commander of the Pacific Fleet. For the Army, Lieutenant General Delos Emmons replaced General Short.

Salvage

Although the Japanese attack inflicted large-scale destruction on Navy vessels and Army aircraft, it did not affect Pearl Harbor's fuel storage, maintenance, submarine and intelligence facilities. After a search for survivors, salvage operations began as divers from the Navy and civilian contractors began to work on the ships that could be refloated. Within 6 months, 5 battleships and 2 cruisers were partially repaired or refloated so that they could be sent to shipyards in Pearl Harbor and on the mainland for extensive repairs.

Assembly of American Carrier Fleet

The American aircraft carriers were untouched by the Japanese attack at Pearl Harbor, and so the Pacific Fleet's ability to conduct offensive operations was not impaired. However, the elimination of the primary battleships left the United States Navy with total reliance on its aircraft carriers and submarines—the very weapons with which the Navy halted and reversed the Japanese advance. 6 of the 8 battleships were repaired and returned to service, but their slow speed limited their deployment, and thus they served mainly in shore bombardment roles. A major flaw of Japanese strategic thinking was a belief the ultimate Pacific Ocean battle would be fought by battleships. Admiral Yamamoto hoarded battleships for a decisive battle that never happened.

Aftermath

Japanese Declaration of War

The Pearl Harbor attack took place before any formal declaration of war was made by Japan. Admiral Yamamoto had originally stipulated that the attack should not start until after Japan had informed the United States that peace negotiations were at an end. The Japanese tried to uphold the conventions of war while still achieving surprise, but the attack began before the notice could be delivered. Tokyo transmitted the message to the Japanese Embassy in Washington, D.C., but transcribing the message took too long for the Japanese Ambassador to deliver it in time. However, the final part of the message neither declared war nor severed diplomatic relations. A declaration of war was printed on the front page of Japan's newspapers in the evening edition on the day of the attack, but it was not delivered to the United States government until the day after the attack.

Relocation of Japanese Americans

A consequence of the attacks on Pearl Harbor was that Japanese American residents and citizens were relocated to internment camps. Within hours of the attack on Pearl Harbor, hundreds of Japanese-American leaders were rounded up and brought to high-security camps. Later, over 117,000 Japanese Americans, including United States citizens, were removed from their homes and transferred to internment camps.

Destruction of the Japanese Fleet

While the attack on Pearl Harbor accomplished its intended objective, it turned out to be diversionary in its effect since the United States Navy decided to abandon defending the

Philippines in response to the outbreak of war. Instead, the United States military concentrated on defeating Germany first while rebuilding its Navy.

At the Battle of the Coral Sea, 70 Japanese aircraft were shot down in a series of battles fought from aircraft carriers, with the Japanese losing the aircraft carrier *Shoho*. At the Battle of Midway, American bombers destroyed 4 Japanese aircraft carriers: the *Akagi*, *Kaga*, *Soryu* and *Hirya* as well as 332 aircraft, with 30,000 Japanese being killed.

Japanese Internment During WWII

Overview

During WWII, the United States government suspended *habeas corpus* and due process, and proceeded to round up over 110,000 Japanese-American citizens and Japanese resident aliens who were residing along the Pacific coast states of Washington, Oregon and California, plus a few in Hawaii. This was a forced relocation and internment from their homes and communities to relocation camps located in the deserts and remote areas of several states. Although they were not charged with any crime, they were made prisoners of the government.

The internment action was triggered by the attack on Pearl Harbor, Hawaii by the naval and air forces of the Japanese Empire in December 1941, that killed or wounded 3,500 Americans as well as destroying or damaging several war ships and military airplanes. Within hours after the attack, FBI agents arrested Japanese teachers, Buddhist priests, Christian ministers, newspaper workers, businessmen, political leaders, and anyone else suspected of having sympathetic ties to Japan. Hundreds of Japanese were shipped off under DOJ orders to detention camps in Santa Fe, New Mexico; Bismarck, North Dakota; Crystal City, Texas; and Missoula, Montana. Many husbands and fathers were arrested and detained in separate camps, and were separated from their families.

All Japanese branch banks and businesses were closed, and the Treasury Department froze all bank accounts that belonged to anyone born in Japan. A mandatory curfew was imposed on all Japanese aliens and Japanese-American citizens, with all being required to carry identification. Severe travel restrictions were also imposed. Both the FBI and the DOJ conducted searches, and seized all items considered to be contraband such as cameras, weapons and short-wave radios. Those who were evacuated were told to discard all their possessions, to sell or lease their businesses, to secure their property or homes, and to pack only what they could carry. The evacuees' baggage was searched upon arrival at the camps, with saws and chisels being confiscated, and Japanese phonograph records and literature being taken away. No pets of any kind were permitted, so these had to be left behind. The evacuees were never told what awaited them, how long they would be gone, or where they were headed.

In 1942, President Franklin Roosevelt signed an executive order to authorize the exclusion of all persons of Japanese descent from 133 designated areas of California, Oregon, Washington and Arizona plus from 135 zones around airports, dams, power plants, railroads, shipyards, harbors and military installations to prevent any possible acts of sabotage or espionage. All Japanese-Americans within the exclusion zones were instructed to secure or sell their houses and possessions, and ordered to report to designated civil control stations. They were registered, placed aboard buses and trains, and taken to temporary assembly centers such as off-season racetracks, unused fairgrounds, and abandoned stockyards. They were then moved to isolated internment camps in Utah, Arizona, Colorado, Wyoming, California, Idaho and Arkansas where they were kept for the duration of the war.

Existing Prejudice Against Japanese People

At the beginning of the 20th century, California experienced a wave of anti-Japanese prejudice with the arrival of new immigrants from Japan. Over 90% of Japanese immigrants to the United States settled in California, where labor and farm competition fed into general anti-Japanese sentiment. In 1905, California's anti-miscegenation law outlawed marriages between Caucasians and Mongolians—a term that was used in reference to the Japanese as well as other ethnicities of East Asian ancestry. They were also excluded from eating in white restaurants and from living in white neighborhoods. In 1906, the San Francisco Board of Education separated the Japanese students from the Caucasian students, and ordered 93 Japanese students in the district to a segregated school in Chinatown.

In 1920, the California Anti-Alien Land Law was enacted to prevent aliens from acquiring, possessing, transmitting or inheriting any property or interest within California. The Oriental Exclusion Law that was passed in 1924 blocked Japanese immigrants from attaining citizenship. Immigrant first-generation Japanese, or Issei, were prohibited from becoming citizens, were forbidden to own land in California, and had several discriminatory laws passed against them that affected their choices of jobs, marriage and education.

Between 1939 and 1941, the FBI compiled the Custodial Detention Index on citizens, enemy aliens and foreign nationals, citing national security as justification. In 1940, the Alien Registration Act was passed by Congress, which required the registration and fingerprinting of all aliens above the age of 14. The act also required aliens to report any change of address within 5 days. Nearly 5 million foreign nationals registered at post offices around the country as a result of this law.

In 1941, President Roosevelt ordered Dr. Henry Field to produce—in the shortest time possible—a list of the full names and addresses of each American-born and foreign-born Japanese persons. They were to be listed by locality within each state, with the 1930 and 1940 census data being used to compile the list. Dr. Field was to contact J. C. Capt, the director of the Census in Suitland, Maryland to tabulate the data. A bank of IBM sorting machines was set up to extract the Orientals from each state from a pack of 110 million punch cards, which were then to be resorted to obtain the Japanese persons only. A total of 127,000 persons of Japanese descent were obtained, which were then turned over to the FBI, the state governors and the military commanders of each state.

Events After the Attack on Pearl Harbor

The attack on Pearl Harbor, Hawaii in 1941, led to a suspicion that Japan was preparing a full-scale attack on the West Coast of the United States. Civilian and military officials had concerns about the loyalty of the ethnic Japanese, although these concerns seemed to stem more from racial prejudice rather than from actual risk. General John DeWitt sought approval to conduct search and seizure operations aimed at preventing alien Japanese from making radio transmissions to Japanese ships. The DOJ declined the request stating that there was no probable cause to support General DeWitt's assertion, especially since the FBI had concluded that there was no security threat.

California Attorney General Earl Warren had begun efforts to persuade the federal government to remove all people of Japanese heritage from the West Coast. The California government dismissed all Japanese-American employees, as did the city of Sacramento. Presidential proclamations were issued designating Japanese, German and Italian nationals as enemy aliens. Information from the Custodial Detention Index was used to locate and incarcerate foreign nationals from Japan, Germany and Italy. Those who were as little as 1/16 Japanese could be placed in internment camps, and even orphaned infants who had a trace of Japanese lineage were included in the program.

President Roosevelt's Executive Order and Other Edicts

The Roberts Commission Report, prepared at President Franklin Roosevelt's request sought to link Japanese-Americans with espionage activity, and to associate them with the bombing of Pearl Harbor. A Presidential Proclamation was issued requiring aliens to report any change of address, employment or name to the FBI. Enemy aliens were not allowed to enter restricted areas, and violators of these regulations were subject to arrest, detention and internment for the duration of the war.

An executive order by President Franklin Roosevelt allowed authorized army commanders to designate military areas at their discretion from which any or all persons could be excluded. These exclusion zones were applicable to anyone that an authorized military commander might choose, whether that person was a citizen or a non-citizen. This power was used to declare that all people of Japanese ancestry were excluded from the entire Pacific coast, including all of California and most of Oregon and Washington.

General John DeWitt issued a public proclamation that declared that such person or classes of persons as the situation may require would be subject to exclusion orders from the entire Pacific coast to about 100 miles inland, and it required anyone who had Japanese ancestry to file a Change of Residence Notice if they planned to move. A second exclusion zone was also designated to further restrict the areas where Japanese-Americans were allowed.

Another executive order by President Roosevelt created the Office of the Alien Property Custodian, and gave it discretionary as well as plenary authority over all alien property interests. Many assets were frozen, creating immediate financial difficulty for the affected aliens, and preventing most of them from moving out of the exclusion zones.

A public proclamation by General DeWitt declared a curfew extending from 8:00 PM to 6:00 AM for all enemy aliens and all persons of Japanese ancestry within the military areas. This nighttime curfew was the first mass-action restricting Japanese-Americans. General DeWitt issued still another proclamation that prohibited all those of Japanese ancestry from leaving military areas for any purpose until and to the extent that a future proclamation or order of this headquarters shall so permit or direct.

General DeWitt issued a Civilian Exclusion Order, ordering all people of Japanese ancestry, whether citizens or non-citizens, who were still living in military areas to report to assembly centers, where they would live until being moved to permanent Relocation Centers. These edicts included persons of part-Japanese ancestry as well. Anyone with at least 1/8 Japanese ancestry was eligible. Korean-Americans were considered to have Japanese nationality since Korea was occupied by Japan, and they were also included.

Exclusion, Removal, and Detention

Approximately 117,000 people of Japanese ancestry were subject to the mass exclusion program, of whom two-thirds were United States citizens. The remaining one-third were non-citizens subject to internment under the Alien Enemies Act. Many of these resident aliens had long been inhabitants of the United States, but had been deprived of the opportunity to attain citizenship by laws that blocked Asian-born nationals from ever achieving citizenship. People of Japanese descent were removed from their homes by the United States Army in California, Oregon, Washington and Arizona as part of the single largest forced relocation in United States history. However, in the other 44 states, Japanese-Americans were allowed to remain in their homes, and many of them worked in production plants in support of the war effort.

Since the Japanese-Americans living in the restricted zone were considered too dangerous to freely conduct their daily business, the military decided it was necessary to find temporary civilian assembly centers to house the evacuees until the relocation centers were completed. The temporary Civilian Assembly Centers' were operated by the Wartime Civil Control Administration where most awaited transfer to more permanent relocation centers that were being constructed by the War Relocation Authority, a civilian agency that was set up to work with the military to carry out the relocation. The Civilian Assembly Centers were frequently located at horse tracks, where the Nisei were sent as they were removed from their communities. Eventually, most were sent to relocation centers, which became known as internment camps. Most of these internment camps were placed on Native American reservations, for which the Native Americans were compensated.

Hawaii Internments

Although there was a strong push to remove and intern all Japanese-Americans and Japanese immigrants in Hawaii, it never occurred. Only 1,800 Japanese nationals and Japanese-Americans from Hawaii—mostly community leaders and prominent politicians—were interned, either in two camps on Oahu or in one of the mainland internment camps. The vast majority of Japanese-Americans and their immigrant parents in Hawaii were not interned because the government had already declared martial law in Hawaii, and this allowed it to significantly reduce the risk of espionage and sabotage by residents of Japanese ancestry. Also, Japanese-Americans comprised over 35% of Hawaii's population, with approximately 160,000 inhabitants—one-third of the population in the islands. Detaining so many people would have been an enormous job in terms of logistics so the War Department concluded that it was impractical due to shipping difficulties and labor shortages. The whole of Hawaiian society was dependent on Japanese productivity, and 5 wealthy families who controlled Hawaii's economy opposed the measure since their sugar cane and pineapple plantations were worked by Japanese field workers. The internment of Japanese-Americans was applied unequally in Hawaii as compared to the rest of the United States—even though they were a lot closer to Japan than the Japanese-Americans on the West Coast.

There were 5 internment camps in Hawaii, all of them being Army facilities. One of the camps was located at Sand Island, Oahu. All prisoners held there were detained under military custody because of the imposition of martial law throughout the Islands. Another Hawaiian camp was the Honouliuli Internment Camp near Ewa, Oahu. The other 3 sites were located at Kilauea Military Camp on Hawaii, Haiku Internment Camp on Maui, and the Kalaheo Stockade on Kauai.

Other Detention Camps

In 1939, when armed conflict by Japan started in East Asia, the FBI and other branches of the DOJ and the armed forces began to collect information and surveillance on influential members of the Japanese community in the United States. After the Pearl Harbor attacks by Japan in 1941, President Roosevelt authorized his attorney general to put into motion a plan for the arrest of individuals on the potential enemy alien lists. Armed with a blanket arrest warrant, the FBI seized these men in 1941. These men were held in municipal jails and prisons until they were moved to DOJ detention camps, separate from those of the WRA. These camps operated under far more stringent conditions and were subject to heightened criminal-style guard, despite the absence of criminal proceedings. The DOJ camps were guarded by Border Patrol agents and were intended for non-citizens.

Detention camps housed Nikkei who were considered to be disruptive or of special interest to the government. Over 2,200 Japanese-Americans and Japanese from 13 Latin American countries were rounded up, transported to the United States and held in internment camps run by the DOJ. 2,500 of these Latin American internees were eventually offered parole relocation to the labor-starved farming community in Seabrook, New Jersey. Many of them became naturalized American citizens after the war.

Citizen isolation centers were set up for those Japanese who were considered to be problem inmates. Detainees who had been convicted of crimes—usually draft resistance—were sent to federal prisons. Some United States Army facilities were used to hold German and Italian detainees as well as Japanese-Americans. Still other camps were used to hold internees. Canadian citizens with Japanese ancestry were also interned by the Canadian government. Forced evacuation and incarceration occurred in Haiti and the Dominican Republic. The internments were not limited to the Japanese as several thousand Americans of German and Italian ancestry as well as Aleutian Island natives in Alaska were classified as enemy aliens and forced to move.

Conditions in the Camps

Japanese internees were housed in tar paper-covered barracks of simple frame construction without plumbing or cooking facilities of any kind. The spartan facilities were based on designs for military barracks, making the buildings poorly equipped for cramped family living. The relocation centers had a barbed-wire-surrounded enclave with un-partitioned toilets, cots for beds, and a budget of 45 cents daily per capita for food rations. Most of the internees lived in 20- by 25-foot apartments that were constructed from real thin materials.

Internees were typically allowed to stay with their families. Because most internees were evacuated from their West Coast homes on short notice and not told of their assigned destinations, many failed to pack appropriate clothing for winters and only took the clothes that they were wearing. In the camps that were in cold areas, temperatures sometimes fell below zero degrees Fahrenheit. A number of persons died or suffered for lack of medical care and inadequate medical facilities as evacuee doctors and nurses worked with minimal equipment and supplies. They were treated as prisoners of war, with no means of appeal.

Psychological injury was incurred by Japanese-Americans who grew increasingly depressed and fearful, experienced monotony, and who were overcome with feelings of helplessness and personal insecurity. Internees were also pressured to use the English language, and to adopt American customs and values. The worst part was seeing their children grow up behind barbed wire and under the scrutiny of armed guards.

Several protests, riots and strikes occurred over living conditions. Armed guards were posted at the camps, with gun emplacements that were pointed inward towards the inmates. There were instances of guards shooting at internees who attempted to walk outside the fences, and several were killed by these sentries—although some camp administrations eventually allowed relatively free movement outside the marked boundaries of the camps.

The worst incident occurred at the internment camp in Tule Lake, California in 1943, when an internee was killed by the guards. Protests were formed and a work strike was called by the internees. The mass demonstration of 5,000 men, women and children greeted National Director Dillon Myer when he visited the site, charging the government with neglect, incompetence and corruption. Army troops armed with tanks, security patrols and FBI agents surrounded the camp, with the protest receiving wide media coverage throughout the nation. Tear gas was used on the crowd, all activities within the camp ceased, and many were arrested and held in the prison stockade where they were kept away from their families and denied medical attention. The army continued its takeover of the Tule Lake facility for the next 6 months, censoring any written accounts by the internees of the incident.

Loyalty Questions and Segregation

Some Japanese-Americans questioned the American government after finding themselves confined in internment, and several pro-Japan groups formed inside the camps. Questionnaires were distributed by the government to everyone to determine their loyalty. The government passed a law that made it possible for an internee to renounce their American citizenship, and 8,000 internees opted to do so. Of those who renounced their citizenship, 1,300 were repatriated to Japan. Many of these individuals would later face stigmatization in the Japanese-American community after the war for having made that choice, although at the time they were not certain what their futures held were they to remain American and interned.

The renunciations had little to do with loyalty or disloyalty to the United States, but were instead the result of a series of complex conditions and factors that were beyond the control of those involved. Prior to discarding citizenship, most of those who renounced their citizenship had experienced the forced removal from homes, loss of jobs, government and public assumption of disloyalty to the land of their birth based on race alone, were subjected to degrading interrogation by the FBI, were terrorized by guards at the camps, and were incarcerated in a segregation center for disloyal Issei or Nisei.

Many of the deportees were Issei who often had difficulty with English and often did not understand the questions that they were asked. Even among those Issei who had a clear understanding were faced with an awkward dilemma: Japanese immigrants were denied United States citizenship at the time, so when asked to renounce their Japanese citizenship, answering "Yes" would have made them stateless persons. However, answering "No" resulted in their being segregated, mostly to the Tule Lake facility, which was a maximum-security center. More than 12,000 Japanese-Americans were sent there, out of which 8,000 renounced their American citizenship and were transported to Japan.

Draft Resistance

When the government circulated a questionnaire seeking army volunteers from among the internees, 33,000 of military-aged male respondents volunteered to serve in the United States Armed Forces—with a promise to restore their rights as American citizens. 20,000 Japanese-American men and many Japanese-American women served in the United States Army. Included in this group were 1,300 Nisei who were former members of the Territorial National Guard in Hawaii and who were sent to Wisconsin for training, as well as 1,500 who volunteered from the Hawaiian Islands to form the 442nd Infantry Regimental Combat Team.

Some of the Nisei proclaimed that the United States government had abridged their rights without due process of law, and that Nisei should cease pursuing appeasement. They formed a Fair Play Committee and maintained that if the government restored their full citizenship rights, they would then comply with selective service requirements. 63 Nisei members from the Heart Mountain internment camp refused to take the military pre-induction physicals for the draft. A federal grand jury indicted all of the resisters. They were tried in Cheyenne, Wyoming, and were found guilty, and each one was sentenced to

3 years in a federal penitentiary, with 30 of them being sent to the McNeil Island Federal Penitentiary in Washington state, and the rest being sent to Leavenworth Federal Penitentiary in Kansas. Seven members who were the leaders of the Fair Play Committee were indicted by the same grand jury, and were tried for conspiring to violate the Selective Service Act, and for counseling Nisei to resist military induction. The 7 leaders of the Fair Play Committee were found guilty, and were sentenced to 4 years at Leavenworth Federal Penitentiary in Kansas.

An appeal was filed on behalf of the 63 Nisei members, but the Appellate Court upheld the convictions. The case was then appealed to the Supreme Court, which refused to review it. Each of the resisters served 27 months of the 3-year sentence. It was not until 1947 that President Harry Truman granted a Presidential Pardon to 315 Nisei draft resisters. All political and civil rights were restored, and their prison records were cleared.

The End of Internment

In 1945, the federal exclusion order was rescinded. The internees left the camps to rebuild their lives at home, although the relocation camps remained open for residents who were not ready or able to make the move back. The freed internees were given $25 and a train ticket to their former homes. While the majority returned to their former lives, some of the Japanese-Americans immigrated to Japan. The last internment camp was not closed until 1946. Japanese taken by the United States from Peru that were being held in the camp in Santa Fe, New Mexico took legal action in 1946 to avoid deportation to Japan.

The Japanese who returned to their pre-war homes often found them vandalized and even marred with racial epithets. Many farms and fields were in shambles from neglect or were lost to new owners. Many internees lost personal property due to the restrictions as to what could be taken into the camps. These losses were compounded by theft and destruction of items placed in governmental storage. The challenges and burdens of resettlement after the internment were shouldered by the Nisei after the internment years. Having witnessed the sacrifices and losses of their Issei parents, the Nisei persevered as active citizens, determined to claim their rightful place in America. The pre-war Japanese-American communities, such as Little Tokyo in Los Angeles and Japantown in San Francisco, were greatly diminished in the post-war period. A significant number of Japanese-Americans chose i to resettle in the East Coast and Midwest states. Many Japanese-Americans faced housing and employment discrimination and were denied access to many recreational and retail services. Many had to start over with their lives, and often had to share housing with friends or relatives, seek rooms in boarding homes or cluster together in trailer parks. Many had to become migrant workers, taking on any jobs that they could find. Despite losses in property, businesses, homes, and communities, most Japanese-Americans rebuilt their lives. The Nisei raised their families, took care of their aging parents, and became active in schools and community activities. In 1959, under the Eisenhower administration, 5,000 Japanese-Americans who renounced their American citizenship during WWII, had their citizenship restored.

WWII—1942

War in Europe

German officials met to discuss the final and complete destruction of 11 million European Jews. The Germans wanted to persuade the European governments to cooperate in what they called the "Final Solution of the Jewish Question." Adolf Eichmann was chosen to carry out the systematic killing of Jews, which was formulated from Adolf Hitler's intent that no other solution existed for Jews—except for extermination. All over Europe Jews were rounded up for deportation, held in camps and then sent by train to 30 concentration camps such as Auschwitz where 6,000 to 16,000 Jews were gassed and burned on a daily basis.

Britain sent 211 bombers against Essen, Germany. The British also sent 234 bombers to strike at the German Baltic port of Lubeck. In response, 45 German bombers struck at Exeter, England, and then again with 60 more bombers. 150 German bombers also attacked Bath, England. The British response consisted of British bombers striking at Rostock, Germany. German bombers retaliated by striking Norwich and York, England. British bombers struck again at Rostock, Germany. More than 1,000 British bombers raided Cologne, Germany—a raid that resulted in the destruction of 250 factories and the loss of 600 acres of housing, making 40,000 people homeless.

An allied raid on Dieppe, France by British and Canadian commandos resulted in 1,000 deaths for the Allies, with 2,000 being captured. The Germans only lost 345 men and had 4 soldiers captured. American bombers raided German positions around Rouen, France. British bombers struck at Dusseldorf, Germany, using 2-ton "block-buster" bombs. British bombers also struck at the naval installations at Naples, Italy, and sank the cruiser *Muzio Attendolo*. British bombers again attacked Dusseldorf, Germany

The Russian Front

Germany's armies suffered a severe winter from 1941 to 1942, and it led to setbacks. The intense fighting plus the snow and bitter cold resulted in a loss of over 1 million casualties for the Germans, just a few months since their assault on Russia had begun. The retreating German forces found themselves 75 miles away from Moscow.

Because there were not enough replacements to make up for these losses, Hitler was forced to rely on Mussolini for help. Augmented by Italian as well as Hungarian and Rumanian troops, German forces were able to reach the outskirts of Stalingrad in 1942. However, Russia still had 1.5 million troops in the north and 500,000 men in the Caucasus region, and they were able to keep the Axis forces in check.

German, Italian and Rumanian forces defeated Soviet forces in the Kerch Peninsula and at Kharkov, and launched an offensive to seize the oil fields of the Caucasus. The Soviets made a stand at Stalingrad, which German forces almost took. A blizzard occurred as

Russian troops mounted an offensive. They surrounded the German Sixth Army at Kalach, which was 40 miles from Stalingrad, and cut it off from being reinforced, nullifying 200,000 German soldiers. The Russian army also broke through the Italian Eighth Army to the North and the Rumanian Third Army to the South.

Africa

In North Africa, the Germans launched an offensive, pushing the British back to positions at the Gazala Line. German General Erwin Rommel struck with his Afrika Corps to drive the British back to the Egyptian border, and marched his troops to within 65 miles of Alexandria, Egypt. Germany captured Libya from the British. But, since General Rommel did not receive any critical supplies or reinforcements, Britain was able to retain Malta and drive off the German Luftwaffe bombers. Three-quarters of General Rommel's supplies were destroyed just as his forces were within sight of the Pyramids in Egypt. The British army stopped the German assault at El Alamein. With no reserves of men, oil or tanks, and with the strafing and bombing of his troops by the British Royal Air Force, General Rommel was forced to retreat. The British then recaptured Libya.

German forces withdrew to Fuka, which was 40 miles away from Alexandria, Egypt. The German forces further retreated to Benghazi, Libya, which was 700 miles away from where General Rommel had started his original advance. His losses were 59,000 men killed, wounded or captured. General Dwight Eisenhower's American and British troops landed at the beaches of Morocco and Algeria with over 100,000 men. Hitler only managed to seize Tunisia by sending 250,000 German and Italian troops.

Naval Actions

German U-boats continued their assault on British and American shipping by sinking more than 700,000 tons of ships—more than could be replaced by the shipyards of the United States, Canada and Scotland. The British merchant ship *Cyclops* was torpedoed off the eastern seaboard of the United States, and 46 Allied merchant ships representing almost 200,000 tons of ships and supplies were sunk off the American coast by German submarines that operated in the Caribbean sea. German submarines sunk a total of 377 merchant ships.

American aircraft carriers launched air strikes on the Japanese Marshall Island bases of Kwajalein, Wotje and Maloelap. The aircraft carrier *Enterprise* was damaged by a Japanese torpedo bomber, but was not sunk. The British submarine *Trident* torpedoed the German cruiser *Prinz Eugen*, killing 50 crewmen and workers.

5 Japanese aircraft carriers in the Indian Ocean sank 3 British cruisers and the destroyer *Tenedos*, killing more than 500 men. The Japanese also bombed the British aircraft carrier *Hermes* and the destroyer *Vampire*, killing 300 men. They sank 23 merchant ships comprising 112,000 tons.

16 American bombers took off from the aircraft carrier *Hornet* and bombed oil and naval installations in Tokyo, Kobe, Yokohama, Nagoya and Yokosuka, with the Japanese aircraft carrier *Ryuho* being hit. At the Battle of the Coral Sea, 70 Japanese aircraft and 66 American planes were shot down in a series of battles fought from aircraft carriers. The American aircraft carrier *Lexington* was badly damaged while the Japanese lost the aircraft carrier *Shoho*. At the Battle of Midway, American bombers destroyed 4 Japanese aircraft carriers. The American aircraft carrier *Yorktown* was also sunk by a Japanese submarine. The Japanese lost 332 aircraft and 30,000 men while the Americans lost 150 aircraft and 7,100 men.

In the Battle of Savo Island, the Japanese forces defeated the Allied forces. One Australian and 3 American cruisers were sunk. The Allied warships and the amphibious force then withdrew from the Solomon Islands. Japanese submarines in the New Hebrides sank the American aircraft carrier *Wasp* and badly damaged the battleship *North Carolina*. At the Battle of Santa Cruz, the American aircraft carrier *Hornet* was sunk and the aircraft carrier *Enterprise* was damaged by Japanese aircraft. At the Battle of Guadalcanal, the United States Fleet destroyed the Japanese fleet by sinking 28 warships and transports.

Far East Operations

Japan invaded the Solomon Islands. Japan also conquered Burma, Malaya, the Dutch East Indies and Singapore. The Japanese had captured Manila, and had also pushed the American and Filipino troops back to the Bataan Peninsula in the Philippines, capturing 76,000 men of whom 12,000 were Americans. The prisoners were marched 65 miles from Mariveles to San Fernando in what became known as the "Bataan Death March" in which 5,000 Filipinos and 600 Americans perished. The survivors were then put into trucks and railroad cars and moved to central Luzon to Camp O'Donnell. Of those who arrived in the prisoner-of-war camps, 16,000 Filipinos and 1,000 Americans died of dehydration, malnutrition, malaria, beriberi, scurvy and dysentery. They were also subjected to extreme brutality that fostered hopelessness in the survivors. Japanese forces landed on Corregidor in the Philippines where the remaining American troops surrendered to the Japanese.

Japan tried to capture Port Mores with an amphibious assault to sever the line of communications between the United States and Australia. The Allies turned back the Japanese naval forces, thus preventing the invasion. The Japanese landed 1,800 men on the islands of Kiska and Attu in the Aleutian chain. Japan then tried to seize the Midway Atoll in an attempt to lure American aircraft carriers into battle so they could be eliminated. The Americans, having broken Japanese naval codes, were aware of the plans and used this critical knowledge to achieve a decisive victory over the Japanese Navy in the Battle of Midway, and they sank 4 Japanese aircraft carriers.

Japan made an attempt to capture Port Moresby by an overland campaign with 16,000 troops in the Territory of Papua, New Guinea, landing at Buna and Gona. The Americans planned a counterattack against Japanese positions in the Solomon Islands, primarily

Guadalcanal by landing 16,000 troops there, as a first step towards capturing Rabaul, the main Japanese base in Southeast Asia. In the fighting, the Japanese won the Battle of Savo Island by sinking 3 American cruisers and one Australian cruiser—with the loss of over 1,000 men.

The battle for Guadalcanal took priority for the Japanese, and troops in New Guinea were ordered to withdraw from the Port Moresby area to the Northern part of Guadalcanal. Guadalcanal became a focal point for both sides with many troops and ships being involved in a battle of attrition. Three American cruisers were sunk, plus one Australian ship. Over 9,000 Japanese soldiers were killed while the American forces lost 1,600 men.

The Japanese attempted to land 10,000 additional men on Guadalcanal, but their effort was stopped by American ships. The Americans lost 2 cruisers, but the Japanese suffered the loss of 2 battleships, a cruiser and 2 destroyers. The Japanese tried again to reinforce their garrison at Guadalcanal and sank the American warship *Juneau*, sank one cruiser, and damaged 3 other cruisers. However, the Japanese transports were forced to turn back.

WWII—1943

War in Europe

An American bombing raid took place at Wilhelmshaven, Germany. Sicily, Italy was invaded by 160,000 Allied troops commanded by General Eisenhower and led by General Patton. With 2,500 ships, 600 tanks and many airplanes, several cities were captured, and Sicily fell to the Allies. 500 American bombers also raided targets in Rome. The Allies lost 25,000 men during the assault while the German and Italian forces lost 167,000 men. Allied forces invaded mainland Italy at Messina, and Italy surrendered— with the ouster and arrest of Premier Mussolini.

Bombing raids by 2,000 Allied bombers were made against Nuremberg. Raids by American bombers were made at Kiel and Dortmund, and British bombers conducted a raid at Friedrichshafen that destroyed an assembly factory of V-2 rockets. More bombing raids were conducted at Hamburg that created a firestorm that killed 42,000 German civilians and left 118,000 of them homeless. The Allies bombed oil fields at Ploesti, Romania, putting 40% of them out of business.

600 British Royal Air Force bombers attacked and badly damaged the V-1 and V-2 rocket construction center at Peenemunde, killing 130 German scientists, engineers and technicians. The British bombed and destroyed 63 more launching sites for the V-1 and V-2 rockets. American bombers struck at Wiener Neustadt in Austria, and also at the German launching site at Eperclecques on the Channel coast.

376 American B-17 Fortress bombers raided the ball bearing plant at Scheinfurt, Germany and an aircraft factory at Regensburg, Germany, but lost 62 aircraft and more than 100 airmen. A British bomber raid over Kassel, Germany destroyed German aircraft and rocket production facilities, and created a firestorm that killed 5,300 civilians. 160 American bombers struck Vermork, Norway and destroyed a hydroelectric power station that was producing heavy water for the German nuclear effort. British bombers raided Berlin, Germany, killing more than 3,000 civilians as well as destroying a tank factory.

The Russian Front

250,000 German troops surrendered to the Soviet Army at Stalingrad, marking the beginning of their retreat. German forces made their last massive attack in Russia at Kursk with 500,000 troops and 17 panzer divisions against a force of 1 million Russian soldiers. The Germans lost one-half of their tanks, and were then confronted with a Russian offensive that drove them out of Orel. The Russians reclaimed Kharkov and Smolensk, and retook Kiev.

Far East

A combined American and Australian attack on Sanananda, New Guinea resulted in 3,000 Japanese being killed. The Japanese were defeated in Guadalcanal and withdrew their troops, losing 9,000 men compared to 2,000 Americans being killed. 188 Japanese warplanes attacked Tulagi and sank the American destroyer *Aaron Ward* and the New Zealand corvette *Moa*. They also attacked Port Moresby.

American forces were sent to land on Attu Island to eliminate Japanese forces from the Aleutians by retaking Kiska Island. The Japanese cruiser *Nachi* and the American cruiser *Salt Lake City* were both badly damaged in the encounter. Soon after the United States began major operations to isolate Rabaul by capturing surrounding islands, and to breach the Japanese perimeter at the Gilbert and Marshall Islands.

At Wewak, New Guinea United States Air Force planes disabled or destroyed 300 Japanese planes, killing 1,500 Japanese pilots and ground crew personnel. United States Marines landed on Bougainville Island in the Solomon Islands. United States Army troops also landed on Makin Island in the Gilbert Islands, with the Marines landing on Tarawa. Both islands were secured, but at the cost of almost 1,100 casualties and over 2,200 wounded for the Americans. American bombers then attacked Formosa and New Guinea. 25,000 Indian prisoners of war held by the Japanese agreed to fight against the British when they were liberated.

Africa

General Rommel and his Afrika Corps defeated American forces at the Kasserine Pass in Tunisia, with the Americans losing 3,000 men and losing 3,000 more to captivity. However, at the Battle of El Guettar Valley in Tunisia, the Americans were victorious under the leadership of General George Patton. When German forces ran out of fuel, the American troops were able to capture Bizerte while the British troops captured Tunis, thus driving German and Italian troops from Tripoli. A total of 250,000 German and Italian troops surrendered to the Allies, with another 250,000 being casualties.

Naval Actions

137 American and Australian fighter planes attacked a Japanese convoy in the Battle of the Bismarck Sea off New Guinea, sinking 8 transports and 4 destroyers while shooting down 25 Japanese planes—with a loss of 3,500 Japanese troops who drowned in the attacks. British destroyers sank the Italian merchant ship, the *Campobasso*, which was taking military supplies in the battle for Tunis. American bombers also sank a second merchant ship, the *San Antonio* that was bringing supplies for the fight in Tunis. American B-24 planes destroyed 43 German U-boats.

WWII—1944

War in Europe

36,000 Allied troops with 3,200 vehicles landed at Anzio, Italy, and captured Rome, Florence and Pisa.

At Lake Tinnsjo, Norway, Norwegian saboteurs blew up the ferryboat *Hydro*, which was carrying the last of Germany's existing supply of heavy water that was needed for their nuclear research.

British and American air forces began an assault of the German Luftwaffe. They destroyed 1,300 German planes, then 2,100 more, and then an additional 2,115. The Allies also began a massive bombing campaign against Germany, especially against aircraft and ball bearing factories as well as port installations within the Brussels-Rostock-Pola triangle area.

German troops occupied Hungary.

The Allied invasion of German-occupied Western Europe called D-Day began on the 5 beaches of Normandy, France. The Allies liberated Cherbourg, France—but at the cost of 22,000 casualties, then they liberated Caen, and finally liberated Paris. Later, they liberated Boulogne and Calais.

The Allies liberated Brussels and Antwerp, Belgium.

The Germans launched the first V-1 rocket to England. Later, the Germans launched the first V-2 rocket to England.

German military leaders attempted to kill Adolf Hitler, but failed.

The Allies entered Germany and captured Aachen. Allied forces launched an airborne assault with 80,000 troops in Arnhem, Holland, but it resulted in failure as 6,000 Allied men were taken prisoner by German forces numbering 250,000 soldiers. More than 19,000 American soldiers and 40,000 German soldiers were killed in the battle.

The Allies entered Greece, and liberated Athens. Later, the Axis forces in Greece surrendered.

Allied forces captured Strasbourg, Germany. Germany launched its last offensive in the Ardennes, thus beginning the Battle of the Bulge. American troops held on to Bastogne, stalling the German offensive. British air raids firebombed oil targets at Heilbronn, Germany in which almost 7,150 German civilians were killed.

The Russian Front

The Russian army crossed the Polish border and captured Rokitno. The German siege of Leningrad ended, and the last German forces at Korsun were destroyed. The Russian Army retook Odessa and Minsk, capturing more than 2,000 tanks and 150,000 German soldiers. The Soviets mounted a massive counter-offensive and expelled Axis forces from the Soviet Union. They then made incursions into Romania.

The Soviet Union bombed Stockholm, Sweden and Helsinki, Finland.

The Soviets launched a strategic offensive in Belarus that resulted in the complete destruction of the German Army that was there. Another Soviet major strategic offensive forced the German troops from the Ukraine and Eastern Poland. The Soviet Union invaded Romania and caused their surrender. The Soviet Union invaded Bulgaria and caused their surrender also. Soviet Union troops entered Yugoslavia and East Prussia. The Soviet army attacked Budapest, Hungary and captured the city.

Allied forces captured Albania.

Far East

Americans made another seaborne landing at Saidor, New Guinea to attack the Japanese. The Japanese lost 1,275 soldiers, but lost 10,000 more as 20,000 of them retreated through the jungle.

American forces landed at 3 of the Marshall Islands with almost 3,750 Japanese being killed at Roi and Namu, and 7,870 Japanese being killed at Kwajalein. At Eniwetok Island in the Marshall Islands, American forces overwhelmed the Japanese defenders, killing more than 2,600 of them.

American bombers and torpedo planes neutralized a major Japanese base on Truk in the Caroline Islands, destroying 15 Japanese warships, 25 merchant ships, and 265 aircraft.

The Japanese attacked Bougainville in the Solomon Islands, but were repelled by American forces, with 5,000 Japanese being killed. The Japanese also launched a major offensive against British positions in Assam, Imphal and Kohima, India.

American forces launched an attack to retake Western New Guinea by assaulting Hollandia and Aitape in which the Japanese lost over 12,800 men.

British forces repelled the Japanese assault at the Battle of Kohima, and stopped any further intrusions by the Japanese.

An American air raid was done at the iron and steel works at Yawata, Japan.

American troops began an assault at Saipan in the Marianas against the Japanese. The Japanese surrendered at Saipan after losing 20,000 soldiers while the Americans suffered over 3,400 casualties. The Americans launched an assault at Guam and Tinian, with the recapture of Guam occurring after several thousand Japanese troops were killed at a cost of over 2,100 American men. Tinian was also captured by the Americans.

The Japanese conquered the province of Henan, China and begun a renewed attack against Changsha in the Hunan province.

British forces repelled the Japanese sieges in Assam, India.

The Japanese captured the city of Hengyang.

American troops landed on Morotai Island in the Moluccas. The Americans also landed on the Palau Islands in the Carolines, with the attack on Peleliu being the costliest amphibious attack, with 13,600 Japanese soldiers dying and over 9,100 Americans being killed. American bombers raided the Philippines and destroyed 405 Japanese aircraft and sank or damaged 103 ships.

More than 100,000 American soldiers landed on the East coast of Leyte Island, and 80,000 Japanese soldiers were killed at the cost of 3,500 American lives.

A massive American air raid on Formosa destroyed 500 Japanese aircraft and 40 Japanese warships. An American task force off Okinawa destroyed more than 100 Japanese aircraft. American B-29 bombers also began a massive bombing campaign against mainland Japan.

The Japanese invaded the province of Guangxi, winning major engagements against Chinese forces at Guilin and Liuzhou.

Naval Actions

The United States Navy defeated the Japanese in the Battle of the Philippine Sea in which more than 400 Japanese airplanes were destroyed, 3 aircraft carriers were lost, with 3 other aircraft carriers being damaged.

The United States Navy defeated the Japanese in the Battle of Leyte Gulf in the Philippines, sinking 36 Japanese warships. The American Navy suffered damages to the aircraft carrier *Intrepid* and 3 other carriers, damages to the battleship *Maryland*, damages to the destroyer *Aulick*, and they lost the aircraft carriers *Princeton* and *St Lo*, plus the cruiser *Birmingham*, the destroyer *Mahan* and the destroyer transport *Ward*.

Near the island of Mindoro, Japanese suicide pilots struck the American cruiser *Nashville* and the destroyer *Haraden*. A ferocious windstorm capsized 3 American destroyers, and killed 720 men.

D-Day: The Invasion of Europe

Overview

President Roosevelt and Prime Minster Churchill ordered the invasion of Normandy, with the agreement of Chief of Staff of the United States Army, George Marshall. Since the United States was supplying three-fourths of the total force, President Roosevelt appointed General Dwight Eisenhower as commander of the operation that would be known as Overlord. The British commander had been designated as General Frederick Morgan since 1943, but General Bernard Montgomery became the chief planner after he took command of the British Eighth Army. The landings in Normandy constituted the Allied invasion of Europe during WWII. The main landings began on June 6, 1944 on a day termed as "D-Day". The assault was conducted in 2 phases: an air assault landing of 24,000 Allied airborne troops who were transported by over 800 C-47 airplanes, and an amphibious landing of Allied infantry and armored divisions on the coast of France. There were also decoy operations that were conducted to distract the German forces from the real landing areas.

The operation was the largest, most difficult and very complicated amphibious invasion, with over 175,000 ground troops being involved. 195,700 Allied naval and merchant navy personnel aboard 6,900 vessels were involved as well as 11,000 airplanes. The invasion required the transport of soldiers and material from Britain by troop-laden aircraft and ships, and included assault landings, paratrooper landings, air fire support, naval interdiction of the English Channel and naval fire support. The landings took place along a 50-mile stretch of the Normandy, France coast that was strategically divided into 5 beach sectors named Utah, Omaha, Gold, Juno and Sword. 50,000 pieces of equipment were transported across the English Channel, including motorcycles, tanks, bulldozers and other types of vehicles—as well as all types of weapons, food, medicines, tents and other supplies.

155,000 British, Canadian and American troops landed on shore. Hitler, who was not convinced that the invasion was the real one, did not commit his full resources to confront the attack. The Allies continued to advance inland, with more than 325,000 Allied soldiers ashore. Eventually, 500,000 Allied soldiers were ashore, and by the end of the operation, nearly 1 million men were ashore linking the 5 beachheads along a 60-mile front that extended 20 miles inland. The human cost was over 6,000 Allied soldiers killed, 9,000 German casualties and 20,000 French civilians killed.

Prelude

German Defenses

In 1942, Hitler had directed that Atlantic coast defenses should be deployed to prevent any invasion from the sea—an Atlantic Wall. He further decreed that a continuous belt of interlocking bombproof concrete structures be erected along the French coast to place defensive armaments such as machine guns, mortar launchers and high-caliber weapon emplacements. Hundreds of thousands of slave laborers and prisoners of war were put to work to construct the Atlantic Wall—a 3,000-mile long stretch along the Atlantic Ocean consisting of fortified gun emplacements, radar installations, observation towers and bunkers that ran from Norway to the frontier of Spain. The strongest German defenses were built at Pas-de-Calais, France because it represented the shortest route between England and France across the English Channel.

Field Marshal General Erwin Rommel, who was in command of the English Channel defenses, had the waterline seeded with 6 million mines and 500,000 obstacles such as angled wooden stakes, concrete cones, logs, steel gates and jagged steel girder hedgehogs that were intended to either blow up landing craft—or tear their bottoms out. He dammed the rivers and let in the sea to flood large areas as a defense against paratrooper landings. The defenses also integrated the cliffs and hills overlooking the beaches, and included tank top turrets and the extensive laying of barbwire and trip wires in front of the hedgerows. General Rommel recognized that the Allies would possess air superiority and would be able to harass his troop movements from the air. He therefore proposed that the armored formations be deployed close to the invasion beaches. His strategy was that it was better to have one Panzer division facing the invasion on the first day, rather than 3 Panzer divisions 3 days later when the Allies would already have established a firm beachhead. He knew that fixed defenses would only hold up an assault, and that it would take a rapid counter attack to defend against the assault.

In contrast, General Von Geyr argued for Panzer formations to be concentrated in a central position around Paris and Rouen, and then deployed against the main Allied beachhead when this had been identified. The strategy difference was brought before Hitler for arbitration, and he imposed an unworkable compromise solution. Only 3 Panzer divisions were given to General Rommel, which were too few to cover all the threatened sectors. The remainder of the Panzers, nominally under General Von Geyr's control, were designated as being in reserve. Thus, only 3 of these Panzer units were deployed close enough to intervene immediately against any invasion of Northern France, while the other 4 Panzer units were dispersed in southern France and the Netherlands. Hitler reserved the authority to move the divisions in reserve, or to commit them to action. Thus, on June 6, 1944—when the invasion took place—many Panzer division commanders were unable to move because Hitler had not given the necessary authorization, and his staff refused to wake him up upon news of the invasion.

Allied Planning

The Allied plan was to first drop paratroopers at night behind the beaches to seize the roads and bridges, and to prevent the Germans from bringing up reinforcements. Then waves of warplanes were to bomb the German defense emplacements that overlooked the landing beaches. Finally, a massive flotilla was to ferry British and American troops to the assigned landing points on the 5 designated beaches. The First Army of the United States under the command of General Omar Bradley would assault the Utah and Omaha beaches. The British and Canadian units of the Second Army of Britain would make their way ashore at the Gold, Juno and Sword beaches.

To land the amphibian forces, landing ships were developed by the British called landing ship, tank (LST) and landing craft, tank (LCT), which were to be used for transporting the men from the ships to the shore. The LST was as big as a light cruiser that was flat-bottomed, with two bow doors that could open to the sides, and with a ramp to allow vehicles to drive to shore. The LCT was a flat-bottomed craft capable of carrying tanks and using a ramp to discharge the cargo on shore. Other vessels that were developed included landing craft, infantry (LCI) to carry about 200 infantry men; landing craft, medium (LCM), and landing craft, vehicle and personnel (LCVP). The Americans took over the task of building these boats.

Two months before the invasion began, General Eisenhower used bombers to destroy the French railway system. In what was referred to as the Transportation Plan, Allied airplanes strafed bridges, rail yards, sidings, stations, sheds, repair shops, roundhouses, turntables, signal systems, switches, locomotives and rolling stock. About 1,700 locomotives and 25,000 wagons were destroyed in the operation. However, the Allied air forces lost 12,000 men and 2,000 planes in doing so.

A week before the planned invasion, 255 minesweepers swept the English coast to clear the English Channel for the 5 separate assault forces. They also marked the areas with lighted buoys spaced at one-mile intervals to guide the ships. They also cleared the areas in which the transports would anchor off the designated beaches.

Initial Attempt

The invasion was set for June 5, 1944, but the weather deteriorated, and General Eisenhower decided to delay the attack for 24 hours because high winds and huge waves made it impossible to launch landing craft, and the low cloud cover prevented the support aircraft from finding their targets on the beaches. The whole convoy was ordered back to England after having traversed 80 miles when they were only 40 miles from the beaches at Normandy.

General Eisenhower conferred with high-ranking staff officers, and the decision to invade was split among his staff, but General Eisenhower's chief meteorologist forecast a brief improvement for June 6, 1944. On that basis General Eisenhower ordered the invasion to proceed.

Preliminary Attacks

Before the main invasion occurred, 18,000 British and American parachutists carried by C-47 transport planes landed in Normandy at midnight on June 6, 1944. Their job was to capture bridges, disrupt German communications, attack defense emplacements, and secure roads. Most of them were scattered over an area 25 miles long by 15 miles wide, with many of them not reaching their reporting points by dawn.

British Airborne Landings

The tactical objectives of the British 6th Airborne Division were as follows:

- To capture intact the bridges of the Bénouville-Ranville crossing
- To defend the crossing against the inevitable armored counter-attacks
- To destroy German artillery at the Merville battery, threatening Sword Beach
- To destroy 5 bridges over the Dives River to further restrict movement of German ground forces from the East.

7,000 paratroopers began landing at midnight on June 6, 1944, and immediately encountered elements of the German infantry. At dawn, a panzer division counter attacked from the South on both sides of the Orne River. By this time the paratroopers had established a defensive perimeter surrounding the bridgehead. Casualties were heavy on both sides, but the 6th Airborne Division troops held the line. Shortly after noon, they were reinforced by commandos, and by the end of D-Day, the 6th Airborne Division had accomplished each of its objectives. Both British and German forces took heavy casualties as they struggled for positions around the Orne River bridgehead. But, British paratroopers overwhelmed the entrenched mechanized infantry in the Battle of Breville. The Germans did not seriously threaten the bridgehead again, and the 6th Airborne Division remained there until it was evacuated.

American Airborne Landings

The 13,400 American paratroopers of the 82nd and 101st Airborne Divisions were less fortunate than the British in completing their main objectives. Numerous factors affected their performance, the primary one being the decision to make the parachute drop at night. As a result, almost one-half of the units were widely scattered and were unable to rally. Efforts of the teams to mark the landing zones were largely ineffective, and the transponding radar beacon systems that were used to guide the 882 C-47 airplanes to the drop zones were flawed.

Three regiments of 101st Airborne paratroopers were dropped first, followed by the 82nd Airborne's drops. Two pre-dawn glider landings brought in anti-tank guns and support troops for each division. On the evening of D-Day 2 additional glider landings brought in 2 battalions of artillery and 24 howitzers to the 82nd Airborne. Additional glider operations delivered the 325th Glider Infantry Regiment to the 82nd Airborne. Still, many of the gliders overshot their open field targets, and landed in the woods or crashed into farmhouses and stone walls.

After 24 hours, only 2,500 troops of the 101st Airborne and 2,000 of the 82nd Airborne were under the control of their divisions, approximately only one-third of the total force that was dropped. The dispersal of the American airborne troops, however, had the effect of confusing the Germans and fragmenting their response. The Germans' defensive flooding also helped to protect the Americans' Southern flank. Paratroopers continued to roam and fight behind enemy lines. Many consolidated into small groups, rallied with non-commissioned officers or junior officers, and became groups of men from different companies, battalions, regiments and divisions. The 82nd Airborne occupied the town of Sainte-Mere-Eglise—the first town that was liberated in the invasion.

The Main Invasion

The Air Bombardment

At dawn on D-Day, the greatest air armada ever assembled flew 3 missions consisting of 14,000 sorties. Their targets were the coastal batteries, but because of the weather—and not wanting to hit their own troops—many of the bombs landed in the meadows instead of on the Atlantic Wall emplacements. Although not one plane was shot down by the Luftwaffe, 113 of the Allied planes were downed by the German land flak batteries—in spite of throwing down foil strips to confuse the German radars.

The Naval Bombardment

The flotilla of cruisers, destroyers and battleships approached the shores of Normandy in preparation for launching the landing crafts that were to go ashore at dawn. A total of 6 battleships, 20 cruisers and 68 destroyers were part of the bombardment group to provide cover for the landings. The warships opened fire with salvos aimed at knocking out the German concrete gun emplacements. The fire support extended beyond the suppression of shore defenses that overlooked the landing beaches, and was also used to break up enemy concentrations of pillboxes, bunkers and redoubts as the troops moved inland.

Sword Beach

The assault on Sword Beach began with an aerial bombardment of the German coastal defenses and artillery sites followed by a naval bombardment that began a few hours later. The first units that reached the beach were the tanks followed closely by the infantry of 8th Brigade. The regular British infantry came ashore with very light casualties. They advanced 5 miles by the end of the day, but failed to make the targets that had been set by General Montgomery. Caen was still in German hands by the end of D-Day, and would remain so until the Battle for Caen that occurred later in 1944.

The 1st Special Service Brigade went ashore in the second wave led by commandos with French troops. The British and French had separate targets, one being a blockhouse and the Casino, and the other being two German batteries, which overlooked the beach. The blockhouse proved too strong for the commandos, but the Casino was taken. The British commandos achieved both battery objectives only to find the gun mounts empty and the guns removed. The commandos withdrew to join the other units of their brigade, moving inland to join the 6th Airborne Division.

Juno Beach

The Canadian forces landed on Juno Beach and faced 2 heavy batteries of guns, as well as machine-gun nests, pillboxes, other concrete fortifications, and a seawall. The first wave suffered 50% casualties. Despite the obstacles, the Canadians were off the beach within hours and began their advance inland. A single troop managed to reach the final objective, but then retreated, having outrun its infantry support. Two fortified positions remained in German hands, and no link could be established with Sword Beach. By the end of D-Day, 30,000 Canadians had landed, and the 3rd Canadian Infantry Division had penetrated further inland, despite having faced strong resistance at the water's edge and from counter attacks on the beachhead by the German panzer divisions.

Gold Beach

At Gold Beach, the casualties were very heavy because the Germans had strongly fortified a village on the beach. However, the 50th Infantry Division overcame these difficulties and advanced to the outskirts of Bayeux. The British commando unit landed and came ashore to proceed inland to make a 10-mile march to attack the coastal harbor of Port en Bessin.

Omaha Beach

The 1st and 29th Infantry Divisions of the United States faced a full complement of 3 German battalions—although they were at reduced strength. However, Allied intelligence was unaware that the complement of defenders had been doubled. Omaha was also the most heavily fortified beach, with high bluffs defended by mortars, machine guns, rifles and artillery. The aerial and naval bombardment of the bunkers proved to be ineffective since cloud cover impaired the American B-17s, with all of their bombs falling 3 miles inland—instead of on the beach or bluff. Difficulties in navigation caused the majority of landings to drift Eastwards, missing their assigned sectors and the initial assault waves of tanks, infantry and engineers took very heavy casualties.

Only a few gaps were blown in the beach obstacles, resulting in problems for subsequent landings. The heavily defended vehicular routes off the beach could not be taken and after the first assault the beach was closed for all but infantry landings. Commanders considered abandoning the beachhead, but small units of infantry supported by naval artillery and the surviving tanks eventually infiltrated the coastal defenses by scaling the bluffs between the strong points. Further infantry landings were able to take advantage of the initial penetrations and 2 isolated footholds were established. American casualties at Omaha Beach numbered 5,000, most of which occurred in the first few hours, while the Germans suffered 1,200 casualties. The beachhead was expanded, and the original D-Day objectives were accomplished within 3 days.

Utah Beach

American casualties on Utah Beach were light out of the 23,000 troops that landed. However, the 4th Infantry Division troops found themselves in the wrong positions because of a current that pushed their landing craft to the Southeast. They came ashore at a sector that was lightly defended, with relatively little German opposition. The 4th Infantry Division was able to press inland over beach exits that had been seized from the inland side by the 101st Airborne Division. The 4th Infantry Division succeeded in linking up with elements of the 101st Airborne Division, and the troops were able to press inward.

The German Response

The Germans noted the existing poor conditions, and believed that no invasion would be possible for several days. Some troops stood down, and many senior officers were away for the weekend. General Rommel took a few days' leave, and dozens of division, regimental, and battalion commanders were away from their posts.

There was no German counter attack since General Rommel's plans were never put in motion. The landings were a surprise, the Germans became confused as the day progressed, and the German command structure fell apart. General Gerd von Rundstedt ordered 2 panzer divisions to move out, which General Fritz Bayerlin had ready to move. But, General Alfred Jodl countermanded the order because it did not have Hitler's approval. Hitler slept until noon, and it was not until late in the day that Hitler finally authorized the movement of the 2 panzer divisions—and then they had to wait for the cover of darkness to avoid being bombed by Allied fighter and bomber planes. Hitler also ordered the launch of V-1 rockets to attack London, England—instead of aiming them where the invasion was happening on the Normandy beaches.

General Rommel did not get word of the attacks until late in the morning, and then had to drive all the way back to the Normandy coast—and reached it at night when the invaders were already past the beaches and moving inland. Without his command, the troops did not take the initiative—and the only existing command structure stayed in their headquarters throughout the day, awaiting orders from the high command to tell them what to do. The bulk of the German armor in France was still in place at the Pas-de-Calais area—waiting for the real invasion. The only German regimental commander at Normandy was Colonel Frederick von der Heydte—who spent most of the day on the defensive, holding crossroads and not being able to launch any counter attacks.

The German failure to fall back and regroup once the Allied forces had infiltrated the line was a major mistake. They could not form counter attacks against the Allied squads, platoons and companies that had made it through the obstacles. Instead, the Germans stayed in their fixed defenses trying to stop the invasion on the beaches. The Allies had constant reinforcements as the day progressed, and the Germans found themselves being surrounded and outnumbered.

The only challenge at sea came from 15 German motor torpedo boats at Utah beach, which sank the American destroyer *Nelson* and the Norwegian destroyer *Svenner*. All of the German *Kriegsmarine* submarines were either in their pens or out in the North Atlantic Ocean. German Admiral Theodor Krancke also canceled all of the German E-boat sea patrols because of the foul weather.

In the air, the German Luftwaffe was non-existent since all of the planes had been either transferred to Germany, redeployed elsewhere or grounded due to fuel shortages. Only one German reconnaissance plane circled the Allied ships—and then went home. Two other planes made an attack on the landings, but after only one pass they fled. There were 8 German bombers that appeared the next day, but by then it was too late.

The Germans intercepted and decoded the message that announced the time set for the Allied invasion of Normandy. Lieutenant Colonel Hellmuth Meyer picked up the messages going to the French underground and correctly interpreted them, warning that the invasion would take place within 48 hours. The message was delivered to General Alfred Jodl, but he did not order an alert since he assumed that Rundstedt had done so— who in turn thought that General Rommel's headquarters had already issued the alarm. Alerts by General Max Pemsel and Major Werner Pluskat were disregarded.

WWII—1945

War in Europe

The Battle of the Bulge ended, with the Americans suffering 77,000 casualties and the Germans losing 120,000 men from the 8 divisions that were thrown into the attack by Hitler. The Germans lost 600 tanks, 1,600 planes and 6,000 vehicles while the Americans lost over 730 tanks.

1,000 German fighters attacked Allied airfields in northern France, Belgium and Holland, destroying over 150 Allied aircraft—but suffered a loss of over 275 German planes. Germany also launched an attack with 18 divisions against the United States 6th Army in Alsace, France.

1,200 British and American bombers firebombed Dresden, Germany and killed over 135,000 Germans, burning over 11 square miles of the city.

Western Allied forces entered Germany and moved to the Rhine River. The Germans lost 350,000 men and the Americans captured almost 300,000 more, as well as their arms and equipment. The Western Allies crossed the Rhine and Ruhr Rivers, encircling a large number of German troops and overrunning the principal jet airfields at Darmstadt and Frankfort—although at the cost of over 20,300 American troops.

The Allies pushed forward in Italy and swept across Western Germany, linking up with the Soviet army on the Elbe River. Benito Mussolini was captured by Italian partisans while trying to escape into Switzerland, and was killed, with his body being strung up from a lamppost in Milan, Italy, and then being cut down into a gutter where vengeful Italians desecrated the body. The remaining German forces in Italy surrendered.

German forces launched their last counter attack on American forces at Uelzen, but were driven back by artillery, tanks and white phosphorous weapons. This was to be the last major battle for the German forces. Nuremberg, Germany fell to the American forces who took 17,000 prisoners. The Americans entered Munich, Germany while the Russians entered Berlin, Germany. The German forces at Baldham and at Rhodes surrendered to the Americans.

In Holland, German forces surrendered. 30,000 German troops on the Channel Islands surrendered.

The Russian Front

3 million German soldiers, 2,000 planes and 4,000 tanks faced 6 million Russian soldiers, 15,500 planes and 13,000 tanks. The Soviets attacked Poland and captured Warsaw, pushing from the Vistula River to the Oder River in Germany, and then overrunning East Prussia. German forces numbering 62,000 men surrendered in Budapest, Hungary after

losing almost 36,000 troops. The Soviets invaded Pomerania and Silesia, and advanced to Vienna, Austria.

Soviet forces went into Berlin, Germany with 3,000 tanks after firing more than 500,000 shells, rockets and mortar bombs. 60 German suicide planes crashed on the Oder River bridges in an attempt to close them, but they were powerless to halt the massive thrust of Soviet troops and armor. The Russian soldiers were savage in their conquest Berlin, and thousands of German women were raped during the conquest, with many of them committing suicide as a result.

Hitler had planned to leave Berlin and travel to Obersalzberg to direct the last stand in his mountain fortress at Barbarossa. Instead, he decided to stay and ordered an all-out counterattack on Russian forces in South Berlin—but German General Felix Steiner never attempted it. When he learned that the Russians had broken through, he gave up the struggle as the Russians made their way to the Chancellery. Chancellor Adolf Hitler committed suicide, and was succeeded by Admiral Karl Doenitz who had his headquarters in Schleswig, Germany. Admiral Doenitz surrendered empowering German Admiral Hans von Friedeburg to surrender to American General Dwight Eisenhower on May 7, 1945. Admiral Doenitz's government at Flensburg was then dissolved.

In Prague, Czechoslovakia the resistance of remnants of the German Army continued, but they surrendered after inflicting the deaths of 8,000 Soviet soldiers. The Germans launched their last counter attack against the Soviet Army near Wansen, Prussia, but were defeated in a fierce combat that resulted in over 470 Russian soldiers being killed. The German forces in Latvia also surrendered. Millions of Germans were expelled westward from Slavic regions as the Soviet army took control of these areas.

The Far East

Japan carried out kamikaze attacks on American ships off Luzon, hitting 53 ships and killing 625 sailors.

Americans landed on Luzon in the Philippines, and retook Manila and Mindanao. The battle for Mindanao cost the lives of more than 13,000 American soldiers.

British and Chinese forces defeated the Japanese in northern Burma, and the British pushed on to Rangoon. American forces also moved toward Japan, taking Iwo Jima. The victory was very costly, with over 6,800 American Marines being killed and 20,000 Japanese defenders perishing. 900 American sailors were killed when a kamikaze attack by a Japanese airplane sank the escort carrier *Bismarck Sea*.

American bombers firebombed Tokyo with napalm bombs and killed between 84,000 and 130,000 Japanese, burning an area of 16 square miles of the city. They destroyed the cities of Nagoya, Osaka, Kobe, Yokohama and Kawasaki. American submarines cut off Japanese imports by patrolling the various ports to ensure that no supplies reached inland.

American forces took Okinawa in one of the costliest battles of the war in the Pacific. More than 107,000 Japanese soldiers died while 20,000 of them were sealed in their caves by American assault teams who used flamethrowers and explosives. American losses were more than 7,600 on land and 4,900 at sea. The losses at sea were mainly due to Japanese suicide pilots who engaged in 1,900 kamikaze attacks, and who were aided by the battleship *Yamato* and the cruiser *Yahagi*, sinking 34 American warships, including the aircraft carrier *Bunker Hill*. 5,000 Japanese aircraft were shot down while the Americans lost more than 760 warplanes. 150,000 local Okinawan civilians were killed, and more than 250,000 people died during this battle.

A typhoon off Okinawa damaged 4 American battleships and 8 aircraft carriers. The battleship *Mississippi* and the cruiser *Louisville* were also damaged by Japanese kamikaze attacks.

Several thousand tons of napalm bombs were dropped by American bombers on Japanese forces on the island of Luzon in the Philippines.

American bombers attacked the Japanese Kure naval base and the airfields at Nagoya, Osaka and Mito. They destroyed 5 Japanese warships, including the aircraft carrier *Amagi* and the cruiser *Tone*. British bombers also attacked Japanese port and oil installations on Sabang Island of Sumatra.

Japanese leaders rejected the Potsdam Declaration, which outlined the terms for peace, and that threatened Japan with complete and utter destruction if it did not agree to an unconditional surrender. The American cruiser *Indianapolis* picked up the special weapon cargo at Hunter's Point, California and sailed to the South Pacific, arriving at Tinian Island with an atomic bomb on board.

The Soviet Union declared war on Japan and invaded Manchuria with a force of 1 million men who were pitted against 700,000 men of the Japanese army. Soviet forces occupied the Sakhalin and Kurile Islands. The Japanese forces continued the struggle, killing over 8,200 Soviet troops while losing 40,000 men.

American bombers dropped their bombs on Saga, Maebashi, Nishinomiya, Mikage, Ube and Imabari on mainland Japan.

The United States dropped the first atomic bomb in Hiroshima in which 80,000 people were killed instantly and 70,000 buildings were destroyed. A second atomic bomb was dropped in Nagasaki in which 40,000 people were killed instantly and 52,000 homes were destroyed.

800 American bombers struck at military installations on the island of Honshu with Torpex bombs. American bombers struck at military targets in Tokyo.

Japan surrendered after Emperor Hirohito cast the deciding vote to do so. Japanese civilian and military leaders signed the surrender agreement, ending the war in the Pacific.

The Japanese garrison at Marcus Island surrendered. The Japanese garrisons at Truk Island in the Carolines, Pagan and Rota in the Marianas, Palau, and Wake Island also surrendered.

Japanese soldiers continued to fight at Burma against the British, resulting in several hundred Japanese being killed—after the peace treaty had already been signed.

Japanese enclaves at Jesselton in Borneo surrendered. Japanese garrisons at Andaman and Nicobar Islands and Japanese naval forces at Mergui, Burma also surrendered. Further surrenders occurred from Japanese forces at Padang, Sumatra and Thaton, Burma.

Naval Actions

A Soviet submarine sank the German ship *Wilhelm Gustloff* in what was the deadliest sinking in maritime history. The sinking killed 10,000 people, most of whom were civilian refugees and wounded German soldiers.

Japanese flying bomb suicide attacks in the Kure-Kobe area damaged the American aircraft carriers *Enterprise* and the *Wasp*.

A German submarine sank 2 merchant ships in what was the last naval attack by the Germans. This ended the submarine war, which killed 27,500 German officers and sailors, caused the loss of 755 of German U-boats, but which sank 2,800 Allied merchant ships and 250 Allied warships.

WWII—Aftermath

The Vanquished

<u>Germany</u>

From Hitler's ascension to power, to the liquidation of Jews, and his assault on neighboring countries, events that culminated in WWII led to the devastation of Germany. Although the British limited the exodus to Palestine to only 13,000 Jews in 1945, almost 100,000 traveled there on their own by clandestine fashion to escape from Europe. The Jews were given a homeland in the Arab territory of Palestine in 1948 with the creation of Israel. In 1952, Germany agreed to pay 3 billion German marks to Israel, and 450 million German marks to Jewish organizations as reparations for the suffering of the Jews at the hands of the Nazis.

Eastern Germany became part of the Soviet bloc along with Poland, Czechoslovakia, Hungary, Yugoslavia, Romania, Bulgaria and Albania—although Yugoslavia broke away in 1948.

In 1955, the Federal German Republic became an independent nation. In the 1960s, Germany began to pay reparations to 11 states that had suffered from German occupation in accordance with the Global Accords of WWII. Germany did not fully recover from the devastation until 1980, and in the aftermath thousands of Germans died of starvation, disease and injuries.

In 1945, a war crimes trial began at Darmsadt for 11 persons accused of participating in the killing of 6 American airmen who had been shot down. 7 were found guilty and 5 of them were hanged.

In 1945, five Germans at Pentonville Prison in London, England were found guilty of the murder of a fellow prisoner, and were hanged. In France, the Nazi French Foreign Minister was found guilty of treason, and was shot by a French firing squad.

In 1945, the Nuremberg trials began to try 22 of the leading Nazis for war crimes, with one of them committing suicide in his cell before the trial began. 11 of remaining 21 were convicted and sentenced to death—with Hermann Goering committing suicide before he was to be hanged. 3 were given life sentences, 4 others were given substantial prison sentences, and 3 were acquitted. Two top Nazis were missing from the trial. One was Heinrich Himmler who had tried to escape in 1945, but was captured by the British—and in whose custody he committed suicide. The other was Martin Bormann who also attempted to escape in 1945, but who committed suicide to avoid being captured by the Russians.

In 1946, 23 physicians and scientists accused of carrying out medical experiments on inmates of concentration camps were also tried, with 16 being found guilty. 7 of them were sentenced to death by hanging, 5 were sentenced to life imprisonment, 2 were sentenced to imprisonment for 25 years, 1 to imprisonment for 15 years, 1 to imprisonment for 10 years, and 7 were acquitted.

In 1945, the trial for the Commandant, 40 guards and the civilian doctor of the Dachau Camp began. Dr. Klaus Schilling who conducted medical experiments was sentenced to death and hanged. At Hameln Prison, 4 Germans who had murdered Jewish children were hanged by the British after a separate trial.

In 1946, the Commandant of Auschwitz, Rudolph Hoess, was hanged. In 1946, 16 Belgians were executed for participating in sadistic tortures. In Prague, a former labor camp prisoner was hanged for cruelties that he perpetrated on his fellow prisoners.

In 1949, a German who had been responsible for shooting down in cold blood British prisoners of war, was tried and hanged at the Hamburg garrison prison. His deputy at the French Gestapo headquarters was found guilty of executing French paratroopers and was also executed.

A trial was held at Frankfurt, Germany between 1962 and 1965 for 20 SS officers who worked at the Auschwitz concentration camp during the war. 17 were convicted, but none received a death sentence.

Italy

Italy became a democratic republic in 1946. It lost its eastern border to Yugoslavia, and divided the territory of Trieste with Yugoslavia. Its government has undergone several changes in leadership throughout the years due to numerous economic crises that it has suffered.

Japan

Japan was devastated by the impact of 2 nuclear explosions. After the surrender of Japan, the nation was placed under Allied occupation. Some of its former military leaders were tried for war crimes before the Tokyo Tribunal, the government educational system was revised, and the tenets of democracy were written into the post-war Constitution of Japan. In 1945, the state Shinto religion was abolished, and in 1946, the Emperor issued an imperial rescript, and announced that he was not a divine being.

In 1946, the Tokyo War Crimes Tribunal was held to try the leaders of Japan who conspired to start and wage war. In 1948, 7 Japanese wartime leaders were sentenced to death and hanged while 16 others were given life imprisonment. 2 defendants died of natural causes during the trial.

The Soviet Union held the Khabarovsk War Crime Trials in which 12 Japanese Army officials were tried for using biological weapons. All 12 were found guilty and sentenced to terms ranging from 2 to 25 years in labor camps.

China conducted its own trials that resulted in 504 convictions and 149 executions.

The Victors

The Soviet Union and the United States emerged from the war as the world's two leading superpowers—a situation that set the stage for the Cold War, which lasted for 45 years.

The United Nations was formed in 1945 in the hopes of preventing another such widespread conflict. The self-determination spawned by the war accelerated decolonization movements in Asia, Africa, and Western Europe began moving towards integration into a union.

The Soviet Union, Britain and France became nuclear powers. The United States moved from 19th place as a military power in 1940 to the most powerful country in 1945. New alliances emerged, with the West forming the North Atlantic Treaty Organization (NATO), and the East creating the Warsaw Pact.

The alliance between the United States and the Soviet Union deteriorated, and the 2 powers established their own spheres of influence. In Europe, the continent was divided by the Soviet "Iron Curtain", which partitioned Germany and Austria.

In Asia, the United States administrated Japan's former islands in the Western Pacific while the Soviets annexed the Sakhalin and the Kuril Islands.

Other Events

Europe

In Greece, civil war broke out between royalist forces and communist forces, with the royalist forces being victorious. Since that time, Greece has experienced much political turbulence and economic downturns.

The East

India broke away from British rule and became an independent country in 1947. However, due to ethnic and religious reasons, two parts broke away from India, leading to the creation of Pakistan in 1947 and Bangladesh in 1971. The partition of India was promulgated in the Indian Independence Act of 1947 that was passed by the British Parliament, which divided India into 3 separate entities: India, Pakistan and Bangladesh. The act also resulted in the dissolution of the British Indian Empire.

The Far East

In 1946, the Republic of the Philippines was inaugurated as an independent country. Burma became independent in 1948, Malaya in 1957, Singapore in 1959, Indonesia in 1945, New Guinea in 1975, and French Indo-China became Vietnam, Laos and Cambodia in 1954.

A civil war ensued in China between nationalist and communist forces. Communist forces led by Mao Zedong were victorious and established the People's Republic of China on the mainland in 1949, while nationalist forces retreated to the island of Taiwan. A government program of oppression under Mao Zedong resulted in the deaths of millions of Chinese.

Korea was divided and occupied between the United States and the Soviet Union. In 1950, war broke out between South Korea, which was backed by the United States, and North Korea, which was backed by the Soviet Union and China. The Korean War resulted in a stalemate and ceasefire in 1953, with South Korea remaining an independent republic in 1945, and North Korea becoming the Democratic People's Republic that was established in 1948.

Africa

Algeria gained its independence from France in 1962. Ethiopia annexed the colony of Italy, Eritrea, and in 1952, the emperor created a federation with Eritrea, which was dissolved in 1962 after the start of the Eritrean War of Independence. Libya became independent in 1951, but in 1969 suffered a coup by a group led by an army officer Muamma Abu Minyar al-Qadhafi who then exiled the king of Libya to Egypt.

The Human Impact of the War

Estimates for the total casualties of the war indicate that 70 million people throughout the world died in the war, with 40 million of them being civilians. Many of these died because of disease, starvation, massacres, and deliberate genocide, including 12 million who died in Nazi concentration camps. Others died in captivity of ailments such as dysentery, cholera, malaria, ulcers, fungal infections, bacterial bone infections and deficiency diseases.

The atrocities of the Holocaust, as well as the Nanking Massacre, in which several hundred thousand Chinese civilians were raped and murdered, plus the use of new weapons—culminating with the atomic bombs dropped on Japan ushered in a new era of cruelty. Other inhumane actions were conducted by the victors, including forced population transfers in the Soviet Union, the Japanese-American internment in the United States, the Soviet massacre of Polish citizens and the firebombing of cities, such as at Dresden, Germany and Tokyo, Japan. 12 million people were employed in the German war economy as forced labor during the war. Japan pressed 18 million people from Far East Asia into forced labor. The Soviet Union labor camps led to the deaths of millions of citizens in occupied countries such as Poland, Lithuania, Latvia, and Estonia—as well as the captured German prisoners of war.

More than 100 million men and women served in uniform. The United States was fortunate in that no American cities were destroyed, and because the relative number of casualties that it incurred in fighting the war—about 405,000—was considerably less than those suffered by other countries. At home, female alcoholism and female juvenile delinquency increased fivefold, and many teenage girls literally became prostitutes by sleeping with anyone in uniform. The birth rate rose—as did the divorce rate.

Industries engaged in defense work expanded as the production of consumer products declined. In 1941, more than 3 million cars were manufactured, but for the rest of the war only 139 more were made. The chronic unemployment ended, personal income doubled, 8 million American women entered the workforce, 16 million men entered the military and 24 million people in search of defense work moved to different areas—such as Washington, Oregon and California, which increased their populations by over one-third. The government spent $321 billion and increased the national debt to $259 billion—and borrowed an additional $185 billion through the sale of war bonds. The number of people paying income taxes rose from 4 million in 1941 to over 40 million in 1945.

Technological Advances

New fighters and bombers were developed during WWII, including the jet engine. Defenses such as anti-aircraft weaponry and radar were invented. Guided missiles were introduced by Germany with their V-1 and V-2 rockets as a means of terrorizing the civilian populations.

At sea, the production of aircraft carriers to quickly move strike forces to any part of the world came into prominence. Improved battleships, destroyers and submarines to serve as escorts and to perform battle duties were produced to add to the arsenals. Anti-submarine weapons were developed such as sonar and homing torpedoes.

The warfare on land changed dramatically, with the tank evolving into a primary weapon having increased speed, armor, mobility and firepower. Instead of just providing support for the infantry, it was used for mobile attacks that negated the use of trench warfare that had been used during WWI. Anti-tank armaments were developed, such as anti-tank guns and mines. Along with these weapons, other innovations included submachine guns and assault rifles. The jeep was invented as a fast, lightweight, all-terrain vehicle.

Other important technologies that were developed during the war years were better communications, advances in cryptology and other methods of deciphering messages. The war marked the beginning of electronic digital computers, and the creation of nuclear reactors.

The Start of the Atomic Age

The New Dilemma

The end of WWII produced a new set of issues and problems, especially the dilemma of how to control nuclear technology. In the United States, reaction to the atomic bomb created a sense of fear among the public that made government-suggested fallout shelters as the way to survive an atomic attack. Government officials focused on the possible impact of the bomb on postwar international relations. The first steps were proposed toward developing a policy on international control of the atom. However, although the Manhattan Project slowed down from its wartime pace, the assembly of additional nuclear weapons continued without abatement. Even though the American nuclear weapons program was transferred to the control of civilians in 1946 with the creation of the Atomic Energy Commission, the United States continued testing atomic weapons, and conducted a series of atomic tests in the Bikini Atoll in the Pacific Ocean. The Cold War began between the Soviet Union and the United States, and the subsequent arms race led other nations to develop nuclear weapons.

The Commitment

Without the leadership of General Leslie Groves and physicist Robert Oppenheimer, as well as that of engineer Crawford Greenewalt of DuPont, plus the revolutionary breakthroughs in nuclear science achieved by Enrico Fermi, Niels Bohr and Ernest Lawrence, the United States would not have produced the atomic bomb for use during WWII. Despite formidable obstacles, the United States was able to combine science, government, universities, the military, and industry into an organization that took nuclear physics from the laboratory to the battlefield to produce a weapon of awesome destructive capability. The effort demonstrated the importance of basic scientific research to national defense, and the Manhattan Project became the organizational model behind the remarkable achievements of American science during the second half of the 20th century. When President John Kennedy announced his goal of putting a man on the moon, it was the Manhattan Project that he invoked for its spirit of commitment and patriotism.

An Unparalleled Feat

The Manhattan Project represents the greatest technological achievement in the history of the world. It was accomplished by the combined efforts of science, industry, labor, the military and the United States, British and Canadian governments. Some of the greatest minds in history were employed in the secret effort to produce the atomic bomb. Only the Apollo Project to send a manned mission to the moon even compares to the magnitude of the organizational and technical skills that were required for such an undertaking. The Manhattan Project will provide the focus and the impetus to create another massive program in the future that requires critical attention—such as the creation of new energy sources for the world or a manned mission to Mars. The development of nuclear technology offers great hope, especially with nuclear fission plants that can significantly reduce the threat of global warming by reducing the reliance on oil and coal—although they do produce a huge amount of radioactive waste.

Economic Recovery

Economic recovery following the war was varied in differing parts of the world, although in general it was quite positive. In Europe, West Germany recovered and doubled production from its pre-war levels by the 1950s. Italy came out of the war in poor economic condition, but by 1950s, the Italian economy was marked by stability and high growth. The United Kingdom was in a state of economic ruin after the war, and continued to experience relative economic decline for decades to follow. France rebounded quite quickly, and enjoyed economic growth and modernization. The Soviet Union experienced a rapid increase in production in the immediate post-war era. In Asia, Japan—in spite of the atomic weapons that caused a terrible devastation—experienced an incredibly rapid economic growth, which led to its becoming one of the most powerful economies in the world by the 1980s. China, following the conclusion of its civil war, was essentially a bankrupt nation. However, by 1953 economic restoration was successful as production resumed pre-war levels. This growth rate persisted, although it was briefly interrupted by the disastrous Great Leap Forward economic experiment. At the end of the war, the United States produced roughly half of the world's industrial output. However, by the 1970s, this economic dominance had lessened significantly.

Creation of the United Nations

In an effort to maintain international peace, the United Nations came into existence in 1945, with its headquarters in New York City, New York. The United Nations Charter established the Security Council to maintain peace, with the 5 responsible members being Britain, the Soviet Union, the United States, China and France—with each of these countries having the power of a veto. The purpose of the United Nations was to stop wars between countries, and to provide a platform for dialogue.

The General Assembly is the main deliberative body of the United Nations. It is composed of all member states, and meets in yearly sessions under a president elected from among the member states. When the General Assembly votes on important questions, a two-thirds majority of those present and voting is required. Important questions that are discussed by the General Assembly include recommendations on peace and security, election of members, the admission, suspension, and expulsion of members, and budgetary matters. All other questions are decided by a majority vote, with each member country having one vote. However, apart from the approval of budgetary matters, resolutions are not binding on the members. The General Assembly may make recommendations on any matters within the scope of the United Nations—except those concerning matters of peace and security that are under the Security Council consideration headed by the 5 permanent members. There are also 10 non-permanent members on the Security Council, which are held for 2-year terms with member states being voted in by the General Assembly.

Bibliography

Adler, Mortimer J., Editor in Chief. *The Annals of America*, Vol. 1-20. Chicago: Encyclopaedia Britannica, Inc., 1976.

Ambrose, Stephen E. *D-Day, June 6, 1944: The Climactic Battle of World War II*. New York: Simon & Schuster Paperbacks, 1994.

_____. *Eisenhower: Soldier and President*. New York: Simon & Schuster Paperbacks, 1990.

Armstrong, Virginia Irving, compiler. *I Have Spoken: American History Through the Voices of Indians*. Athens: Swallow Press, 1971.

Auchincloss, Louis. *Woodrow Wilson*. New York: Penguin Group, 2000.

Badger, Anthony. *The New Deal: The Depression Years, 1933-1940*. Chicago: Ivan R. Dee, 1989.

Benson, Bill and M. J. Beckman. *The Law That Never Was*. Washington, D.C.: Constitutional Research Associates, 1985.

Bernanke, Ben S. *Essays on the Great Depression*. Princeton: Princeton University Press, 2000.

Blum, John Morton. *Woodrow Wilson and the Politics of Morality*. Boston: Little, Brown and Company, 1956.

Bond, L.E. *Statue of Liberty: Beacon of Promise*. Santa Barbara: Albion Publishing Group, 1990.

Bonnifield, Paul. *The Dust Bowl: Men, Dirt and Depression*. Albuquerque: University of New Mexico Press, 1979.

Brands, H. W. *Woodrow Wilson*. New York: Henry Holt and Company, 2003.

Brown, Dee. *Bury My Heart at Wounded Knee: An Indian History of the American West*. New York: Holt, Rinehart & Winston, 1970.

Brown, E. E. *The Life and Public Services of James A. Garfield*. Boston: D. Lothrop and Company, 1881.

Chickering, Rodger. *Imperial Germany and the Great War, 194-1918*. Cambridge: Cambridge University Press, 2004.

Connant, Jennet. *109 East Palace: Robert Oppenheimer and the Secret City of Los*

Alamos. New York: Simon & Schuster, 2005.

Cooper, John Milton Jr. *Woodrow Wilson: A Biography.* New York: Alfred A. Knopf, 2009.

Cooper, Michael L. *Dust to Eat: Drought and Depression in the 1930s.* New York: Clarion Books, 2004.

Daws, Gavan. *Shoals of Time: A History of the Hawaiian Islands.* Honolulu: The University Press of Hawaii, 1968.

Dean, John W. *Warren G. Harding.* New York: Henry Holt and Company, 2004.

DiNunzio, Mario R., Editor. *Theodore Roosevelt: An American Mind.* New York: Penguin Books, 1994.

Du Bois, W. E. B. *Black Reconstruction in America: 1860-1880.* Cleveland: The World Publishing Company, 1935.

Dorsheimer, William. *Life and Public Services of Grover Cleveland.* Philadelphia: Hubbard Brothers, 1884.

Egan, Timothy. *The Worst Hard Time: The Untold Story of Those Who Survived The Great American Dust Bowl.* New York: Houghton Mifflin Company, 2006.

Eichengreen, Barry. *Golden Fetters: The Gold Standard and the Great Depression, 1919-1939.* Oxford: Oxford University Press, 1992.

Esherick, Joseph W. *The Origins of the Boxer Uprising.* Berkeley: University of California Press, 1987.

Everett, Marshall. *Complete Life of William McKinley and Story of His Assassination.* Memorial Edition, 1901.

Foner, Eric. *Reconstruction: America's Unfinished Revolution, 1863-1877.* New York: HarperCollins Publishers Inc., 1988.

Friedman, Milton and Anna Jacobson Schwartz. *A Monetary History of the United States, 1867-1960.* Princeton: Princeton University Press, 1963.

Galbraith, John Kenneth. *The Great Crash: 1929.* Boston: Houghton-Mifflin Company, 1954.

Garraty, John A. and Mark C. Carnes, Editors. *American National Biography,* Vol. 1-24. New York: Oxford University Press, 1999.

Gilbert, Martin. *The Second World War: A Complete History.* New York: Henry Holt and Company, 1989.

Gillette, William. *Retreat From Reconstruction: 1869-1879.* Baton Rouge: Louisiana State University Press, 1979.

Grady, John Randolph. *The Life and Public Services of the Great Reform President, Grover Cleveland.* Cincinnati: W. H. Ferguson Company, 1892.

_____. *The Life and Public Services of Adlai E. Stevenson.* Cincinnati: W. H. Ferguson Company, 1892.

Graham, Amy. *A Look at the 18th and 21st Amendments: The Prohibition and Sale of Intoxicating Liquors.* Berkeley Heights: Enslow Publishers, Inc., 2008.

Green, Robert. *Profiles of the Presidents: Benjamin Harrison.* Minneapolis: Compass Point Books, 2004.

Greene, Julie. *The Canal Builders: Making America's Empire at the Panama Canal.* New York: Penguin Press, 2009.

Harris, Jonathan. *A Statue for America: The First 100 Years of the Statue of Liberty.* New York: Macmillan Publishing Company, 1985.

Hersey, John. *Hiroshima.* New York: First Vintage Books, 1946.

Hoebeke, Christopher Hyde. *The Road to Mass Democracy: Original Intent and the Seventeenth Amendment.* New Brunswick: Transaction Publishers, 1995.

Hoyt, Edwin P. *James A. Garfield.* Chicago: Reilly & Lee Co., 1964.

Inada, Lawson Fusao, editor. *Only What We Could Carry: The Japanese American Internment Experience.* Berkeley: Heyday books, 2000.

Jeffers, Paul H. *An Honest President: The Life and Presidencies of Grover Cleveland.* New York: Harper-Collins Publishers, 2000.

Johnson, Allen and Dumas Malone, Editors. *Dictionary of American Biography,* Vol. I-X. New York: Charles Scribner's Sons, 1930.

Josephy, Alvin M. Jr. *The Congress of the United States.* New York: American Heritage Publishing Co., 1975.

Keller, Ulrich. *The Building of the Panama Canal: In Historic Photographs.* New York: Dover Publications, Inc., 1983.

Kelly, Cynthia C., editor. *The Manhattan Project: The Birth of the Atomic Bomb in the Words of its Creators, Eyewitnesses and Historians.* New York: Black Dog and Leventhal Publishers, Inc., 2007.

Knauer, Kelly, editor. *America: An Illustrated Early History, 1776-1900.* New York: Time Books, 2007.

Langellier, John P. *Uncle Sam's Little Wars: The Spanish-American War, Philippine Insurrection, and Boxer Rebellion, 1898-1902.* Philadelphia: Chelsea House Publishers, 1999.

Langley, Lester D. *The Banana Wars: United States Intervention in the Caribbean, 1898-1934.* Wilmington: Scholarly resources, Inc., 2002.

Latham, Frank B. *The Panic of 1893.* New York: Franklin Watts, Inc., 1971.

Leuchtenburg, William E. *Herbert Hoover.* New York: Henry Holt and Company, 2009.

Lyons, Eugene. *Herbert Hoover: A Biography.* Garden City: Doubleday & Company, Inc., 1948.

Matthiessen, Peter. *In the Spirit of Crazy Horse.* New York: Penguin Books, 1983.

McCullough, David. *The Path Between the Seas: The Creation of the Panama Canal, 1870-1914.* New York: Simon & Schuster Paperbacks, 1977.

McElvaine, Robert S. *The Great Depression: America, 1929-1941.* New York: Three Rivers Press, 1984.

Meyer, G. J. *A World Undone: The Story of the Great War, 1914-1918.* New York: Delta Books, 2006.

Miller, Nathan. *FDR: An Intimate History.* Garden City: Doubleday & Company, Inc., 1983.

_____. *Theodore Roosevelt: A Life.* New York, HarperCollins Publishers, Inc., 1992.

Morgan, H. Wayne. *William McKinley and His America.* Kent: The Kent State University Press, 2003.

Morris, Richard B. and Jeffrey B. Morris, Editors. *Encyclopedia of American History.* New York: Harper Collins, Publishers, 1996.

Murray, Robert K. *The Harding Era: Warren G. Harding and His Administration.* Newtown: University of Minnesota Press, 1969.

Nelson, Michael, Editor. *The Presidency*. New York: Smithmark Publishers, 1996.

Perret, Geoffrey. *Ulysses S. Grant: Soldier & President*. New York: Random House Inc., 1997.

Preston, Diana. *The Boxer Rebellion*. New York: Berkley Books, 1999.

Pringle, Henry. *William Howard Taft: The Life and Times, Volume One*. Newtown: American Political Biography Press, 1939.

_____. *William Howard Taft: The Life and Times, Volume Two*. Newtown: American Political Biography Press, 1939.

Reeves, Thomas C. *Gentleman Boss: The Life and Times of Chester Alan Arthur*. Newtown: American Political Biography Press, 1975.

Rhodes, Richard. *The Making of the Atomic Bomb*. New York: Simon & Schuster, 1986.

_____. *Dark Sun: The Making of the Hydrogen Bomb*. Simon & Schuster, 1995.

_____. *The Politics of Upheaval: The Age of Roosevelt*. Boston: Houghton Mifflin Company, 1960.

Russell, Francis. *The Shadow of Blooming Grove: Warren G. Harding in His Times*. New York: McGraw-Hill Book Company, 1968.

Santella, Andrew. *Profiles of the Presidents: Chester A. Arthur*. Minneapolis: Compass Point Books, 2004.

Schlesinger Jr., Arthur M. *The Almanac of American History*. Greenwich: Brompton Books Corporation, 1993.

Schlup, Leonard Clarence. *The Political Career of the First Adlai E. Stevenson*. Urbana-Champaign: University of Illinois, PhD Dissertation, 1973.

Severn, Bill. *William Howard Taft: The President Who Became Chief Justice*. New York: David McKay Company, 1970.

Shirer, William L. *The Rise and Fall of the Third Reich: A History of Nazi Germany*. New York: Simon & Schuster Paperbacks, 1959.

Sievers, Harry J. *Benjamin Harrison: Hoosier Warrior, 1833-1865*. Chicago: Henry Regnery Company, 1952.

_____. *Benjamin Harrison: Hoosier Statesman*. Newtown: American Political

Biography Press, 1996.

Sobel, Robert. *Coolidge: An American Enigma*. Washington, D.C.: Regnery Publishing, Inc., 1998.

Stallings, Frank L. *Black Sunday: The Great Dust Storm of April 14, 1935*. Austin: Eakin Press, 2001.

Toland, John. *Infamy: Pearl Harbor and its Aftermath*. Garden City: Doubleday & Company, 1982.

Trumbull, Robert. *Nine Who Survived Hiroshima and Nagasaki*. Rutland: Charles E Tuttle Company, 1957.

Wallace, Lew. *Life of General Ben Harrison*. Philadelphia: Hubbard Brothers, Publishers, 1888.

Ward, Geoffrey C. and Ken Burns. *The War: An Intimate History, 1941-1945*. New York: Alfred A. Knopf, 2007.

Welch Jr., Richard E. *Response to Imperialism: The United States and the Philippine-American War, 1899-1902*. Chapel Hill: The University of North Carolina Press, 1979.

Werstein, Irving. *Turning Point for America: The Story of the Spanish American War*. New York: Julian Messner, 1964.

White, William Allen. *A Puritan in Babylon: The Story of Calvin Coolidge*. Glouchester: The MacMillan Company, 1938.

Williams, Charles Richard. *The Life of Rutherford Birchard Hayes, Volumes I and II*. Boston: Houghton Mifflin Company, 1914.

www.ingramcontent.com/pod-product-compliance
Lightning Source LLC
Chambersburg PA
CBHW080458110426
42742CB00017B/2925